Teacher's Book

Magdalena Kondro

Macmillan Education
Between Towns Road, Oxford OX4 3PP
A division of Macmillan Publishers Limited
Companies and representatives throughout the world

ISBN 978-0-230-53380-6

Text © Macmillan Publishers Limited 2010
Design and illustration © Macmillan Publishers Limited 2010

All rights reserved; no part of this publication may be reproduced, stored in a retrieval system, transmitted in any form, or by any means, electronic, mechanical, photocopying, recording, or otherwise, without the prior written permission of the publishers.

Note to Teachers
Photocopies can be made, for classroom use, of pages 102–129 without the prior written permission of Macmillan Publishers Limited. However, please note that the copyright law, which does not normally permit multiple copying of published material, applies to the rest of this book.

Text by Magdalena Kondro
Test CD by Barbara Mackay

Original design by D & J Hunter
Page make-up by D & J Hunter; Expo Holdings; Julian Littlewood
Illustrated by Kathy Baxendale, Mark Davis, Karen Donnelly, Gillian Martin, Julian Mosedale, Julia Pearson
Cover design by Designers Collective

These materials may contain links for third party websites. We have no control over, and are not responsible for, the contents of such third party websites. Please use care when accessing them.

Student's Book acknowledgements
Text © Colin Granger and Katherine Stannett 2010
Original design by Wild Apple Design
Page make-up by Giles Davies
Illustrated by Adrian Barclay, Russ Daff, Wes Lowe, Chris Pavely, Baz Rowell, Mark Ruffle, Simon Rumble, Martin Sanders, Jorge Santillon, Lisa Smith, Simon Smith, Mark Turner and Gary Wing

The authors and publishers would like to thank the following for permission to reproduce their photographic material:
Alamy/ blinkwinkel p70(c), Alamy/ Rob Cousins p72(br), Alamy/ Shaun Cunningham pp6(br), 89(11), Alamy/ Gist Images pp84(tr), 89(15), Alamy/ Jeff Greenberg pp7(tr), 14(b), 58(tr), 88(2), Alamy/ Iconotec p77(cocoa), Alamy/ Janine Wiedel Photolibrary p41(t), Alamy/ David Kadlubowski p64(j), Alamy/ Jim Lane p22(c), Alamy/ Lenscap p45(tr), Alamy/ Mediablitzimages UK Ltd p41(b), Alamy/ Motoring Picture Library p77(car), Alamy/ Nordic Photos p64(c), Alamy/ Owaki/Kulla pp68(tl), 88(12a), Alamy/ PCL p47, Alamy/ Photodisc p87(c), Alamy/ Emil Pozar p77(hair), Alamy/ Simon Reddy p82(cl), Alamy/ Doug Steley p68(b), 89(12d), Alamy/ Steppenwolf pp68(c), 89(12b), Alamy/ Travelshots.com p64(f), Alamy/ Rob Walls p23(b), Alamy/ Doug Wilson p64(e);
Brand X/ pp64(i), 68(tl insert), 70(br), 87(tl);
Corbis/ pp17, 64(a), 77(grass), Corbis/ Atlantide Phototravel p84(br), Corbis/ Neville Elder p72(bl), Corbis/ Brooke Fasani p48(bc), Corbis/ Image Source p87(bl), Corbis/ Rob Lewine pp72(l), 89(13), Corbis/ Lawrence Manning p45(tl), Corbis/ Gideon Mendel pp70(bl), 75, Corbis/ Robert Michael p29(t), Corbis/ Michael Prince pp6(tr), 14(c), 58(b), 88(1);
Digital Stock/ p64(b), Digital Stock/ Corbis p64(h);
Fotolibra/ Mark Fearon pp68(t), 89(12c), Fotolibra/ Robert Ho p82(br), Fotolibra/ Avi Kallan p77(wood);
Getty Images/ pp 24(l), 24(r), 88(4), Getty Images/ Blasius Erlinger p22(t), Getty Images/ Sylvain Grandadam p7(br), Getty Images/ VEER Third Eye Images p58(3);
Image Source/ pp23(cl), 64(d), 64(g), 68(b insert), 68(c insert);
Lodgepole Gallery and Tipi Village, USA p85;
Lonely Planet/ David Creedy p6(bl);
Macmillan Publishers Ltd/ David Tolley p45(bl);
Macmillan Readers cover/ *Nelson Mandela* Getty/Tom Stoddart p87
NationalGeographicStock.com/ Dean Conger/photo illustration by Macmillan Publishers Ltd p84(c);
NPL/ Jane Burton p22(b);
PA Photos/ p25(b);
Photodisc pp13, 23(tl), 58(2), 68(t insert), 72(tr), 77(sand);
Photolibrary/ age fotostock p82(tl), Photolibrary/ Liane Cary p29(c), Photolibrary/ Fresh Food Images pp38, 77(omelette), Photolibrary/ Garden Picture Library p82(tr), Photolibrary/ Dennis Macdonald p58(1), Photolibrary/ Mauritius p77(water), Photolibrary/ Red Chopsticks pp6(tl), 14(t), 58(tl, 88(10), Photolibrary/ Zen Shui pp45(br), 69, Photolibrary/ Stockbyte p73, Photolibrary/ Wave Royalty Free p70(t);
Punchstock/ Digital Vision p23(cr), Punchstock/ Thinkstock p49;
Rex Features/ Alix/Phanie p77(plastic), Rex Features/ Nick Cunard pp48(c), 48(bl), Rex Features/ IBL p88(9), Rex Features/ Image Source p23(tr), Rex Features/ Elinor Jones p53, Rex Features/ Ken McKay p25(t), Rex Features/ Richard Young p91;
Stockbyte/ pp29(b), 82(bl), 87(r).

Commissioned photography by:
Paul Bricknell pp8, 18, 26, 46, 56, 57, 62, 82 (portrait), 83, 88(8).

These materials may contain links for third-party websites. We have no control over, and are not responsible for, the contents of such third-party websites. Please use care when accessing them.

Whilst every effort has been made to locate the owners of copyright material in this book, there may have been some cases when the publishers have been unable to contact the owners. We should be grateful to hear from anyone who recognises copyright material and who is unacknowledged. We shall be pleased to make the necessary amendments in future editions of the book.

Printed and bound in Thailand

2014 2013 2012 2011 2010
10 9 8 7 6 5 4 3 2

Hot Spot Teacher's Book 3

Contents

Introduction to Hot Spot iv
Student's Book contents 2

Teacher's notes T6

Module 1
Lesson 1 *Where I live* T6
Lesson 2 *Charlie's busy week* T8
Lesson 3 *The cheapest shirts in town* T10
Lesson 4 *Looking after your pet* T12
Review T14
Extra Special T16

Module 2
Lesson 5 *Sports day* T18
Lesson 6 *What were you doing?* T20
Lesson 7 *Amazing stories* T22
Lesson 8 *My hero* T24
Review T26
Extra Special T28

Module 3
Lesson 9 *In my life* T30
Lesson 10 *An amazing life* T32
Lesson 11 *My latest news* T34
Lesson 12 *Sumeo's story* T36
Review T38
Extra Special T40

Module 4
Lesson 13 *The talent show* T42
Lesson 14 *Helpful Herbert* T44
Lesson 15 *The festival* T46
Lesson 16 *The Brit School* T48
Review T50
Extra Special T52

Module 5
Lesson 17 *How are you feeling?* T54
Lesson 18 *I'm worried* T56
Lesson 19 *You should say thank you* T58
Lesson 20 *Survival* T60
Review T62
Extra Special T64

Module 6
Lesson 21 *DIY disasters* T66
Lesson 22 *My home* T68
Lesson 23 *The eco-village* T70
Lesson 24 *The eco-family* T72
Review T74
Extra Special T76

Module 7
Lesson 25 *Rules of the road* T78
Lesson 26 *My secret identity* T80
Lesson 27 *My amazing year* T82
Lesson 28 *Amazing places* T84
Review T86
Extra Special T88

Grammar summary key T90

Resource section 91

Activity Book answer key 130

Introduction

Who is *Hot Spot* for?

Hot Spot is a communicative English course designed for **young teenagers**. It addresses the needs of this age group and will take students from beginner to low-intermediate level. *Hot Spot* is designed to **bridge the gap** between the **upper primary and lower secondary sectors**. The course is designed with both the student and teacher in mind and gives continual tips and support to help teachers with today's **mixed-ability classes**.

What are the main aims of *Hot Spot*?

- To provide relevant, **stimulating**, **age-specific materials** that help sustain **students' motivation** and make the focus of the English lessons the students themselves
- To help students **remember the language** learnt in class
- To **encourage students** to take an active part in their English class by **providing opportunities** in every lesson for students to communicate about themselves and their own world
- To provide **culturally-rich content** about the world with a focus on the UK and other English-speaking countries

What are the components of *Hot Spot*?

- Student's Book with CD-ROM
- Activity Book
- Teacher's Book interleaved with Student's Book pages
- Test CD (included with the Teacher's Book)
- Photocopiable supplementary materials in the Teacher's Book
- Class Audio CDs
- Teacher's Resource Website www.macmillanenglish.com/hotspot

How is the Student's Book organized?

The teaching material is divided into seven theme-based modules.

Each module is sub-divided into six lessons:

- Three core **Language input** lessons
- A core **Integrated skills** lesson
- A **Review** lesson
- An optional **Extra special** lesson which also includes a **Mini-project**

What are the key features of the Student's Book?

- Traditional and transparent **grammar syllabus** with a gradual progression
- **Personalisation** of the material to help students use new language to describe themselves, classmates, family and friends
- A good balance of all **four skills** in each lesson
- A variety of **pronunciation** activities
- **Check your English** activity at the end of each lesson
- **Integrated skills** lesson with cross-cultural focus
- **Recurrent characters** to help engage students
- **Songs** and **games** to help stimulate learning
- **Writing** and **Study tips** in each module
- **Real English** highlights common expressions in dialogues
- **Remember!** reminds students what to watch out for in grammar practice
- **Story extracts** at the back of the book encourage extensive reading

How many teaching hours are there in the Student's Book?

Hot Spot provides up to **90 hours of teaching per level**. This includes supplementary materials and ideas in the Teacher's Notes, the Activity Book, Photocopiable materials, the CD Rom and Grammar summary section at the back of the Student's Book, as well as the Teacher's Resource website.

For teachers with fewer teaching hours per week, *Hot Spot* provides four core lessons per module (three language input lessons and an integrated skills lesson), making a total of **42 core hours** in Student's Book 3. Each *Hot Spot* lesson provides materials for two 45 minute lessons. These lessons are divided into Part 1 and Part 2 in the Teacher's Notes.

How much revision is in *Hot Spot*?

Each module of *Hot Spot* has a **Review lesson** which comprehensively revises and consolidates all language introduced in the Student's Book. There are ten pages of **further practice material** for each module in the **Activity Book** and the Teacher's Notes also provide additional ideas for revision.

How is grammar covered?

One of the aims of *Hot Spot* is to make **grammar more accessible** for students. The organisation of the course makes it possible for grammatical areas to be broken up into small, manageable chunks enabling students to master one area before moving on to the next. **Grammar is always fully contextualised** in photos, pictures, dialogues and texts.

Grammar spot boxes which highlight specific grammar points appear throughout the modules on the lesson pages. Furthermore the back of the Student's Book has a comprehensive illustrated **Grammar summary**.

How is vocabulary taught?

Hot Spot places a **strong emphasis on vocabulary**. The course aims to make the acquisition of new language easier for students by providing **illustrations** of most

new words within the teaching material. These illustrations can be used by the teacher in **Picture search** activities to pre-teach vocabulary or by the students to discover meaning without recourse to translation or explanation.

Vocabulary is **recycled** throughout the course and students are encouraged to use techniques such as word maps, collocation, association, imagery and memory games to help memorise new words.

How is the Teacher's Book organised?

- **Interleaved notes.** Next to each Student's Book page there is a page of comprehensive Teacher's Notes providing teachers with step-by-step lesson notes and important additional information and ideas.
- **Photocopiable worksheets** with teaching notes for each lesson
- **Grammar summary** with answers
- **Activity Book** answer key
- **Tests** on a CD at the back of the Teacher's Book. There are tests for each module as well as a middle and end test. There are two versions of each test, **Test A** and **Test B**, which can be edited to suit individual classes.

What are the key features of the Teacher's Book?

- **Lesson summary** which gives an overview of the grammatical and lexical aims of the lesson and references to additional activities in the Activity Book and in the Photocopiable Resource material
- Closed-book **Warm-up activities** designed to motivate students at the start of each lesson
- **Teaching tips** ranging from peer correction to memorisation
- **Mixed-ability activities** to help classes with students who finish quickly and also for those who need more support
- **Dyslexia tips** with suggestions on how to help dyslexic students
- **Extra activity suggestions** to help support the activities in the Student's Book
- **Cultural** information
- **Tapescripts** for the listening material
- **Answers** to the activities in the Student's Book
- **Homework** suggestions
- Comprehensive teaching notes for the **Photocopiable worksheets**

What are the key features of the Activity Book?

- The *Hot Spot* Activity Book plays an important role in **consolidating and recycling the language** presented in the Student's Book.
- The Activity Book has a **Learning diary** in every module, which can be used by the students independently to check if they have achieved all the learning objectives.
- For every module in the Activity Book there are **Fast finisher** activities designed to be used by students who have finished a task before other students in the class.
- Each module of the Activity Book has **Extra practice** activities designed to be used by students who need additional practice or by students who need to catch up after missing lessons.
- The Activity Book also has a **Story** which exploits the language learnt by placing it in a fun and engaging context.
- The Activity Book has a **Word list** organized in lexical sets, which can be used for further study and vocabulary revision.

How does *Hot Spot* tie into the Common European Framework (CEF)?

Hot Spot has clear links to the **CEF** with features such as:

- Various **writing tasks** which students can put in to the **Language Portfolio**
- A wide range of **speaking activities** which meet the **Speaking skills requirements** (both production and interaction)
- **Mini-projects** in each module which help to develop **student autonomy and responsibility**
- Specific **Cross-cultural** and **skills** lessons in each module
- **Self-assessment tools** in both the Student's Book and the Activity Book
- **Review lessons** written using CEF **"Can do"** descriptors.

Upon completion of *Hot Spot* 3, students can expect to be at CEF Level A2.

Essential *Hot Spot* teaching tips

Starting the lesson

Develop a set of routine activites to allow students to settle and get ready for the new lesson. Start by taking the register. Getting students to confirm their attendance with a word from a given category, e.g. *animals*, different for each lesson, will provide a quick revision activity. After returning and correcting homework, move to a warm-up activity. Each lesson in the *Hot Spot* Teacher's Book begins with a warm-up designed to interest and involve students before opening their books.

Lesson objectives

Tell students the objective of the lesson to help them understand what they are working towards. In the *Hot Spot* Student's Book the objectives for each lesson can be found next to the lesson titles.

Setting up activities

Before each activity, make sure that students have been introduced to the necessary language to complete the activity. After a lead-in, e.g. a dicussion, studying visual materials or vocabulary items, organize the students so that they can do the activity. This may involve putting them in pairs or groups or rearranging the seating.

Giving instructions

Keep instructions as short as possible, use examples or demonstrate the task with a student. Split up long instructions to give at different stages of the activity. Get students to repeat the instructions back to you to check understanding.

Group and pair work

Students struggle with pair or group activities if they cannot express what they want to say. Before the task revise the phrases you expect students to use and if necessary, put these on the board. It is impossible for you to monitor all groups and pairs at once. Therefore, to encourage students to work effectively, inform them that after the activity you will choose a pair or group to re-do the task in front of the class.

Giving feedback

Monitor students' work as they are doing pair or group work activities and take notes on their performance. After the activity give feedback on the content and the language; do not focus on just the mistakes, praise students for their achievements too. Discuss the mistakes with the whole class without revealing who made each one.

Correcting mistakes

Let students know if the purpose of the activity is accuracy or fluency and correct mistakes accordingly. Concentrate primarily on the target language when correcting. In controlled practice activities correct mistakes on the spot. Give students a chance to correct themselves: signal the mistake through facial expression and use hand signals to indicate the type of error, e.g. point back over your shoulder for the past tense. In freer tasks take notes so as not to destroy the flow of conversation. After the activity put the mistakes on the board to discuss with the whole class. Encourage peer correction to show students that they can learn from one another.

Mixed-ability classes

Try the following ideas if you have students at different levels in your class:

- For each group or pair work activity decide if it is better to put students of similar levels together or to mix different level students.
- Give fast finishers extra activities, e.g. from the *Fast finisher* section of the *Hot Spot* Activity Book.
- Encourage weaker students to preview what is coming up next in the coursebook at home so that they can be more prepared.
- Assign weaker students extra revision exercises for homework, e.g. from the *Extra practice* section of the *Hot Spot* Activity Book.
- Recognise your students' strengths and weaknesses, and get weaker students to answer questions in areas where they feel more confident.

Discipline

Students tend to behave badly when they are not challenged enough, or the activity is too long or too difficult. Set time limits to keep the pace, give fast finishers extra tasks and be prepared to finish an activity early if it clearly does not work for your class. Keep watching the classroom to anticipate misbehaviour. When you are writing on the board or helping individuals, give disruptive students additional tasks or make them responsible for the discipline in the classroom. If this does not help, have a quiet word with the troublemaker and if necessary ask them to sit out of the next activity. This is less embarrassing for the students than speaking in front of the class, and less disruptive to other students.

Ending the lesson

Review the objective of the lesson and ask students if they feel they have achieved it. Set the homework and finish the lesson with a short fun activity. This can be any language game, or get students to say a 'password' – any new word or a sentence with a new structure they have learnt in the lesson.

Dyslexia tips

Hot Spot Teacher's Book provides additional support for teaching dyslexic students. Helpful tips precede activities which dyslexic students are likely to find difficult. These tips provide teachers with ideas on how they can further encourage their students.

This page provides a summary of strategies that can be used to help dyslexic students in your lessons.

Characteristics of dyslexic students

Dyslexic students may have some or all of these characteristics:

- easily distracted
- short attention span
- poor short term memory
- poor reading skills
- weak reading comprehension skills
- poor spelling
- poor handwriting
- difficulty in remembering sequences, including instructions
- slow to complete tasks
- slow and often inaccurate copying (e.g. from the board)

They may also face repeated failure on a daily basis and can have very low self-esteem and extreme lack of confidence.

How can teachers help?

- Be understanding and sympathetic towards students' difficulties.
- Show that you are willing to help.
- Accept and respect **all** their efforts.
- Bear in mind that dyslexic students are often highly intelligent despite their difficulties.

Main strategies for teaching dyslexic students

- Sit dyslexic students at the front of the class where they can see the board and hear the teacher most easily.
- Give new information more than once and check that it has been understood in a way that does not embarrass the student.
- Teach in short chunks and change activities frequently to keep attention and motivation.
- Keep spoken instructions short, simple and in the correct sequence.
- Give information on a sheet to be stuck into books rather than being copied from the board.
- Give instructions for homework in writing, preferably on a handout.
- Be very cautious about asking dyslexic students to read aloud as this can cause great anxiety. Keep reading activities within small ability groups or pairs.
- Give students sufficient time to complete each task or make the task shorter according to abilities.
- Reward for content and effort. When marking, focus on one or two mistakes for correction rather than marking all errors, as this is very discouraging.
- Revise frequently and in different ways to help transfer information from short to long term memory. One third of each lesson should consist of revision.
- Allow students to demonstrate knowledge orally.
- All teaching should be multi-sensory. That is, students should see, hear and be able to touch or do something with the information being taught.
- Allow students to experience success and avoid tasks that may lead to failure. Don't ask your dyslexic student to do anything you are not sure they will be able to do.

Dyslexia and language learning

Learning a language can be broken down into two elements: comprehension (listening and reading) and production (speaking and writing). Normally, comprehension develops first and students require confidence in order to be able to produce spoken or written language. Dyslexic students find reading and writing particularly difficult. Thus slowing their production.

- Ask questions that only need a nod, simple action or a *yes/no*, *true/false* response to show understanding.
- Give new information in small chunks followed by plenty of practice.
- Keep written work to a minimum.
- English spelling is exceptionally difficult for dyslexic students. Accept a phonic equivalent of the word in written work and allow students to use wall displays, vocabulary lists and individual word cards for independent writing.
- Use objects and pictures as much as possible to teach vocabulary and grammar. Students will memorise more if they are able to see, touch, hold, wear, smell or even taste as appropriate.
- Use singing, chanting and rapping to practise vocabulary and grammar. These are particularly helpful as an aid to long term memory.
- Help students' listening comprehension by speaking slowly and in short chunks. When using recordings, pause and repeat frequently.
- When doing a listening comprehension, get students to use drawing instead of writing to indicate understanding (this is particularly useful for descriptions and stories).
- Help students' reading comprehension by underlining the main meaning-carrying words in a text. For listening comprehensions, give these words a slight emphasis.
- Students are likely to be most comfortable in pairs or small ability groups for reading and speaking activities.
- Don't expect production from your dyslexic students straight away.

Remember: The most significant factor affecting the learning of dyslexic students is their teacher's attitudes towards them and their difficulties.

Contents

LESSON	OBJECTIVES	GRAMMAR	COMMUNICATION
MODULE ONE: Me and my world			
1 **Where I live** *Pages 6–7*	• Talking about the place where you live	Present simple	**Vocabulary:** *Everyday actions and things* **Pronunciation:** *Tongue twister*
2 **Charlie's busy week** *Pages 8–9*	• Talking about future arrangements	Present continuous Possessive pronouns	**Vocabulary:** *Actions* **Pronunciation:** *Pronoun chant* **My English file:** *Plans for the week*
3 **The cheapest shirts in town** *Pages 10–11*	• Talking about and comparing your things	Comparative and superlative adjectives	**Vocabulary:** *Shopping*
4 **Looking after your pet** *Pages 12–13*	• Skills: general knowledge		**Reading:** *Pet quiz* **Listening:** *Finding missing words* **Speaking:** *Asking and answering questions* **Writing:** *Looking after your pet*
Module review	*Pages 14–15*		
Extra special *Pages 16–17*	• Mystery European adventure • **Mini-project:** *Me and my world*		
MODULE TWO: Playing games and sports			
5 **Sports day** *Pages 18–19*	• Talking about the past • Talking about sports	Past simple	**Vocabulary:** *Sports* **Pronunciation:** *Tongue twister*
6 **What were you doing?** *Pages 20–21*	• Describing past actions	Past continuous	**Vocabulary:** *Garden objects and actions* **Pronunciation:** *Weak forms of **was** and **were***
7 **Amazing stories** *Pages 22–23*	• Telling a story in the past	Past continuous and past simple	**Vocabulary:** *Everyday objects* **My English file:** *Your amazing story*
8 **My hero** *Pages 24–25*	• Skills: cross-cultural		**Reading:** *My hero* **Listening:** *Relaying information* **Speaking:** *Listening for mistakes* **Writing:** *My hero*
Module review	*Pages 26–27*		
Extra special *Pages 28–29*	• Mini-play • **Mini-project:** *Sports at my school*		

LESSON	OBJECTIVES	GRAMMAR	COMMUNICATION
MODULE THREE:	**Experiences and news**		
9 In my life *Pages 30–31*	• Talking about experiences	**Present perfect:** *ever, never*	**Vocabulary:** *Everyday objects and actions* **Pronunciation:** *-ed endings*
10 An amazing life *Pages 32–33*	• Talking about experiences you have had in your life	**Present perfect and past simple**	**Vocabulary:** *Everyday objects and actions* **Song:** *Have you Ever Seen the Rain?*
11 My latest news *Pages 34–35*	• Announcing news	**Present perfect:** *just* **Present perfect and past simple**	**Vocabulary:** *Email and text language* **My English file:** *My latest news*
12 Sumeo's story *Pages 36–37*	• Skills: cross-cultural		**Reading:** *Tuvalu fears* **Listening:** *Answering questions* **Speaking:** *Asking and answering questions* **Writing:** *Funafala*
Module review	*Pages 38–39*		
Extra special *Pages 40–41*	• What's just happened? • **Mini-project:** *My latest news …*		
MODULE FOUR:	**Dancing, acting, singing**		
13 The talent show *Pages 42–43*	• Making predictions	**Future predictions:** *will*	**Vocabulary:** *Talent show* **My English file:** *Predictions*
14 Helpful Herbert *Pages 44–45*	• Making offers and requests	**Requests:** *can, could* **Offers:** *will*	**Vocabulary:** *Musical instruments* **Pronunciation:** *Intonation of requests*
15 The festival *Pages 46–47*	• Making and responding to suggestions	**Suggestions:** *How about, let's, would you like to*	**Vocabulary:** *Entertainment*
16 The Brit School *Pages 48–49*	• Skills: cross-cultural		**Reading:** *The Brit School* **Listening:** *Finding missing words* **Speaking:** *Acting out an interview* **Writing:** *Why I want to go to the Brit School*
Module review	*Pages 50–51*		
Extra special *Pages 52–53*	• In the year 2030 • **Mini-project:** *Festival FactFile*		

LESSON	OBJECTIVES	GRAMMAR	COMMUNICATION
MODULE FIVE: Good advice			
17 How are you feeling? *Pages 54–55*	• Talking about illness • Talking about future possibilities	First conditional	**Vocabulary:** *Illness* **Pronunciation:** *Tongue twister*
18 I'm worried *Pages 56–57*	• Talking about possible events	**Possibility:** *may*	**Vocabulary:** *Camping objects* **My English file:** *Next school holiday*
19 You should say thank you *Pages 58–59*	• Giving advice • Talking about customs	**Obligation and advice:** *should/shouldn't*	**Vocabulary:** *Customs* **Song:** *I have a dream*
20 Survival *Pages 60–61*	• Skills: general knowledge		**Reading:** *What should you do?* **Listening:** *Finding missing words* **Speaking:** *Asking and answering questions* **Writing:** *Survival situation*
Module review	*Pages 62–63*		
Extra special *Pages 64–65*	• Round the world jigsaw • **Mini-project:** *How to keep fit*		
MODULE SIX: House and home			
21 DIY disasters *Pages 66–67*	• Talking about what is going to happen	**Future predictions:** *going to*	**Vocabulary:** *DIY objects, phrasal verbs*
22 My home *Pages 68–69*	• Talking about where you live	**Determiners:** *too much/too many (not) enough*	**Vocabulary:** *Everyday objects and places* **My English file:** *Where you live* **Pronunciation:** */uː/ and /ʌ/*
23 The eco-village *Pages 70–71*	• Using large numbers • Talking about processes	Present passive	**Vocabulary:** *Large numbers and processes*
24 The eco-family *Pages 72–73*	• Skills: cross-cultural		**Reading:** *My life* **Listening:** *Listening for mistakes* **Speaking:** *Acting out an interview* **Writing:** *Your unusual life*
Module review	*Pages 74–75*		
Extra special *Pages 76–77*	• Mini-play • **Mini-project:** *General knowledge quiz*		

LESSON	OBJECTIVES	GRAMMAR	COMMUNICATION
MODULE SEVEN: Travelling			
25 Rules of the road *Pages 78–79*	• Talking about rules • Giving directions	**Obligation:** *must/mustn't*	**Vocabulary:** *Road features and traffic signs*
26 My secret identity *Pages 80–81*	• Giving information about yourself and others	**Present perfect:** *for/since*	**Vocabulary:** *Personal information*
27 My amazing year *Pages 82–83*	• Describing recent experiences • Talking about future plans	**Present perfect** **Past simple** **Future plans:** *going to*	**Vocabulary:** *Everyday objects* **Pronunciation:** *Tongue twister* **My English file:** *This year and next year* **Song:** *We are the champions*
28 Amazing places *Pages 84–85*	• Skills: cross-cultural		**Reading:** *Holiday emails* **Listening:** *Listening for the correct word* **Speaking:** *Choosing a holiday* **Writing:** *Holiday email*
Module review	*Pages 86–87*		
Extra special *Pages 88–89*	• Hot Spot end of book quiz • Mini-project: *The important times in my life*		

Songs *Pages 90–91*	• **Module 3:** *Have You Ever Seen the Rain?* • **Module 5:** *I Have a Dream* • **Module 7:** *We are the Champions*
Extra reading *Pages 92–97*	• **Module 2:** *Robinson Crusoe* • **Module 4:** *The Adventures of Tom Sawyer* • **Module 6:** *Jane Eyre*

REFERENCE

Grammar summary
Pages 98–106

Word lists
Pages 107–111

1 Where I live

Lesson objective

Talking about the place where you live

1 Presentation

a 1.02 Listen and read. What is special about the places where Sun and Lukas live?

My name is Sun and I live in Dongguan County in China. People call Dongguan the *home of swimming* because many of China's top **divers** and swimmers come from here. There are good places to swim in the **creeks** along the Zhu River. Farmers sometimes swim to their fields because it is quicker than walking to the nearest bridge.

This is my e-pal Lukas. He lives in the Yukon in Canada and in the summer he sometimes sees bears in his garden. He always **claps** his hands when he leaves the house. He does this because bears usually walk away when they hear humans. Lukas doesn't have to worry in the winter because bears **hibernate** from October to April.

b Read again. Can you guess what the words in blue mean?

2 Comprehension

Read again. Answer these questions.

1 Dongguan County

1 Where does Sun live?
2 What do people call Dongguan?
3 Why do farmers sometimes swim to their fields?
4 Where does Lukas live?
5 What does Lukas sometimes see in his garden?
6 When do bears hibernate?

Grammar spot
Present simple

I **live** in Dongguan County in China.
Lukas **lives** in the Yukon in Canada.
What **do** people **call** Dongguan County?
Where **does** Lukas **live**?

Grammar page 98

1 Where I live

Grammar
- present simple; question words

Vocabulary
- everyday activities; lifestyles; countries

Optional materials
- bilingual dictionaries; timer or stopwatch

Optional Activity Book activities
- Fast finishers p60, Extra practice p61

Photocopiable activity
- *Getting to know you* p102

PART 1

Teaching tip: *The first lesson*

The first lesson is very important as the foundation of the whole course. You may consider the following suggestions for first lesson activities and procedures:

- If you are teaching a new class, introduce yourself and say a few things about your hobbies, family and pets in English. Encourage students to do the same. Allow two minutes for each introduction, using an egg timer or stopwatch if necessary.
- Inform students about the rules and procedures in the classroom, e.g. taking attendance, collecting homework, tests, discipline etc.
- Introduce students to the Student's Book and summarise the material they are going to be studying in the school year.
- Play a few whole class games, e.g. *Find somebody who* … Choose activities that students of all abilities are able to complete successfully, so that they develop a positive attitude.

Introduction

Ask students to stand in a circle. Name a country, e.g. *Australia*. The first student names one thing they associate with this country, e.g. *a kangaroo* and says the name of another country, e.g. *The USA* for the second student to make their association. The second student then adds another country and so on round the circle. Students are not allowed to repeat any countries.

1 Presentation

a) [1.02] Point to the first picture and introduce Sun to students. Ask them to guess where she lives on the basis of the large photo. Then introduce Sun's friend, Lukas, and ask students to guess where he lives. Do not reveal the answers yet. Play the CD and ask students to follow the text in their books to check their predictions and find out what is special about the places where the teenagers live. Elicit the answers, allowing students to select the facts they find the most special.

Tapescript
see Student's Book Activity 1a

b) Ask students to read the text again and try to guess the meaning of the words in bold from the context. Elicit the students' ideas and provide explanation if necessary. Explain any other words students do not understand, using the photos, mime or giving definitions.

Elicit or explain, using L1 if necessary, that *hibernation* is a deep sleep that helps animals save energy and survive the winter when food is difficult to find. During hibernation the body temperature drops and breathing slows down to save energy coming from body fat.

2 Comprehension

Students read the questions. Then they read the text in Activity 1a again to find the answers. Students compare their answers in pairs. Check the answers with the whole class.

Mixed-ability classes
Fast finishers check how many things they can name in the photos in Activity 1a.

Extra activity
Ask the class the following questions: *What is the name of the region where you live? What is the region famous for?* Elicit students' ideas. Teach students the English name of their region if there is one.

Tapescript
see Activity 1

Answer key
1 Dongguan County (in China) **2** the home of swimming **3** because it's quicker (than walking to the nearest bridge) **4** the Yukon (in Canada) **5** bears **6** in winter/from October to April

Grammar spot
Ask students to read the example sentences and questions. Then review the use and form of the present simple, which was introduced in *Hot Spot Student's Book 1 and 2.*
Ask students to find more examples of the present simple in Activity 1 and Activity 2. Point out the position of adverbs of frequency *always, usually* and *sometimes* within a sentence in the present simple. Refer students to the **Grammar summary** on page 98 for more information on the present simple.

Cultural information
Dongguan is located in the Zhu (Pearl) River Delta in the south of China. Criss-crossed with water canals and reservoirs, it was originally a farming area producing rice, lychees, bananas and seafood. In the last few decades, Dongguan's industry has been expanding rapidly, making Dongguan a rich and populous city and county.
The Yukon is a territory in the north-west of Canada. Its climate is arctic with long cold winters. The main attractions are Aurora Borealis/the Northern Lights, dog sledding, kayaking and viewing the wildlife, including bears and moose.

3 Grammar practice

a Make questions with *do* or *does*.

1 Where ____ Sun live?
2 Where ____ you come from?
3 What ____ bears do in winter?
4 Where ____ your friends go swimming?
5 Why ____ Lukas not have to worry about bears in winter?

b Then ask and answer with a classmate.

Where does Sun live?

She lives in Dongguan County.

Remember!
Remember the -(e)s!

Where do you live?
I live in …

Where do**es** he live?
He live**s** in …

4 Class poll

a What is special about where you live? Work in a small group and write ideas. Use a dictionary to help with new vocabulary. Then write your ideas on the board.

There is a big forest and lots of sawmills.
Lots of people work on farms.
You can sometimes see deer.

b What are the best three ideas? Vote with your classmates.

5 Pronunciation

a 1.03 Listen to this tongue twister.

/h/
Hedgehogs have to hibernate in their homes but humans have houses and don't have to.

b 1.04 Listen again and repeat. How fast can you say it?

6 Listening

a 1.05 Listen to Rachel. Is her life different from yours?

My name's Rachel and I'm Amish.

b 1.05 Listen again. Then write answers to the questions below. Use the words in the box.

the USA   a simple, traditional life
horse-drawn buggies   on their farms
TVs, computers and mobile phones

1 Rachel lives in the USA.

1 Where does Rachel live?
2 What kind of life do Amish people like?
3 What have they not got?
4 How do they travel?
5 How do they help their neighbours?

7 Check your English

a How much can you remember? Make sentences with the present simple.

1 Sun (live) …
2 People (call) Dongguan …
3 Lukas (live) …
4 Lukas (not worry) …
5 The Amish people (live) …
6 The Amish people (travel) …

b Do these things:

1 Write the name of a top diver or swimmer.
2 Draw a creek.
3 Clap your hands.
4 Think of two animals that hibernate.
5 Think of the name of one of your neighbours.
6 Think of something traditional in your country.

❸ Grammar practice

a) Refer students to the **Remember!** box to review the different form for the third person singular.

Complete the first question with the whole class as an example. Students complete the remaining questions individually.

b) Read out the example dialogue with a confident student. Then students ask and answer the questions in pairs. Ask a pair of students to repeat their dialogue to the whole class.

Answer key

1 does/She lives in Dongguan County. **2** do/students' own answers **3** do/hibernate **4** do/students' own answers **5** does/ He doesn't have to worry about bears in winter, because they hibernate from October to April.

Dyslexia tip: *Ending the lesson*

Dyslexic students are often distracted, especially towards the end of the lesson. It is useful to devote the last few minutes to reviewing the key issues students have studied in the lesson. If you decide to assign homework, do it orally and get the whole class to repeat it chorally. Then ask three different students, including dyslexic students, to repeat the assignment before you write it on the board for students to copy.

Homework suggestions

1 Activity Book page 4-5, Activities 1-3

2 Students write three questions to ask their classmates about the house where they live, their street and their neighbours. They can ask and answer the questions in pairs at the beginning of the next lesson.

PART 2

Introduction

Divide students into groups of five. Write the following topics on the board: *food, meals, houses, work, school, sports, transport.* Ask students to come up with at least three things which surprise them about foreign countries they visit or see on TV. Students can use the topics on the board or their own ideas, e.g. *In Thailand people eat rice soup for breakfast* or *In Ireland people drive on the left.* Elicit the groups' ideas and ask students what they think foreigners find surprising about their own country.

❹ Class poll

a) Divide the class into groups of four. They should write down what is special about their town or region. Go through the example before they begin writing. Distribute dictionaries to look up new words. Set a time limit of five minutes.

b) Elicit different groups' ideas onto the board. Read them out and get students to vote for the best three ideas by raising their hands. Each student can vote for three ideas only. Count the votes and announce the winners.

Extra activity

In pairs, students imagine that a foreign exchange student is going to visit them for a weekend. They write an itinerary for his/ her visit, including any special local customs or attractions.

❺ Pronunciation

a) [1.03] Ask students: *What's the difference between a house and a home?* If necessary, explain that *a house* is a building, whereas *a home* is a place where someone lives permanently with their family.

Explain that in some languages we do not pronounce the initial sound /h/, but in English we nearly always pronounce it when it is the first sound of the word. Exceptions include *hour* and *honest*.

Play the CD and ask students to follow the tongue twister in their books.

Tapescript

see Student's Book Activity 5a

b) [1.04] Play the CD again and ask students to repeat the tongue twister. Then encourage them to practise saying the tongue twister as fast as they can.

Tapescript

see Activity 5a

❻ Listening

[1.05] Introduce Rachel. Explain that the larger photo shows how people in her community live. Ask the class to make guesses about their lives.

Play the CD for students to check their guesses. Then ask them to write the answers to the questions, using the words in the box. Point to the photo to explain *horse-drawn buggies.* Students compare their answers in pairs before you check them with the whole class.

Tapescript

My name's Rachel and I'm Amish. I live in the USA but I'm different to many American children. Amish people like to live a simple, traditional life and we haven't got things like TVs, computers and mobile phones. We also haven't got cars. We travel in horse-drawn buggies! Many Amish people are farmers and I spend a lot of time helping my parents on the farm. We also like to help our neighbours. Our neighbours come to our farm to help us and we go to their farms to help them.

Answer key

1 Rachel lives in the USA.
2 Amish people like a simple, traditional life.
3 They haven't got TVs, computers and mobile phones.
4 They travel in horse-drawn buggies.
5 They help their neighbours on their farms.

❼ Check your English

a) Students make present simple sentences about the places and people from the lesson and compare their answers in pairs. Check the answers with the whole class.

Answer key

1 Sun lives in Dongguan County in China. **2** People call Dongguan the 'home of swimming'. **3** Lukas lives in the Yukon in Canada. **4** Lukas does not have to worry about the bears in winter (because they hibernate). **5** The Amish people live in the USA. **6** The Amish people travel in horse-drawn buggies.

b) Students read the instructions and complete the task. Individual students demonstrate their answers to the whole class.

Answer key

students' own answers

Photocopiable activity

Getting to know you, p102; instructions p92

Homework suggestions

1 Activity Book page 5, Activities 4-6

2 Students write the top five things they miss about their home and hometown when they go on holiday.

2 Charlie's busy week

1 Presentation

a 1.06 Listen and read. Today is Monday. When are Charlie and his friends practising the sketch?

Mel Here are the scripts. This is yours, Charlie, and this is mine. So when can we practise the sketch?
Charlie Let's see. I'll look in my diary on my mobile.
Sophie How about tomorrow after school?
Charlie No, I'm sorry, I can't. I'm seeing the dentist on Tuesday.
Mel Okay. Are you free on Wednesday?
Charlie No, I'm going out with my family. We're going to the cinema.
Sophie Right. How about on Thursday?
Charlie Let's see. No, I'm afraid not. My sister's playing netball for the school team on Thursday and I'm watching the match.
Mel So that leaves Friday. Are you free on Friday?
Charlie Let's see. Oh no! We're going away for the weekend on Friday and we aren't coming back until Sunday night.
Sophie But that's terrible! We're performing the sketch in class next Monday.
Charlie How about now?
Mel What? You're free now?
Charlie Yes.
Sophie Great! Let's practise the sketch right now. We haven't got a moment to lose.

b 1.06 Listen again. Then read the dialogue with your classmates.

Real English

Let's see.
How about tomorrow?
No, I'm afraid not.
We haven't got a moment to lose.

2 Comprehension

When is Charlie doing what? Match the words in A with the times in B.

1 seeing the dentist – Tuesday

	A		B
1	seeing the dentist	a	Sunday night
2	going to the cinema	b	Wednesday
3	watching netball	c	Friday
4	going away	d	right now
5	coming back	e	next Monday
6	performing the sketch	f	Thursday
7	practising the sketch	g	Tuesday

2 Charlie's busy week

Grammar
- present continuous for future arrangements; possessive pronouns; demonstrative pronouns *this, these*

Vocabulary
- days of the week; everyday activities

Optional materials
- one Post-it™ note per student

Optional Activity Book activities
- Fast finishers p62, Extra practice p63

Photocopiable activity
- *Plans* p103

PART 1

Introduction

Review the days of the week. Then ask students to work in pairs and test each other on how many times they can say the days of the week backwards, i.e. *Sunday, Saturday, Friday, etc.* within two minutes.

Dyslexia tip: *Seating plan*

A lot of dyslexic students have problems concentrating if there is a lot of noise and visual clutter. It is best to seat them away from windows and the door. Seats in rows with the focus on the teacher often work better for dyslexic students than other arrangements with students facing their classmates. Some students will benefit from sitting right in front of the teacher's desk, but others are distracted by classmates behind them, so you need to seat them at the back of the classroom.

1 Presentation

a) [1.06] Introduce the characters in the picture: Charlie, Mel and Sophie. Explain that they are classmates and they have to perform a sketch together. Elicit or explain that a *sketch* is a short, humorous play. Point out that it is Monday in the story. Ask students to listen to the dialogue and find out when the three friends are practising the sketch. Play the CD through.

Elicit that the characters are practising the sketch right now. Find out if students can guess the meaning of the following words: *netball, free, until, in class, right now.* Provide explanation if necessary.

Refer students to the **Grammar spot** at the top of the next page and elicit or explain the present continuous for future arrangements. Go over the examples and point out the time expressions referring to the future.
Remind students that we can also use *to be going to* to talk about future plans, but the present continuous describes arrangements which have already been fixed. Then tell the class one of your personal future arrangements, e.g. *I'm meeting a friend this evening,* and encourage them to ask questions about it, e.g. *Which friend are you meeting?*

Refer students to the **Grammar summary** on page 98 for more information on the present continuous for future arrangements.

Point to **Real English.** Demonstrate the meaning of the phrases by asking students to do different tasks and getting them to choose a phrase to respond with, e.g. *Can you clean the classroom windows tomorrow? (I'm afraid not/Let's see); There's a fire in the building, you need to leave now (We haven't got a moment to lose).* To practise *How about (tomorrow)?* explain that you are very busy and you cannot find the time to exercise next week. Get individual students to suggest different times when you could do sports, e.g. *How about tomorrow/Saturday morning?* Give true or false excuses, using the present continuous.

Tapescript
see Student's Book Activity 1a

b) [1.06] Play the CD again. Divide students into groups of three and ask them to read the dialogue aloud, each student taking one role. Students then read the dialogue again, changing roles.

Extra activity

Ask students if they perform plays or sketches in class or as part of their extracurricular activities. If any students answer *yes*, ask them to share their experiences with the whole class, e.g. how long it takes them to learn the text, how often they practise with other members of the cast, if they are afraid to perform, etc.

2 Comprehension

Students match Charlie's future arrangements in box **A** with the times in box **B**. Allow them to look at the dialogue in Activity 1a to help them with the task. Check the answers with the whole class.

Mixed-ability classes

Fast finishers rank the plans in box A 1–7 from the most to the least exciting ones, in their opinion.

Answer key

1 seeing the dentist – Tuesday
2 going to the cinema – Wednesday
3 watching netball – Thursday
4 going away – Friday
5 coming back – Sunday night
6 performing the sketch – next Monday
7 practising the sketch – right now

Grammar spot
Present continuous for future arrangements

I'**m seeing** the dentist on Tuesday.
My sister'**s playing** netball for the school team on Thursday.
What **are** you **doing** on Wednesday?
I'**m going out** with my family.

Grammar page 98

3 Grammar practice

a Write questions using the present continuous.

1 When is Charlie seeing the dentist?

1 When/Charlie/see the dentist?
2 When/Charlie and his family/go/to the cinema?
3 When/Charlie's sister/play/netball?
4 When/Charlie and his family/go/away for the weekend?
5 When/they/come/back?
6 When/Mel, Charlie and Sophie/practise/their sketch?
7 When/they/perform/their sketch?

b Now ask and answer the questions.

When is Charlie seeing the dentist?

He's seeing the dentist on Tuesday.

4 Speaking

a Invent some plans for the week. Choose one day when you don't have any plans. Don't show your classmate.

Monday – I'm meeting my friends.
Tuesday – I'm watching TV.
Wednesday – I'm going to the park.
Thursday –
Friday – I'm doing my homework.
Saturday – I'm shopping.
Sunday – I'm visiting my grandparents.

b Now find out which day your classmate is free. Ask and answer questions.

Are you free on Friday?

No, I'm not. I'm doing my homework.

How about on Monday?

No, I'm afraid not. I'm meeting my friends.

5 Pronunciation

a 1.07 Listen to this chant.

I've got yours and you've got mine.

She's got his and he's got hers.

We've got theirs and they've got ours.

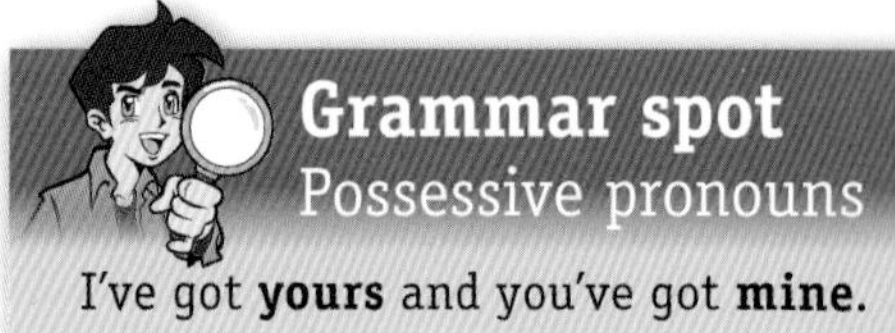

b 1.07 Listen again and repeat. Notice the intonation of speech.

Grammar spot
Possessive pronouns

I've got **yours** and you've got **mine**.

Grammar page 98

My English file

Write about your true plans for the rest of the week.

I'm playing basketball tomorrow.
I'm going shopping on Saturday morning.

6 Check your English

a Complete with the present continuous of these verbs.

help hang out wash go watch do have

A: What [1]_____ you _____ this evening?
B: I [2]_____ a shower and [3]_____ my hair. And then my sister and I [4]_____ our favourite TV programme at nine o'clock.
What about you? Are you [5]_____ with your friends?
B: No, I'm not. My brother [6]_____ away tomorrow and I [7]_____ him get ready.

b Collect things from your classmates and put them on a desk. Can you remember who the things belong to? Make sentences.

This is his.

These are theirs.

❸ Grammar practice

a) Go through the example. Ask students to write questions in the present continuous, using the prompts. Students compare their answers in pairs. Ask individual students to read out the questions.

Answer key

see Activity 3b

b) Read out the example dialogue with a confident student. In pairs, students ask and answer questions from Activity 3a about the characters from the dialogue in Activity 1a. Encourage them to respond in full sentences.

Answer key

1 When is Charlie seeing the dentist? He's seeing the dentist on Tuesday. **2** When are Charlie and his family going to the cinema? They're going to the cinema on Wednesday. **3** When is Charlie's sister playing netball? She's playing netball on Thursday. **4** When are Charlie and his family going away for the weekend? They're going away on Friday. **5** When are they coming back? They're coming back on Sunday night. **6** When are Mel, Charlie and Sophie practising their sketch? They're practising their sketch right now. **7** When are they performing their sketch? They're performing their sketch next Monday.

Homework suggestions

1. Activity Book page 6, Activities 1-2
2. Students imagine what Sophie from Activity 1 is doing this week and write seven sentences about her arrangements, using the present continuous.

PART 2

Introduction

Give each student a Post-it™ note. They should draw pictures of two activities they are doing after school today, e.g. a computer screen to represent *surfing the Internet* and a little child with blocks to show *playing with my little brother.* Students stick the Post-it™ notes to their fronts, get up and mingle. They look at their classmates' drawings and try to identify the activities by asking, e.g. *Are you writing emails after school today?* Set a time limit of five minutes. Then students should form groups with people who have similar plans.

Teaching tip: *Mingling*

Mingling is a way of organising pairwork in which students stand up and walk around, interacting with other students in turn, one at a time, usually to ask and answer questions. If you have a large class, you can do a mingling activity in groups, with students remaining seated. Another way is to have students mingle with students in their row, if they are sitting in rows. Set a time limit for mingling activities so that students keep their conversations short and try to speak to as many different students as possible.

❹ Speaking

a) Students invent different plans for themselves for the week and leave one day without a plan. They should not show their plans to their classmates. Go through the example first.

b) Divide the class into pairs. They ask each other questions about the plans from Activity 4a to find when their classmate is free. The student who finds out the answer using fewer questions than their partner wins the game. Demonstrate the task by reading out the example with a confident student.

Photocopiable activity

Plans p103; instructions p92

❺ Pronunciation

a) [1.07] Focus students' attention on the pictures and play the CD. Refer students to the **Grammar spot** to explain possessive pronouns. Make sure students understand that unlike possessive adjectives, possessive pronouns are not followed by nouns. You may wish to review possessive adjectives to contrast them with possessive pronouns, e.g. *my–mine, your–yours*, etc.

Demonstrate the pronouns by picking up objects belonging to yourself and various students and saying, e.g. *This notebook is mine; These glasses are yours.* Then repeat the procedure silently and elicit the sentences from the whole class. Refer students to the **Grammar summary** on page 98 for more information on possessive pronouns.

Tapescript

see Student's Book Activity 5a

b) [1.07] Play the CD again and ask students to repeat the sentences. Then students close their books and try to repeat the sentences from memory.

Tapescript

see Activity 5a

My English file

Students write at least five sentences in the present continuous about their true plans for the rest of the week. Go through the examples first. Set a time limit of six minutes. Monitor students' work, providing help.

When students have finished the task, they exchange their notebooks in pairs and read each other's sentences.

Extra activity

Students copy their sentences from **My English file** and add two false sentences to the list of plans. In different pairs, students exchange their sentences and try to guess which two are false.

❻ Check your English

a) Students match the verbs to the gaps and write them in the present continuous form, adding the correct form of the verb *be*. They compare their answers in pairs before you check them with the whole class.

Answer key

1 are (you) doing **2** 'm having **3** I'm washing **4** are watching **5** hanging out **6** is going **7** 'm helping

b) A volunteer collects small objects from classmates and puts them on your desk. Individual students take turns to come to the desk, choose five objects and identify who they belong to, using possessive pronouns. Go through the example first.

Homework suggestions

1. Activity Book page 7, Activities 3-5
2. Students imagine that they are journalists and want to interview their favourite celebrity who is very busy. They write a phone conversation in which they try to arrange a meeting with the celebrity. They should use the dialogue in Activity 4b as a model.

3 The cheapest shirts in town

1 Guessing

Look at the pictures. Choose the correct words.

1 The boy wants *to buy some jeans/to buy a shirt.* 2 He *wants to/doesn't want to* buy a cheap shirt.

2 Presentation

a 1.08 Listen and read. Which shirt does Oscar buy?

1

Oscar	Phoebe, do you like this shirt?
Phoebe	No. I don't like the pattern.
Oscar	But look. They're the cheapest shirts in town!
Phoebe	Yes, but they look horrible.

2

Phoebe	What about these?
Oscar	Yes, but how much are they?
Phoebe	They're £29.
Oscar	£29! They're much more expensive than the shirts in the sale.
Phoebe	Yes, but these shirts are much nicer.

3

Phoebe	What about these? They're cheaper than the blue shirts.
Oscar	What size are they?
Phoebe	They're large.
Oscar	No, those shirts are too big.

4

Oscar	Come on, Phoebe. I'm going to buy this. It's the right size and the right price.
Phoebe	But you can't buy that! It's the same as the shirt you've got on!
Oscar	Yes, and I like the shirt I've got on – that's why I'm buying it.

Real English

They're large.
It's the right size and the right price.

b 1.08 Listen again. Then read the dialogue with a classmate.

3 The cheapest shirts in town

Grammar
- comparative and superlative adjectives; adverb *much* with comparative adjectives; demonstrative pronouns *this, that, these, those*

Vocabulary
- shopping; clothes; colours; adjectives

Optional Activity Book activities
- Fast finishers p64, Extra practice p65

Photocopiable activity
- *Clothes* p104

PART 1

Introduction

Ask students to imagine that an English family is moving to their town/district/area and they want to know the best places to shop for the following products: fruit and vegetables, groceries, clothes and cosmetics. In groups of four, students discuss which places in their town or their area they can recommend, including reasons. Set a time limit of four minutes. Elicit suggestions from all the groups.

❶ Guessing

Ask students to study the pictures in Activity 2 and make guesses about what is happening in them. Then students read the sentences and choose the correct phrase to describe the situation in the pictures. Check the answers with the whole class.

Answer key

1 The boy wants to buy a shirt. **2** He wants to buy a cheap shirt.

❷ Presentation

a) [1.08] Introduce Oscar and Phoebe, using the pictures. Elicit that they are shopping for clothes. Ask students to listen and read the dialogue to find out which shirt Oscar buys. Play the CD.

Elicit that Oscar buys a shirt which is the same as he is wearing. Check if students know or can guess the meaning of the following words and phrases: *pattern, in the sale, too big, the same as, the shirt you've got on.* If necessary, provide explanation. Elicit or explain that prices in the shop are in British pounds.

Make sure students understand what Phoebe and Oscar mean when they use *this, that, these, those,* e.g. *What about these?* = the blue shirts (under picture 2). Explain that the characters do not say the nouns because they know which shirts the other person is talking about.

Point out that *this/that* and *these/those* refer to singular and plural nouns respectively. Elicit or explain that we use *this/these* when we stand close to the object/objects and *that/those* when we are further away from the object/objects.

Point to **Real English** and draw large jeans on the board with a label reading *L* to demonstrate *They're large.* Then point to a well-fitting item of clothing you are wearing, invent a reasonable price you paid for it and say: *It's the right size and the right price.*

Refer students to the **Grammar spot** and the **Remember!** box on the next page to review the comparative and the superlative of adjectives, which students practised in *Hot Spot Student's Book 2,* and point out that we can use *much* to make comparatives stronger. Go through the examples and elicit the rules for comparatives and superlatives of one syllable or two syllable adjectives ending in *-y* and two syllable or longer adjectives. Refer students to the **Grammar summary** on page 99 for more information on comparatives and superlatives.

Extra activity

Elicit onto the board the different sizes that appear on T-shirt labels: XS, S, M, L, XL. Explain that they stand for *extra small, small, medium, large and extra large.*

Tapescript

see Student's Book Activity 2a

b) [1.08] Play the CD again. Students read the dialogue in pairs twice, changing roles.

Mixed-ability classes

Fast finishers cover the text and invent their own version of the dialogue between Phoebe and Oscar using their own ideas.

Dyslexia tip: *Alternatives to reading aloud*

Dyslexic students may display various erratic behaviours when reading aloud, e.g. omission of words, reading one word at a time, substituting words or inappropriate sounds for letters, reversing sounds within a syllable, reading in a flat way without understanding the text, repeating the same sentences, etc. It can be frustrating and embarrassing for them to read aloud in front of their classmates. Instead, you can put a dyslexic student with a pair/group of non dyslexic students reading a dialogue aloud and ask him/her to perform one of the following alternative tasks:

- take the role of a narrator and introduce each scene before the other classmates read their parts
- listen and then summarize orally the text that has been read
- present his/her opinion on the text having listened to it
- give feedback to the classmates on their performance.

Cultural information

The British currency is the pound sterling = GBP (Great British Pound). Its symbol is £. The pound is divided into 100 pence. The singular of *pence* is *penny.* The symbol for the penny is *p* and an amount of 60p is pronounced *sixty* /pi:/ rather than *sixty pence.* English banknotes are accepted throughout the UK. Scotland and Northern Ireland issue their own banknotes which can be used within these countries respectively, but only Bank of England notes are accepted as legal tender in other countries of the UK.

Tapescript

see Activity 2a

3 Comprehension

Answer these questions about the dialogue in Activity 2.

1 Why doesn't Phoebe like the yellow shirt?
2 Why doesn't Oscar like the blue shirt?
3 What's wrong with the green shirt?
4 Why does Oscar like the brown shirt?

Grammar spot
Comparative/superlative

Comparative
These shirts are **cheaper** than the blue shirts.
These shirts are **more expensive** than the shirts in the sale.

Superlative
These are **the cheapest** shirts in town.
These are **the most expensive** shirts in town.

We can make comparatives stronger with **much**:
These shirts are **much** nicer.

Grammar page 99

4 Grammar practice

a Look at the pictures and make sentences using the comparative.

1 The yellow ball is bigger than the white ball.

1 yellow ball/white ball (big)
2 yellow ball/brown ball (small)
3 brown vase/green vase (cheap)
4 green vase/orange vase (expensive)

b Look at the pictures again and make sentences using the superlative.

1 The white ball is the smallest.

1 white ball (small)
2 brown ball (big)
3 brown vase (cheap)
4 green vase (expensive)

Remember!

The spelling changes in comparative and superlative adjectives:

big	bi**gg**er	bi**gg**est
tid**y**	tid**i**er	tid**i**est

5 Speaking

Make true sentences about things in the classroom with:

more interesting/most interesting
smaller/smallest older/oldest nicer/nicest
more comfortable/most comfortable
worse/worst tidier/tidiest messier/messiest
more beautiful/most beautiful better/best

This book is more interesting than this book.

6 Check your English

Complete the sentences about these T-shirts. Use the comparative or the superlative of the adjectives in brackets.

1 The red T-shirt is _____ than the green T-shirt. (expensive)
2 The green T-shirt is _____ than the blue T-shirt. (cheap)
3 The blue T-shirt is the _____ (big).
4 The green T-shirt is the _____ (small).
5 The blue T-shirt is the _____ (expensive).

❸ Comprehension

Students answer the questions about the dialogue in Activity 2a. Then they compare their answers in pairs. Check the answers with the whole class.

Extra activity

In pairs, students discuss which shirt in the pictures they think is the best and explain their reasons.

Answer key

1. (She thinks) it looks horrible.
2. Because it is much more expensive than the shirt in the sale.
3. It is too big.
4. It is the right size and the right price/the same as the shirt he has got on.

Homework suggestions

1. Activity Book pages 8-9, Activities 1-4
2. Students imagine they are shopping for clothes with their friend and write their dialogue, using Activity 2a as a model. They can illustrate the dialogue with drawings or pictures of clothes cut out from magazines.

PART 2

Introduction

Write the following sentences on the board and ask students to complete them so that two are true and one is false for them:

The oldest object in my house is …
The most unusual object in my house is …
The largest object in my house is …

In groups of four, students take turns to read out their sentences for their classmates to guess which one is false. Then they themselves correct the false sentence. Groups share the most interesting answers with the whole class.

❹ Grammar practice

a) Students look at the picture and make comparative sentences about the balls and the vases, using the prompts. Go through the example first. If necessary, refer students to the **Grammar spot**. Encourage students to use *much* to make comparatives stronger.

Refer students to the **Remember!** box to explain the spelling changes of one syllable adjectives with a consonant-vowel-consonant pattern and two syllable adjectives ending in *-y* in the comparative and the superlative. Go through the example before students begin writing. Students compare their answers in pairs. Individual students read out their sentences.

Extra activity

Divide students into groups of four and ask them to write down the names of two countries. Students take turns to make sentences comparing the two countries, e.g. their size, weather, people. Each student makes at least one sentence.

Answer key

1. The yellow ball is bigger than the white ball.
2. The yellow ball is smaller than the brown ball.
3. The brown vase is cheaper than the green vase.
4. The green vase is more expensive than the orange vase.

b) Students make superlative sentences about the objects in Activity 4a.

When students have compared their answers in pairs, ask individual students to read out their sentences.

Answer key

1. The white ball is the smallest.
2. The brown ball is the biggest.
3. The brown vase is the cheapest.
4. The green vase is the most expensive.

❺ Speaking

In groups of three, students make true comparative and superlative sentences about different objects in the classroom, using the adjectives provided. Make sure students understand all the adjectives. Monitor their work. Elicit sentences for each adjective from different groups.

Mixed-ability classes

For less confident students write on the board the objects they can talk about using each adjective, e.g. *messier/messiest – desk, nicer/nicest – poster.*

Extra activity

Think of an object in the classroom. Students try to guess which object you have on your mind by asking up to ten *Yes/No* questions with comparative adjectives, e.g. *Is it bigger than the blackboard? Is it heavier than the chair?* If they cannot guess, reveal the object. Students repeat the game in groups of four, taking turns to think of an object.

Teaching tip: *Turn taking*

In group activities students often interrupt each other or they lose track of whose turn it is to speak. You can help students wait patiently and remember or decide whose turn it is by using a visual and tactile reminder, e.g. a rubber ball. Only the person holding the object can talk and when they have finished, they pass the ball to the person sitting next to them or roll the ball to a group member of their choice. Students should make sure that everyone has a chance to speak in their group so they can raise their hand if they have already spoken. If you see someone is talking for too long, make eye contact with them and place your finger over your mouth to signal it is someone else's turn to speak.

❻ Check your English

Students complete the sentences about the picture with the adjectives in brackets in the comparative or the superlative. Students compare their answers in pairs. Individual students read their sentences to the whole class.

Answer key

1. more expensive
2. cheaper
3. biggest
4. smallest
5. most expensive

Photocopiable activity

Clothes p104; instructions p92

Homework suggestions

1. Activity Book page 9, Activities 5-7
2. Students write sentences in which they compare three different cars, TV programmes or celebrities of their choice, using comparative and superlative adjectives.

4 Looking after your pet

1 Reading

a 1.09 Listen and read the quiz. Find these words. Do you know or can you guess what they mean?

treat bone aquarium sawdust stroke swish teach mice feed

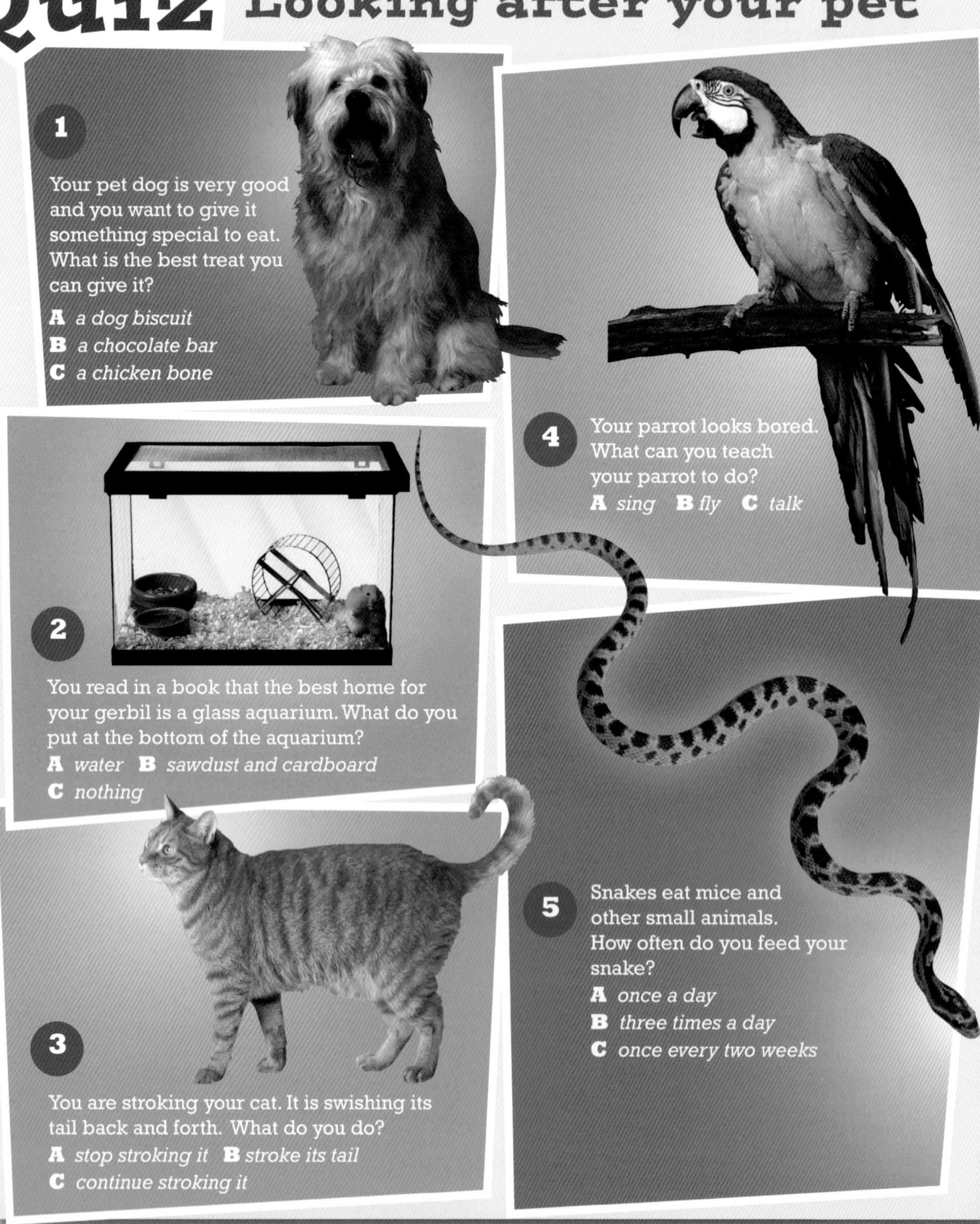

Quiz Looking after your pet

1 Your pet dog is very good and you want to give it something special to eat. What is the best treat you can give it?

A *a dog biscuit*
B *a chocolate bar*
C *a chicken bone*

2 You read in a book that the best home for your gerbil is a glass aquarium. What do you put at the bottom of the aquarium?

A *water* **B** *sawdust and cardboard*
C *nothing*

3 You are stroking your cat. It is swishing its tail back and forth. What do you do?

A *stop stroking it* **B** *stroke its tail*
C *continue stroking it*

4 Your parrot looks bored. What can you teach your parrot to do?

A *sing* **B** *fly* **C** *talk*

5 Snakes eat mice and other small animals. How often do you feed your snake?

A *once a day*
B *three times a day*
C *once every two weeks*

b Now complete the quiz. Write your answers.

4 Looking after your pet

Photocopiable activity
- *What's my word?* p105

PART 1

Introduction

Divide the class into five groups. Give each group one of the following verbs: *fly, jump, swim, run, bite.* Groups make a list of pets which can do their activity, e.g. *fly – parrot, budgerigar, beetle, dove, pigeon.* Help with English translation of the names if necessary. Set a time limit of three minutes and ask the groups to read out their lists. Get students to raise their hand if they hear a pet they have or had in the past.

1 Reading

a) [1.09] Focus attention on the pictures in the quiz. Elicit the names of the pets and ask students if they know how to look after these pets. Explain that they can test their knowledge by completing the quiz, but they first need to make sure they understand all the questions. Ask students to read the words in the box. They should listen and read the quiz to find the words in the box and try to guess their meaning. Play the CD.

Students compare their ideas in pairs. Check the answers with the whole class and drill the pronunciation of the words.

Ask students if they know/can guess the meaning of the following phrases: *at the bottom, back and forth, once every two weeks.* Provide explanation if necessary.

Extra activity

Students write their own sentences with the words in the box.

Tapescript

see Student's Book Activity 1a

b) Ask students to read the quiz again and choose the correct answers. Do not check the answers at this stage.

Mixed-ability classes

Put fast finishers in groups to discuss why they have chosen their answers, e.g. 1A – because a dog biscuit is the healthiest.

Extra activity

Divide students into groups of four. Students say who out of all the people they personally know has the friendliest/the most unusual/the most aggressive pet and describe the pets briefly. Groups share the most interesting answers with the whole class.

Teaching tip: *Multiple choice questions*

Teach students the following strategies for taking multiple choice quizzes or tests:

- read through the text quickly and answer the easiest questions first
- read through the text again and answer more difficult questions
- you may cover the answers, read the questions and try to answer them yourself. Then choose the option that matches your own answer the best
- you can treat the optional answers as true or false, read each of them and decide which one is true
- remember that you are looking for the best answer, it does not have to be true all the time in all circumstances without exceptions
- eliminate the incorrect answers
- always guess when there is no penalty for wrong answers
- read through the text once more to review both questions and the answers.

2 Listening

a 1.10 Listen to the answers to the quiz. Are your answers correct?

b 1.10 Listen again. What are the missing words?

1 Chicken bones are too s_____ and d_____.
2 Gerbils can make nests under the s_____ and c_____.
3 Cats are feeling a_____ or u_____ when they swish their t_____.
4 R_____ the same w_____ everyday until your parrot can s_____ it.
5 Don't f_____ your snake m_____ often than this.

3 Speaking

a Think of a pet animal and write the name on a piece of paper. Don't show your classmates.

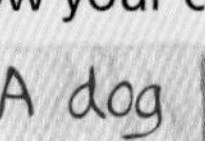

b Guess what your classmate's pet animal is. Ask questions with *Do ...? Is ...? Can ...? Has ...?*

Do you give your pet biscuits?

Yes, I do.

Is your pet bigger than a mouse?

4 Writing

a Read below. Can you guess what kind of animal it is?

> **Looking after my pet**
>
> I talk to him every day.
> I clean his cage every week.
> I feed him small pieces of fruit and seeds.
> I give him fresh water every day.
> I put toys in his cage.

b Now choose an animal and write about how you look after it. Then get your classmates to guess what animal it is.

> Looking after my pet
>
> I feed her once a day.
> I give her biscuits and pet food.
> I take her for a walk twice a day.

Who am I? game

Play with your classmates.

1 Think of a famous person.

2 Write the person's name on a piece of paper.

3 Your classmates have 20 questions to guess who you are.

4 Answer their questions with short answers.

❷ Listening

a) [1.10] Students listen to the answers to the quiz in Activity 1 and check if their own answers were correct. Play the CD. Award students one point for each correct answer. Find out who scored the most points.

Tapescript and Answer key

1 The best treat for your dog is *a)* a dog biscuit. Chocolate is bad for dogs. Chicken bones are too small and dangerous.
2 The best thing to put at the bottom of the aquarium is *b)* sawdust and cardboard. Gerbils can make nests under the sawdust and cardboard. This is where they sleep at night.
3 *a)* Stop stroking your cat. Cats are feeling angry or unhappy when they swish their tails.
4 You can teach your parrot to *c)* talk. Spend time with your parrot and repeat the same word every day until your parrot can say it.
5 Feed your snake *c)* once every two weeks. Don't feed your snake more often than this.

b) [1.10] Play the CD again and ask students to complete the missing words. In pairs, students compare their answers. Play the CD once more for students to check the answers. Write the answers on the board for students to check the spelling.

Mixed-ability classes

For less confident students write the missing words in mixed order on the board.

Tapescript and Answer key

see Activity 2b

Homework suggestions

1 Activity Book page 10, Activity 1
2 Students write a quiz question and three answers about another pet. Only one answer should be correct. At the beginning of the next lesson students can exchange their questions in pairs and choose the correct answers.

PART 2

Introduction

Draw a simple picture of a hungry shark in the waves, ten steps leading down to the water and a stick figure over the first step. Think of a pet students know, preferably an unusual one and draw a dash for each letter of its name, e.g. _ _ _ _ _ _ (gerbil). Students guess and call out the letters one at a time. If the letter is part of the name, write it over the correct dash, and if it is not, erase the stick figure and draw it on the next step, moving closer towards the shark. Keep a record of all the letters suggested on the board. Students try to guess the word before the stick figure reaches the water. Students cannot say full words. If they think they know which pet it is, they should call out the correct letters of its name.

❸ Speaking

a) Students think of a pet animal and write its name on a piece of paper without showing their classmates.

b) Divide students into groups of five. They take turns to answer up to ten *Yes/No* questions from their classmates to guess the animal. Go over the example questions and the dialogue first. If their classmates do not manage to guess the pet, they reveal the answer. Then it is another student's turn to answer questions about their pet. If students have come up with the same names of pets, ask them not to reveal this fact and still get their classmates to make guesses.

Find out which pets different students chose and if their classmates managed to guess them.

❹ Writing

a) Students read the text and try to guess what animal it refers to. Elicit or explain the meaning of the words *cage, pieces of, seeds.* Elicit ideas for the mystery animal, e.g. gerbil, hamster, rat, mouse.

Cultural information

In English pets are often referred to as *he/she* and *it* is generally used in reference to wild animals.

b) Students choose a pet and write at least three sentences about how they look after it. Go through the example first. Students write draft texts and then make copies. Monitor their work, providing help.

Divide students into groups of five. Students take turns to read out their texts and make guesses about their classmates' animals. Finally, they exchange and read each other's texts in pairs. If they notice any mistakes in their friend's text, they should point these out orally.

Mixed-ability classes

Fast finishers write texts about looking after two different pets.

Photocopiable activity

What's my word? p105; instructions p93

Who am I? game

Students each think of a famous person and write that person's name on a piece of paper. Make sure they choose someone all their classmates know. They should not show the name to anyone.

Divide the class into four groups. Within their groups students imagine they are the famous person whose name they have written down. Their group members can ask up to 20 questions to guess the name of the person. Go through the example questions first.

Homework suggestions

1 Activity Book page 10, Activity 2
2 Students imagine they are their own pet or a pet of someone they know well and they describe how they look after their owners, e.g. *I warn him when somebody is at the door, I help him eat his meals, etc.*

Module 1 Review

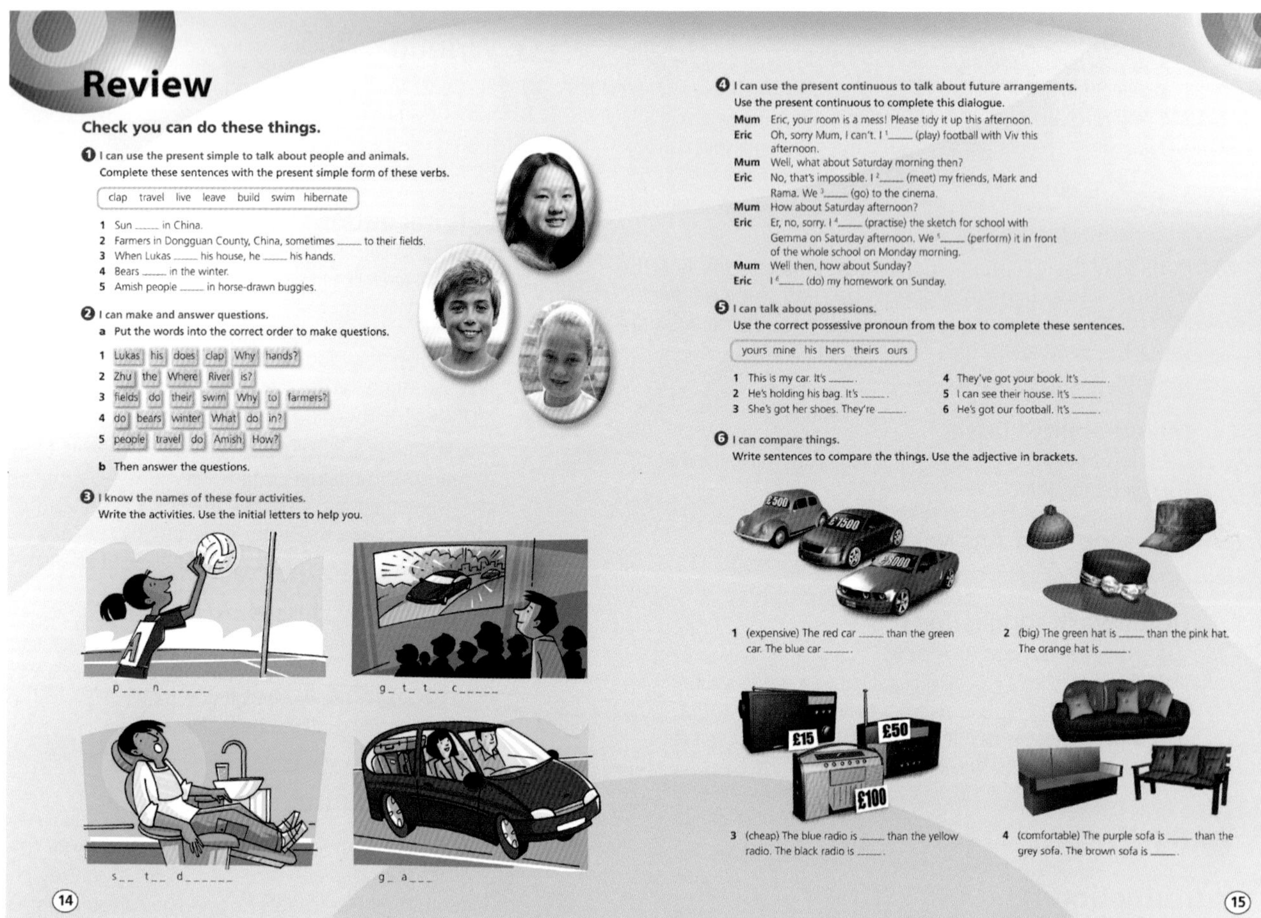

Review

Check you can do these things.

1 I can use the present simple to talk about people and animals.
Complete these sentences with the present simple form of these verbs.

clap travel live leave build swim hibernate

1 Sun ___ in China.
2 Farmers in Dongguan County, China, sometimes ___ to their fields.
3 When Lukas ___ his house, he ___ his hands.
4 Bears ___ in the winter.
5 Amish people ___ in horse-drawn buggies.

2 I can make and answer questions.
a Put the words into the correct order to make questions.

1 Lukas his does clap Why hands?
2 Zhu the Where River is?
3 fields do their swim Why to farmers?
4 do bears winter What do in?
5 people travel do Amish How?

b Then answer the questions.

3 I know the names of these four activities.
Write the activities. Use the initial letters to help you.

p___ n______
g_ t_ t__ c_____
s__ t__ d______
g_ a___

4 I can use the present continuous to talk about future arrangements.
Use the present continuous to complete this dialogue.

Mum Eric, your room is a mess! Please tidy it up this afternoon.
Eric Oh, sorry Mum, I can't. I [1]___ (play) football with Viv this afternoon.
Mum Well, what about Saturday morning then?
Eric No, that's impossible. I [2]___ (meet) my friends, Mark and Rama. We [3]___ (go) to the cinema.
Mum How about Saturday afternoon?
Eric Er, no, sorry. I [4]___ (practise) the sketch for school with Gemma on Saturday afternoon. We [5]___ (perform) it in front of the whole school on Monday morning.
Mum Well then, how about Sunday?
Eric I [6]___ (do) my homework on Sunday.

5 I can talk about possessions.
Use the correct possessive pronoun from the box to complete these sentences.

yours mine his hers theirs ours

1 This is my car. It's ___.
2 He's holding his bag. It's ___.
3 She's got her shoes. They're ___.
4 They've got your book. It's ___.
5 I can see their house. It's ___.
6 He's got our football. It's ___.

6 I can compare things.
Write sentences to compare the things. Use the adjective in brackets.

1 (expensive) The red car ___ than the green car. The blue car ___.
2 (big) The green hat is ___ than the pink hat. The orange hat is ___.
3 (cheap) The blue radio is ___ than the yellow radio. The black radio is ___.
4 (comfortable) The purple sofa is ___ than the grey sofa. The brown sofa is ___.

14 15

Optional revision

Before your students start this Review, you may want to direct them to the Grammar summary at the back of their coursebooks and to the Lexical sets at the back of their Activity Books. This will remind them of the main grammar and vocabulary in the module. Give them ten minutes to read through those in small groups and ask you any questions they may have.

- Activity Book: Refer your students to page 85: *Adjectives*; *Animals and Pets*; *Clothing*
- Grammar summary: Refer your students to pages 98–99 sections 1–4

Module 1 Review

The purpose of this section is revision and consolidation of the material studied in Module 1.

Completing the activities

Go over all the activities with the class, explaining rubrics and giving examples to make sure students know what to do. There are written and oral tasks, but you may decide yourself how they should be completed by students. Generally students should do the writing tasks individually and the oral tasks in pairs, testing each other's knowledge. Make sure they do not treat the *Review* as a formal test, but complete the activities in a friendly, stress-free atmosphere. Fast finishers can write down the answers to the oral tasks.

Checking answers

When students have finished, check the answers with the whole class by asking volunteers to copy their answers onto the board or to say them aloud. If necessary, explain the more difficult issues, ask additional questions about the activities and solve any problems that arise.

Self-evaluation

Tell students to evaluate themselves. They should tick the activities where at least half of their answers were correct.

Feedback

Ask students which activities were difficult, which were easy and if there is anything they would like to review. Make a note of common language problems to go over in future lessons.

Answer key

❶ **1** lives
2 swim
3 leaves … claps
4 hibernate
5 travel

❷ **a)** **1** Why does Lukas clap his hands?
2 Where is the Zhu River?
3 Why do farmers swim to their fields?
4 What do bears do in winter?
5 How do Amish people travel?

b) **1** Because bears go away when they hear humans.
2 It is (in Dongguan County) in China.
3 Because it is quicker to swim than walking to the nearest bridge.
4 They hibernate.
5 They travel in horse-drawn buggies.

❸ **1** play netball
2 go to the cinema
3 see the dentist
4 go away

❹ Students fill in the gaps with the verbs in brackets in the present continuous. Remind students to use contractions as it is an informal conversation.

Answer key

Mum: Eric, your room is a mess! Please tidy it up this afternoon.
Eric: Oh, sorry Mum, I can't. *I'm playing* (play) football with Viv this afternoon.
Mum: Well, what about Saturday morning then?
Eric: No, that's impossible. *I'm meeting* my friends, Mark and Rama. We*'re going* to the cinema.
Mum: How about Saturday afternoon?
Eric: Er, no, sorry. *I'm practising* the sketch for school with Gemma on Saturday afternoon. We*'re performing* it in front of the whole school on Monday morning.
Mum: Well then, how about Sunday?
Eric: *I'm doing* my homework on Sunday.

❺ **1** mine **2** his **3** hers **4** yours **5** theirs **6** ours

❻ **1** is more expensive … is the most expensive
2 bigger … the biggest
3 cheaper … the cheapest
4 more comfortable … the most comfortable

Extra activity

Students stand or sit in a circle. Say: *fast*. The first student makes a comparative sentence with the adjective, e.g. *A moped is faster than a bike*. The next person thinks of something faster than the previous student mentioned and makes a comparative sentence, e.g. *A car is faster than a moped*. Students continue the game round the circle. When a student cannot think of a faster object, they make a superlative sentence, e.g. *A space shuttle is the fastest*. Then repeat the game with another adjective, e.g. *dangerous, small, expensive*.

Module 1 Tests (A and B) are on the Tests CD

Learning diary

You can refer students to page 11 of the Activity Book for further review, more study tips and self-assessment activities.

Extra special

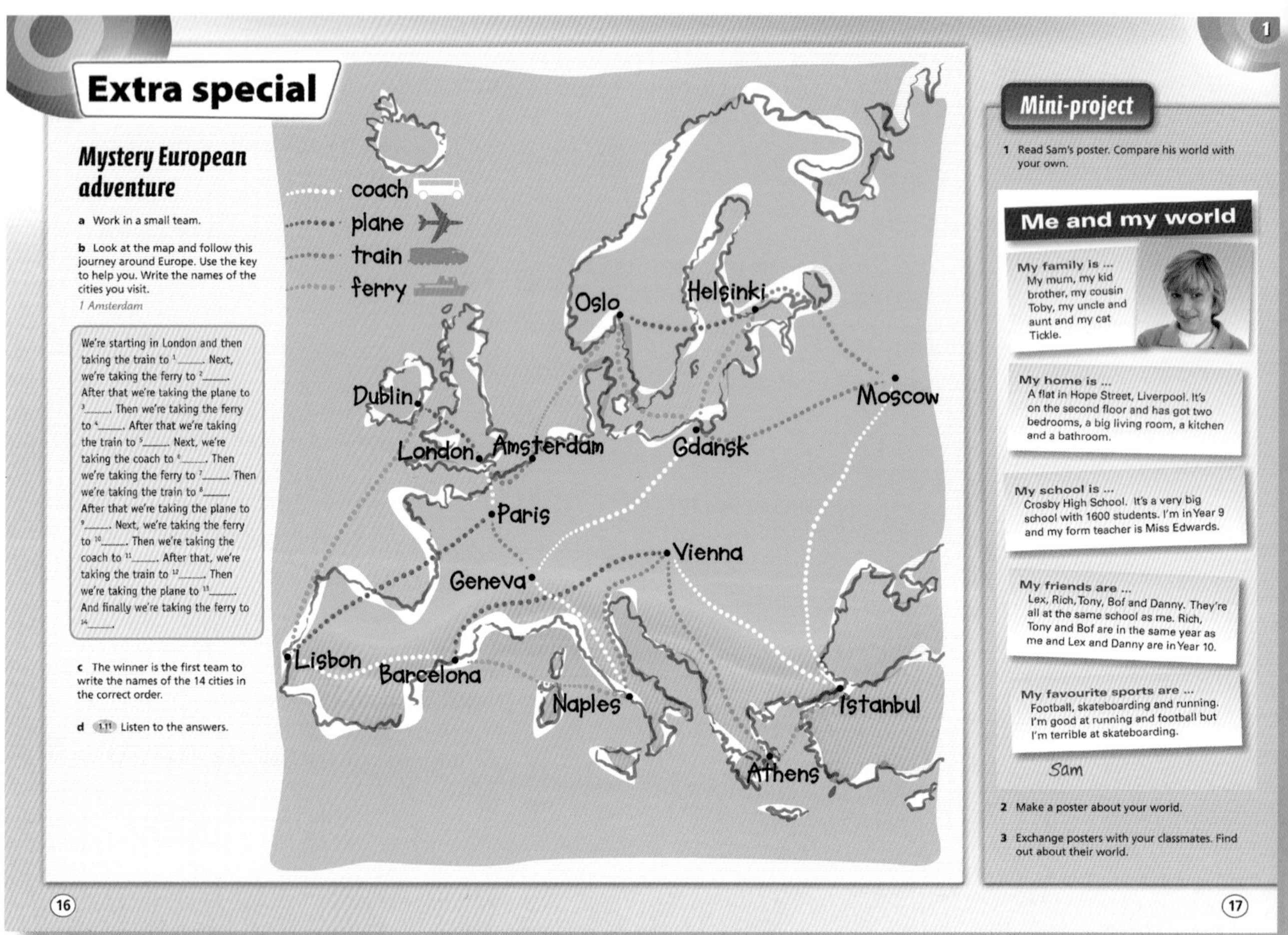

Extra special

Mystery European adventure

a Work in a small team.

b Look at the map and follow this journey around Europe. Use the key to help you. Write the names of the cities you visit.

1 Amsterdam

We're starting in London and then taking the train to [1]_____. Next, we're taking the ferry to [2]_____. After that we're taking the plane to [3]_____. Then we're taking the ferry to [4]_____. After that we're taking the train to [5]_____. Next, we're taking the coach to [6]_____. Then we're taking the ferry to [7]_____. Then we're taking the train to [8]_____. After that we're taking the plane to [9]_____. Next, we're taking the ferry to [10]_____. Then we're taking the coach to [11]_____. After that, we're taking the train to [12]_____. Then we're taking the plane to [13]_____. And finally we're taking the ferry to [14]_____.

c The winner is the first team to write the names of the 14 cities in the correct order.

d 1.11 Listen to the answers.

16

Mini-project

1 Read Sam's poster. Compare his world with your own.

Me and my world

My family is ...
My mum, my kid brother, my cousin Toby, my uncle and aunt and my cat Tickle.

My home is ...
A flat in Hope Street, Liverpool. It's on the second floor and has got two bedrooms, a big living room, a kitchen and a bathroom.

My school is ...
Crosby High School. It's a very big school with 1600 students. I'm in Year 9 and my form teacher is Miss Edwards.

My friends are ...
Lex, Rich, Tony, Bof and Danny. They're all at the same school as me. Rich, Tony and Bof are in the same year as me and Lex and Danny are in Year 10.

My favourite sports are ...
Football, skateboarding and running. I'm good at running and football but I'm terrible at skateboarding.

Sam

2 Make a poster about your world.

3 Exchange posters with your classmates. Find out about their world.

17

Optional materials

- a large map of Europe, Post-it™ notes

Extra activity

Stick a large map of Europe on the board with magnets. In groups of five, students make a list of all the European countries they have been to, marking how many students have visited each place. Help with the English names of the countries if necessary. Group representatives come to the map with their lists and stick Post-it™ notes on each country their group members visited, e.g. if three students have visited France, they should stick three Post-it™ notes onto the French territory. Find out which countries the most students have visited. Elicit all the means of transport students used to get to each destination.

Mystery European adventure

a) Divide the class into groups of three or four students.

b) Point to the map in the book and explain that they are going to follow a journey around Europe. Refer students to the key to explain the coloured lines denoting the mode of transport used. Ask students to read the instructions **a–c**. Point out that the aim of the game is to write the names of the fourteen cities which students visit in the correct order.

c) Teams read the text, follow the route on the map and write the names of the cities. The first team to finish calls out *Stop.* Other teams must stop writing. Ask the first team to read out their list of cities. If the cities are correct, the team wins the game. If they are not, let other teams continue working until one team makes a correct list.

d) [1.11] Play the recording for teams to check their answers.

Extra activity

Divide students into groups of four. Ask them to make a list of the countries where the cities on the map are. Set a time limit of five minutes. The group with the complete or the longest correct list wins the game. Additionally, you can ask students which cities on the map are not capital cities.

Answer key

1 Amsterdam
2 Oslo
3 Helsinki
4 Gdansk
5 Moscow
6 Istanbul
7 Athens
8 Vienna
9 Barcelona
10 Naples
11 Geneva
12 Paris
13 Lisbon
14 Dublin

Cultural information

There are over 50 countries and territories in Europe. The total number differs depending on various categorisations. As of 2009 The Council of Europe has 47 members and the European Union consists of 27 states. A few countries including Russia and Turkey are transcontinental, i.e. their territory lies on more than one continent, in this case Europe and Asia.

Mini-project

1. Explain to students that a boy called Sam has made a project about his world. Focus attention on the headings and elicit the topics he writes about. Ask students to read Sam's project. Clarify any vocabulary if necessary.
2. Students work individually and make a poster about their own world. They can choose the same topics as in the example or add their own ideas, e.g. their pets, favourite clothes, school subjects, etc. Students should write about at least five topics. Encourage them to make a draft copy first. Let students illustrate their project. Monitor their work.
3. In groups of three or four, students exchange and read each other's posters. Ask students to report to the class anything interesting they have found out about their group members.

Mixed-ability classes

Fast finishers work in pairs or small groups. They take turns to name the topics of their project for their classmate/s to guess what they have written on these topics. Finally, they exchange and read each other's projects to check if they guessed correctly.

Extra activity

Put students into pairs. On the board write: *1 person, 1 CD with music, 1 film or video game, 1 book, equipment for 1 sport.* Say: *Imagine you are going to a desert island for one year. You can take with you only what is on the board.* Students choose what they would take in each category. Then they present and explain their choices in pairs. Ask students to report to the class their classmate's most surprising choices.

Teaching tip: *Approach to personalisation*

Personalisation is crucial in the classroom as it allows students to bond better if they know more about each other and prepares them for authentic situations when they are going to talk about themselves and their experiences. However, students should be allowed to skip any topics they find too personal or sensitive. It is also vital to respond to the content of students' personalisations and not just concentrate on the form or the errors.

Lesson objectives
- Talking about the pas
- Talking about sports

5 Sports day

1 Vocabulary

1.12 Match the sports with the pictures.

swimming race javelin 100-metre race obstacle course long jump

2 Presentation

1.13 Listen and read. Why is Charlie unhappy?

Charlie Hello.
Mel Hi Charlie! How was Sports day?
Charlie Oh, not so good. What a disaster!
Mel But you're really good at sport! What happened?
Charlie I ran fast and I won the 100-metre race.
Mel Brilliant!
Charlie My team swam well in the swimming race. We didn't win, but we got a medal.
Mel Cool!
Charlie I threw the javelin 28 metres and everyone cheered.
Mel Well done!
Charlie I jumped 4.8 metres and I broke the school long jump record!
Mel Wow, Charlie, that's amazing!
Charlie The last race was the obstacle course. I didn't see the rope and I fell over …

3 Comprehension

1.13 Listen and read again. Answer these questions.

1 The swimming race.

1. In which sport did Charlie win a medal?
2. How far did Charlie throw the javelin?
3. How far did Charlie jump?
4. What was the last race?
5. What happened to Charlie in the last race?

5 Sports day

Grammar
- past simple

Vocabulary
- sports; distances; everyday activities

Optional materials
- a soft ball/crumpled newspaper

Optional Activity Book activities
- Fast finishers p68, Extra practice p69

Photocopiable activity
- *Last week* p106

PART 1

Introduction

Ask students to stand in a circle to play a game of *hot potato*. Name a category: *Sports* and throw a soft ball or a crumpled newspaper to a random student. The student has ten seconds to name any sport, e.g. *volleyball* and then throws the ball/ newspaper to another student who names a different sport and so on. If someone cannot name a sport within the allotted time or they repeat the sport already mentioned, they are out of the game. Set a time limit of three minutes. You can repeat the game for another category, e.g. *sports equipment*.

1 Vocabulary

[1.12] Ask students to look at the words in the box and listen as you play the CD. Then they try to match the words with the pictures in Activity 2. They should make guesses about new vocabulary.

Students work individually on the task and then compare their answers in pairs. Play the CD again and get students to call out the letter of the corresponding picture. Make sure everybody understands all the words now and drill the pronunciation.

Mixed-ability classes

Fast finishers check if they can name the sports equipment necessary for the sports in Activity 1. Elicit their ideas when everyone has finished working on Activity 1.

Extra activity

Put students into groups of four to brainstorm all the sports disciplines they practise during PE lessons or as extracurricular activities. Elicit the lists from different groups onto the board. Ask students about example results in each sport/discipline on the board, e.g. football – 2:0 (two–nil), and teach them how to read out the results in English.

Tapescript

see Student's Book Activity 1

Answer key

swimming race – **b**
javelin – **c**
100-metre race – **a**
obstacle course – **e**
long jump – **d**

2 Presentation

[1.13] Explain that students are going to listen to a dialogue between Charlie and Mel. Find out if students remember from Module 1 that these characters are classmates. Ask them to listen and read the dialogue to find out why Charlie is unhappy. Play the CD and elicit the answer.

The past simple was introduced in *Hot Spot Student's Book 2*. Refer students to the **Grammar spot** at the top of the next page to review the use and form of the past simple. Ask students to find more examples of the past simple in the dialogue. Refer students to the **Grammar summary** on page 99 for more information on the past simple. Review the verb *be* in the past.

Check if students know or can guess the meaning of the following words and phrases: *not so good, disaster, brilliant, medal, school record, rope, fell over, twisted, ankle, no more, oops.* If necessary, provide explanation.

Tapescript

see Student's Book Activity 2

Cultural information

A Sports Day is an event organised by most primary schools in Britain in warmer months of the academic year. Students take part in different sports competitions and winners get medals or prizes. Typical Sports Day activities in primary schools include sack races, relay races and obstacle races. In secondary schools, students compete in traditional track, field and aquatic sports.

3 Comprehension

[1.13] Students listen and read the dialogue in Activity 2 again to find the answers to the questions. Play the CD.

Students compare their answers in pairs. Check the answers with the whole class. You can then ask students to read the dialogue in pairs twice, changing roles.

Mixed-ability classes

Fast finishers should rewrite the answers in full sentences.

Extra activity

Divide students into groups of four and ask them to tell their classmates briefly about any of their own sports accidents, revealing what happened, where and when. Monitor the activity, providing help. Ask volunteers to share their stories with the whole class.

Tapescript

see Activity 2

Answer key

1 The swimming race.
2 28 metres
3 4.8 metres
4 The obstacle course.
5 He twisted his ankle and broke his arm.

Grammar spot
Past simple

I **jumped** 4.8 metres and I **broke** the school record!
We **didn't win** but we **got** a medal.

Grammar page 99

Study tip
Past simple

Add irregular verbs to your verb table.

break – broke *get – got*
win – won *fall – fell*
swim – swam *run – ran*

4 Grammar practice

a What did they do on Sports Day? Look at the chart. Make sentences about Charlie's friends.

Ryan didn't swim in the swimming race. He ran in the 800-metre race.

	swimming race	800-metre race	javelin
Ryan	✗	✓	✗
Sophie	✗	✓	✓

	long jump	obstacle course	medal
Ryan	✓	✓	✓
Sophie	✓	✗	✗

b Work in pairs. Ask and answer about Ryan and Sophie.

Did Ryan swim in the swimming race?

No, he didn't.

5 Listening

1.14 Listen to Charlie talking about his weekend. Put the phrases in the correct order.

Last weekend, Charlie …

___ bought a tennis racket
___ looked at a bike
___ read a book
_1_ watched TV
___ talked about cycling
___ visited an exhibition
___ did his homework
___ went to his uncle's

6 Speaking

a What did you do last weekend? Read the questions and write answers about yourself.

Did you buy anything?
What did you buy?
Did you read a book or a magazine?
Did you watch TV?
What did you watch?
Did you visit a friend/a relative?
What did you talk about?
Did you do your homework?

b Work in pairs. Find out about your friend's weekend. Ask the questions above and make notes.

c Tell another classmate about your friend's weekend.

Last weekend, Sophie bought a CD. She …

7 Pronunciation

a 1.15 Listen to this tongue twister.

/v/ /w/
Victoria Wells won one hundred volleyball victories and was wonderful at windsurfing.

b 1.16 Listen again and repeat. How fast can you say it?

8 Check your English

Use the past simple of the verbs in brackets to complete Mel's diary.

Last Saturday I [1]_____ (visit) Charlie and then we [2]_____ (go) to the new café in town for lunch. After lunch, I [3]_____ (buy) some trainers and Charlie [4]_____ (get) a DVD of his favourite film. Then we [5]_____ (go) to Charlie's house and [6]_____ (watch) the DVD.

Study tip

Elicit from students that there are regular and irregular verbs in the past simple and that regular verbs take the *-ed* ending in positive sentences. Ask students to find irregular verbs in Activity 2 and note them down. Encourage them to add irregular verbs to their list as they come across them.

Homework suggestions

1 Activity Book pages 12–13, Activities 1–3
2 Students write positive or negative sentences with the irregular verbs from the **Study tip** in the past simple.

PART 2

Introduction

Divide students into groups of three. Two students in each group keep their books closed. The third student looks at Activity 2 and says the infinitive of the regular and irregular verbs in the dialogue at random. The first student to say the past simple of the named verb gets a point. Students should finish the game after ten verbs have been mentioned. The person with the most points wins.

4 Grammar practice

a) Explain that Charlie's friends, Ryan and Sophie, also took part in the Sports Day events. Ask students to look at the chart and make sentences about what Ryan and Sophie did and did not do. Go through the example first. Elicit the sentences from different students.

b) Review questions and short answers in the past simple. Divide students into pairs. One student in each pair closes the book and answers the other person's questions about Ryan from memory. Then students change their roles and ask and answer questions about Sophie. They can award each other points for correct answers. Demonstrate the task first by reading out the example with a confident student.

5 Listening

[1.14] Students listen to Charlie talking to Mel and find out what he did last weekend. Play the CD. Then students read the phrases and put the events in the correct order. Play the CD again for students to check the answers. Ask a volunteer to read out the events in the correct order.

Tapescript

Mel: So what did you do last weekend, Charlie? No sport, eh?
Charlie: No, I didn't do any sport! I stayed at home on Friday night and watched TV.
Mel: What did you watch?
Charlie: Football. On Saturday morning I did my homework and then I read a book about swimming.
Mel: What about in the afternoon?
Charlie: On Saturday afternoon I went to my uncle's. We talked about cycling and we looked at his bike. It's amazing.
Mel: And on Sunday?
Charlie: On Sunday morning I bought a new tennis racket. After lunch, I went to our local museum with my sister.
Mel: Museum! You at a museum! No way!
Charlie: It was great! We visited an exhibition about the Ancient Greek Olympics!
Mel: So last weekend, you watched football on TV, read a book about swimming, talked about cycling, looked at a bike, bought a tennis racket, and went to an exhibition about the Olympics. Hmm. No sport at all!!

Answer key

1 watched TV,
2 did his homework,
3 read a book,
4 went to his uncle's,
5 talked about cycling,
6 looked at a bike,
7 bought a tennis racket,
8 visited an exhibition

Photocopiable activity

Last week p106; instructions p93

6 Speaking

a) Students read the questions and write true answers in note form about their last weekend. Set a time limit of four minutes.

b) In pairs, students ask and answer the questions from Activity 6a to find out about each other's weekends. Encourage them to take notes.

c) Students work in different pairs. Using their notes, they tell each other about the last weekend of the friend they interviewed in Activity 6b. Go through the example first.

Extra activity

Tell students about your last weekend. Ask them to interrupt you with as many questions as possible, e.g. *T: I went to the cinema. SS: Which film did you see?* If students manage to ask you ten questions before you finish, they win the game.

7 Pronunciation

a) [1.15] Point out the English pronunciation of *v* and *w* and ask students to compare that with their L1. Play the CD and ask students to read the tongue twister in their books.

Tapescript

see Student's Book Activity 7a

b) [1.16] Play the CD again and ask students to repeat it. Then encourage students to practise saying the tongue twister as fast as they can.

Tapescript

see Activity 7a

8 Check your English

Students complete the text with the verbs in brackets in the past simple. Students compare their answers in pairs. Check the answers with the whole class.

Answer key

1 visited
2 went
3 bought
4 got
5 went
6 watched

Homework suggestions

1 Activity Book page 13, Activities 4–5
2 Students imagine that last weekend was their dream weekend. They write at least six sentences about what they did, using Activity 8 as a model.

Lesson objective
Describing past actions

6 What were you doing?

1 Vocabulary

1.17 Find these things in the picture.

hammock clothes line flowerbed bone flowerpot

2 Presentation

1.18 Look at the picture and listen to Martha Gloom. Why is she angry?

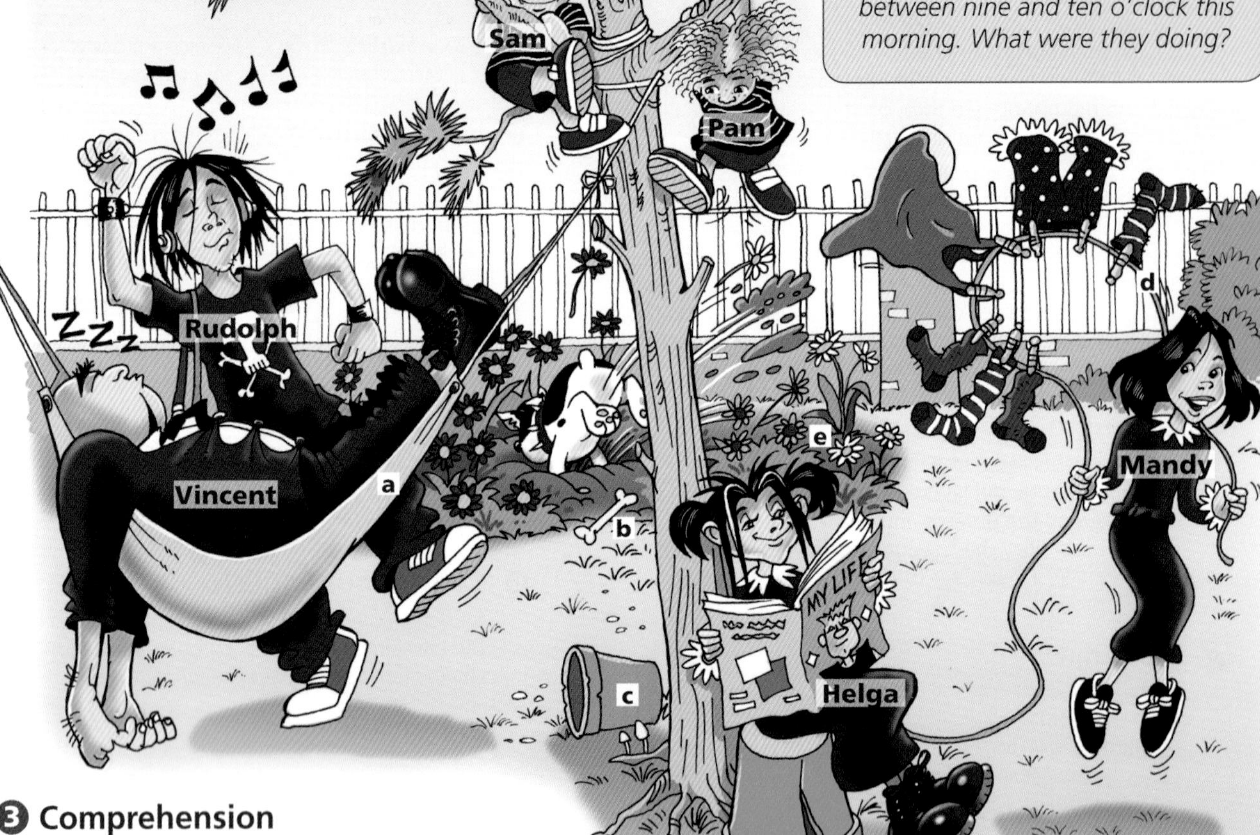

3 Comprehension

a Look at the picture again. What were the Glooms doing this morning? Write the name.

1 Helga

1. ______ was reading a magazine.
2. ______ was listening to music.
3. ______ were climbing a tree.
4. ______ was sleeping in a hammock.
5. ______ was skipping.
6. ______ was burying a bone.

b 1.19 Listen and check.

Grammar spot
Past continuous

He **was listening** to music.
They **were climbing** a tree.

Grammar page 100

6 What were you doing?

Grammar
- past continuous

Vocabulary
- objects in the garden; routine and garden actions; time

Optional materials
- a selection of magazine photos showing busy scenes with people doing a variety of activities; a DVD of a well-known film or TV series

Optional Activity Book activities
- Fast finishers p70, Extra practice p71

Photocopiable activity
- *Find out the truth* p107

PART 1

Introduction

Ask the class to brainstorm all activities people can do in the garden. Write their ideas on the board. Then ask students to look at the picture in Activity 2 and check if they thought of any activities the characters are doing.

Teaching tip: *Starting the lesson*

To help students focus on the lesson from the very beginning allow a minute for them to sit down and prepare their books and other materials. Then signal the start of the lesson using an egg timer or playing a CD with students' favourite music for a few seconds. Establish eye contact with students who are still fidgeting or not paying attention.

❶ Vocabulary

[1.17] Focus students' attention on the words in the box and play the CD. Ask students to find the objects in the large picture in Activity 2. Encourage them to make guesses about new words.

Students compare their answers in pairs. Check the answers with the whole class. Make sure everybody understands all the words now and drill the pronunciation.

Tapescript

see Student's Book Activity 1

Answer key

hammock – **a**
clothes line – **d**
flowerbed – **e**
bone – **b**
flowerpot – **c**

❷ Presentation

[1.18] Point to the pictures and ask students: *Do you remember the Gloom family from Hot Spot Student's Book 1 and 2?* Elicit that the Glooms are an unusual family and find out if students remember any details about them. Then point to Martha and ask students to guess why she is angry. Encourage them to study the pictures to find the answer.

Students listen and read Martha's words to check their guesses. Play the CD and elicit that she is angry because there is a hole in the garden. Explain that to find out who made the hole she needs to find out what everybody was doing this morning in the garden.

❸ Comprehension

a) Students study the picture in Activity 2 again and complete the sentences with the correct names to show what everyone was doing in the garden in the morning. Clarify any vocabulary, using the picture. Check the answers with the whole class.

b) [1.19] Play the CD for students to check their answers and then refer them to the **Grammar spot** to elicit or explain the form and use of the past continuous. Go over the examples and point out, using the picture in Activity 2, that these actions were unfinished, in progress at a specific time in the past. Point out the form of the verb *be* for different persons. Refer students to the **Grammar summary** on page 100 for more information on the past continuous.

Extra activity

Bring to class a selection of magazine photos showing busy scenes with people doing a variety of activities. Divide the class into groups of three and give each group one picture to study for one minute. When the time is up, ask one student in each group to take the picture and position it in such a way that their group members cannot see it, e.g. hide it behind a book. The remaining group members take turns to make past continuous sentences from memory about what the people in the picture were doing. The student looking at the picture checks the answers and awards a point for each grammatically and factually correct statement. Set a time limit of three minutes. The winner is the student with the most points.

Dyslexia tip: *Disruptive behaviour*

Some dyslexic students are inattentive and/or hyperactive, which results in disruptive classroom behaviour. It is best to discuss the behaviour in private, and in class to use non-verbal warning signals to make students focus on the assigned task, e.g. wave your hand, tap them gently on their shoulder or put a Post-it™ note on their desk.

Tapescript and Answer key

1 Helga was reading a magazine.
2 Rudolph was listening to music.
3 Sam and Pam were climbing a tree.
4 Vincent was sleeping in a hammock.
5 Mandy was skipping.
6 Bonehead was burying a bone.

4 Grammar practice

a 1.20 Look at the picture in Activity 2 and listen to Vincent. Then correct his mistakes. Use the phrases in the box.

1 Helga wasn't mowing the lawn. She was reading a magazine.

mow the lawn   water the plants   hang up the washing   play with toys   sleep

1 Helga ____. **2** Rudolph ____. **3** Mandy ____. **4** Sam and Pam ____. **5** Bonehead ____.

b 1.21 Listen and check.

Grammar spot
Past continuous

Negative
Helga **wasn't mowing** the lawn.
Sam and Pam **weren't playing** with toys.

Questions
Were you **having** a shower? Yes, I **was**.
Was she **doing** her homework? No, she **wasn't**.

Grammar page 100

5 Speaking

a Complete the chart about what you were doing yesterday. Use these or your own ideas.

sleep   eat breakfast/lunch/dinner/a snack
do homework   play football/tennis
talk on the phone   watch TV   get up
have a shower   have a lesson

7.30 am	*I was eating breakfast.*
10.00 am	
11.30 am	
5.30 pm	
8.00 pm	
10.00 pm	

b Work in pairs. Find out what your classmate was doing yesterday.

Were you having a shower at 7.30 yesterday?

No, I wasn't. I was eating breakfast.

6 Pronunciation

1.22 Listen and practise saying the weak forms of *was* /wəz/ and *were* /wə/.

1. I **was** playing tennis yesterday.
2. They **were** doing their homework.
3. Sarah **was** working with him.
4. We **were** eating breakfast.

7 Game

a Work in pairs. Look at the picture in Activity 2 for one minute.

b Now close your books. Ask and answer about the Glooms.

Was Rudolph mowing the lawn?

No, he wasn't. He was listening to music.

Correct!

8 Check your English

Choose the correct words and make sentences.

1. I *was/were* doing my homework at six o'clock last night.
2. *Was/Were* they watching TV yesterday afternoon?
3. Sara and Fred *wasn't/weren't* playing tennis this morning, they *was/were* taking the dog for a walk.
4. Last Sunday afternoon we were *sit/sitting* on the beach, *eat/eating* ice cream.

❹ Grammar practice

a) [1.20] Point to Vincent in the picture in Activity 2 and elicit that he was sleeping in his hammock this morning. Ask students to listen to Vincent telling Martha about the morning. Play the CD and elicit that Vincent made mistakes and that students need to correct him.

Refer students to the **Grammar spot** to introduce negative sentences in the past continuous. Then ask students to look at the pictures illustrating Vincent's words and compare them with the picture in Activity 2 which shows what was really happening.

Students correct Vincent by making negative and positive sentences as in the example. Then they compare their answers in pairs.

Tapescript

Martha: Vincent, were you looking after the children this morning?
Vincent: Yes, of course I was!
Martha: What were they doing?
Vincent: Well … um … Helga was, um, mowing the lawn. And, er, er … Rudolph was watering the plants. Mandy was, um … she was helping me. We were hanging up the washing. Sam and Pam, they were playing with their toys. And Bonehead was sleeping.

b) [1.21] Play the CD for students to check their answers.

Tapescript and Answer key

1. Helga wasn't mowing the lawn. She was reading a magazine.
2. Rudoph wasn't watering the plants. He was listening to music.
3. Mandy wasn't hanging up the washing. She was skipping.
4. Sam and Pam weren't playing with their toys. They were climbing a tree.
5. Bonehead wasn't sleeping. He was burying a bone.

Homework suggestions

1. Activity Book page 14, Activities 1–3
2. Students choose four family members or friends and write past continuous sentences about what they think these people were doing at 7 p.m. the previous day.

PART 2

Introduction

Review telling the time in English by drawing a clock on the board with its hands in different positions. Then ask students to choose and write down three times which are important to them. In pairs, they show each other the times and explain the meaning, e.g. *My favourite TV show starts at 6.30 p.m.*

❺ Speaking

a) Go over the everyday activities in the box and make sure students remember all of them. Ask students to complete the chart about what they were doing yesterday at these times. They should write true sentences in the past continuous. They can use the phrases in the box if these are relevant and/or their own ideas.

Mixed-ability classes

For less confident students demonstrate the task by completing the chart about you on the board as an example. Fast finishers can think of their favourite activity of the previous day and add another time when they were doing that, e.g. 6.00 – I was surfing the Internet.

b) Go over the **Grammar spot** to introduce questions and short answers in the past continuous. Refer students to the **Grammar summary** on page 100 for more information on the past continuous.

Divide the class into pairs. Students make guesses about what their friend was doing yesterday and ask questions to check their ideas. Demonstrate the task by reading out the example with a confident student.

Extra activity

In pairs, students choose a celebrity and imagine what this person was doing yesterday at the times in the chart in Activity 5a. Then ask students to report their ideas to the whole class.

Photocopiable activity

Find out the truth p107; instructions p93

❻ Pronunciation

[1.22] Explain that some words in English have two different pronunciations, according to whether they are stressed or not. Demonstrate the strong and the weak form of ***was*** and ***were***. Explain that within a sentence in the past continuous we normally use the weak form.

Play the CD, pausing after each sentence for students to repeat. Then ask students to practise saying the sentences individually.

Tapescript

see Student's Book Activity 6

❼ Game

a) Divide students into pairs. Student A looks at the picture in Activity 2 for one minute.

b) Student A closes the book. Student B asks questions about the picture and says if Student A's answers are correct or incorrect. After four questions students change roles and repeat the game with Student B answering the questions. Demonstrate the task first by reading out the example with a confident student.

Extra activity

Play a DVD with a short scene from a well-known film or TV series. Turn the film off and ask students to write four past continuous questions about what different characters were doing. In pairs, students exchange and answer the questions from memory. Play the DVD again for students to check the answers.

❽ Check your English

Students choose the correct words to make past continuous sentences. They compare their answers in pairs before you check them with the whole class.

Answer key

1. was
2. Were
3. weren't … were
4. sitting … eating

Homework suggestions

1. Activity Book page 15, Activity 4–5
2. Students choose a special photo of their family or friends. They write a short description of where the people were and what they were doing at the moment of taking the photo.

7 Amazing stories

1 Presentation

1.23 Listen and read. Match the photos with the emails.

TRUE STORIES PAGE

Have you got an amazing story for us?
Send an email to Teen Dreams and tell us your stories.

1

Hi Teen Dreams!

Last Wednesday I was playing football with my school. It was a very important match and the score was 1-1. I was running towards the ball when I fell. My football boot came off and flew through the air. It hit the ball and the ball went into the goal. Just then, the referee blew his whistle and the game ended. Our team won the match! My football boot was the hero of the match! It was very funny!

Tony

2

Dear Teen Dreams!

Last Saturday morning, my mum was mowing the lawn and my dad was at work. I was doing my homework in my room when I heard our dog, Bobo. He was barking loudly in the kitchen. I ran into the kitchen and saw a lot of smoke. The saucepan was on fire and Bobo was trying to tell me. I called my mum and we put out the fire. Bobo saved our lives! We were very lucky.

Sally

3

Hi Teen Dreams!

I was shopping with my friend. We were looking at some CDs in a music shop. I was listening to some music when I heard a loud noise. It sounded like an alarm. I shouted, 'Fire! Fire!' and everyone started to run out of the shop. Then I realised that it wasn't an alarm, it was the music. It was so embarrassing!

Freya

2 Comprehension

Can you remember? Try to answer these questions from memory.

Sally Bobo Tony Freya

1 Sally

1 Who was doing their homework?
2 Who was listening to music?
3 Who shouted, 'Fire! Fire!'?
4 Who was playing football?
5 Who was barking loudly?

Grammar spot
Past continuous and past simple with *when*

I **was running** towards the ball ***when*** I **fell**.

I **was listening** to some music ***when*** I **heard** a loud noise.

Grammar page 100

7 Amazing stories

Grammar	**Optional Activity Book activities**
• past continuous and past simple with *when*	• Fast finishers p72, Extra practice p73
Vocabulary	**Photocopiable activity**
• sports, kitchen and shopping words	• *The missing bag* p108

PART 1

Introduction

Elicit from students what teenage magazines and websites they read. Ask them to name different sections and features the magazines and websites have. Find out if readers send their emails and what they usually write about. Explain that in this lesson students are going to read some unusual emails sent by readers of a magazine *Teen Dreams*.

❶ Presentation

[1.23] Focus attention on the photos and ask students to make guesses about what the stories they illustrate are going to be about. Ask students to listen and read the stories and match them to the correct photos. Play the CD. Then check the answers with the whole class.

Tapescript

see Student's Book Activity 1

Answer key

1 b **2** c **3** a

Extra activity

Ask students to guess which story most of their classmates like best. They should note down their guess. Then ask the class to vote for the best story by raising their hands. Students can only vote once and they do not have to vote for the same story they have marked as their classmates' favourite. Count the votes. Find out how many students predicted the correct result.

❷ Comprehension

Ask students to read the questions and to try to answer them from memory, using the names in the box. Let students read the texts in Activity 1 again and check their answers. Elicit the answers.

Answer key

1 Sally
2 Freya
3 Freya
4 Tony
5 Bobo

Check if students know or can guess the following new words and phrases: *came off, air, goal, blew, barking, loudly, smoke, put out, saved, sounded, realised, embarrassing.* If necessary, provide explanation.

Extra activity

Divide students into pairs and ask them to write five more comprehension questions about the texts in Activity 1. They can ask about various details, not necessarily just the names of the characters. Set a time limit of four minutes. When students have finished, ask them to exchange their questions with another pair and write the answers from memory.

Grammar spot

Go through the examples and elicit or explain the use of the past continuous and the past simple with *when.* Explain that each sentence contains two actions. Elicit that the past continuous phrase describes a longer, incomplete action and the past simple phrase describes a shorter, complete action that interrupted the other one.

Ask students to find more examples of this grammar point in Activity 1. You can write the examples on the board, using different colours for each tense (see *Teaching tip: Colour coding* below). Refer students to the **Grammar summary** on page 100 for more information on the two tenses joined within one sentence by ***when***.

Teaching tip: *Colour coding*

To help students learn tenses you can colour code them. Assign one colour to each tense they are learning and stick to it throughout the year when writing examples on the board. This way students learn to associate a particular colour with one tense. Encourage students to use the same colours in their notes. Develop your own colour codes for tenses, making sure you choose colours students are likely to have in their pencil cases and using contrasting colours for tenses that students confuse, e.g. blue for the past simple and orange for the past continuous.

❸ Grammar practice

a Use the past continuous or past simple of the verbs in brackets to complete this story.

1 was watching
2 heard

I [1]_____ (watch) TV when I [2]_____ (hear) a strange noise outside. I [3]_____ (go) into the garden. I [4]_____ (look) around the garden when a cat [5] _____ (run) into my house. I [6]_____ (run) after the cat when the doorbell [7]_____ (ring). It [8]_____ (be) my neighbour, Fred. He [9]_____ (look) for his cat. I [10]_____ (talk) to Fred when the cat [11]_____ (run) out of my house and into Fred's garden.

b 1.24 Listen and check.

❹ Vocabulary

Find words from the emails in Activity 1 to match these pictures.

1 whistle

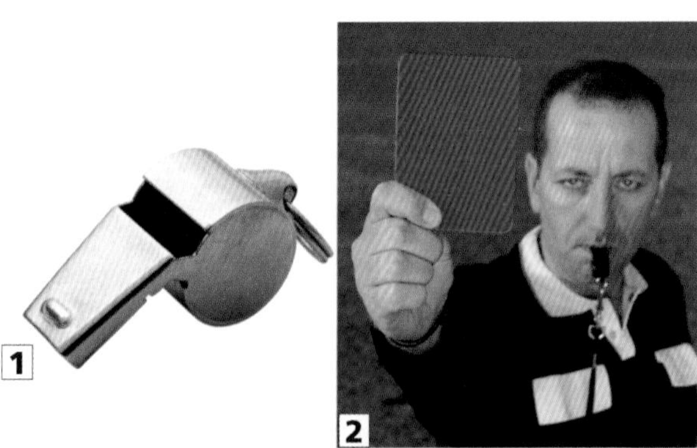
1
2

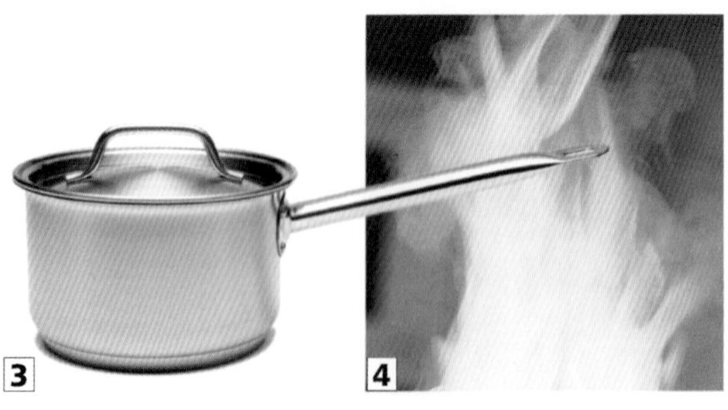
3
4

5

❺ Writing

a Look at the phrases below and complete Ted's letter to Teen Dreams. Use the past continuous and the past simple.

1 I was at home in the morning

a
at home in the morning/get ready

b
very late/really angry/get into car

c
walk/start/point

d
wear

Hello Teen Dreams

This is my true story. I [1]_____ and I [2]_____ for school. I [3]_____ and my mum [4]_____ with me. I [5]_____ very quickly. I [6]_____ into the classroom when my friend [7]_____ to laugh. He [8]_____ at my feet. I [9]_____ my slippers! How embarrassing!

Ted

b 1.25 Now listen and check.

My English file

Make up your own amazing story.

- Where were you?
- What were you doing?
- What happened?

I was in my room listening to music. My sister…

❻ Check your English

Use the prompts to make sentences with *when*.

1 I was walking the dog when I found a purse.

1 walk the dog/find a purse
2 eat a sandwich/break my tooth
3 ride my bike/fall off
4 do my homework/fall asleep

❸ Grammar practice

a) Students complete the story with the past continuous or the past simple of the verbs in brackets and compare their answers in pairs. Individual students read out the story, one sentence each.

b) [1.24] Play the CD for students to check their answers.

Extra activity

Before students begin Activity 4, write a few key words from the story on the board, e.g. *noise, garden, cat, doorbell, neighbour*. In groups of four, students predict what the story is about on the basis of these words. They check their ideas by completing Activity 4.

Answer key

1 was watching **2** heard **3** went **4** was looking **5** ran **6** was running **7** rang **8** was **9** was looking **10** was talking **11** ran

Mixed-ability classes

To help less confident students, reveal that the past simple appears six times in the story and the past continuous five times. Fast finishers can continue the story of the missing cat by adding one or two more events.

Homework suggestions

1 Activity Book pages 16–17, Activities 1–3
2 Students choose one email from Activity 1 and write four questions to its author. The questions should relate to the stories, e.g. *What did you do next? What was your friend doing?*

PART 2

Introduction

Write the following questions on the board: *What was happening when you arrived at school today? What was happening when you came into the classroom?* Divide students into pairs. They should take turns to ask and answer the questions on the board. Encourage students to make full sentences with the past continuous, the past simple and *when*, e.g. *Two students were playing with a yoyo and the Maths teacher was talking on the phone when I arrived at school this morning.*

❹ Vocabulary

Students find words in the emails in Activity 1 to label the pictures. Elicit the words and drill their pronunciation.

Answer key

Email 1 1 whistle 2 referee
Email 2 3 saucepan 4 on fire 5 alarm

Extra activity

Students write their own sentences with the words from Activity 4.

❺ Writing

a) Explain that the text under the pictures is an email from Ted to *Teen Dreams* describing an embarrassing story. Students look at the pictures to guess what happened to Ted.

Students complete Ted's story with the phrases in the past simple or the past continuous. They should insert the verb *be* in the past where necessary. The phrases are in the same order as in the text. When students have finished writing, they compare the answers in pairs.

Mixed-ability classes

Fast finishers imagine what Ted did next after noticing he was wearing his slippers. When everybody has completed Activity 5a, fast finishers share their ideas with the whole class.

b) [1.25] Play the CD for students to check their answers.

Tapescript and Answer key

Hello Teen Dreams
This is my true story. I was at home in the morning and I was getting ready for school. I was very late and my mum was really angry with me. I got into the car very quickly. I was walking into the classroom when my friend started to laugh. He pointed at my feet. I was wearing my slippers! How embarrassing!
Ted

My English file

Students imagine and write down their own amazing story. They can also write a true story if they want to. Go through the instructions and the example first. Students write at least six sentences, using the past simple and the past continuous. Set a time limit of ten minutes. Monitor students' work, providing help.

When students have finished the task, they exchange their notebooks in pairs and read each other's stories. Individual students report their classmate's stories to the whole class.

Extra activity

Ask students to think of a true funny or unusual incident that happened to them or somebody they know. Give students three minutes to prepare to tell the story. Help with key vocabulary. Then students choose a classmate, tell them their story and listen to theirs. Next they change partners and retell each other the last story they heard. Repeat twice, with students each time telling the last story they have heard. Then each student repeats the last story they heard to the whole class. The person whose story it was says what changes have been made to the original story.

Teaching tip: *Students' lives as a resource*

Personal experiences of students are a useful resource in the classroom, stimulating the class to listen attentively and respond. Students are genuinely interested in each other's lives and they will develop their fluency if given opportunities to share their own stories and discuss their classmates' experiences. Organise activities in which students tell their stories to the whole class and allow their classmates to ask questions. You could have a few minutes every week for students to share their recent adventures with the class in English.

Photocopiable activity

The missing bag p108; instructions p94

❻ Check your English

Students use the prompts to make sentences with the past continuous, the past simple and ***when.*** Students compare their answers in pairs. Individual students read their sentences to the whole class.

Answer key

1 I was walking the dog when I found a purse.
2 I was eating a sandwich when I broke my tooth.
3 I was riding my bike when I fell off.
4 I was doing my homework when I fell asleep.

Homework suggestions

1 Activity Book page 17, Activities 4–5
2 Students describe two surprising moments in their favourite films or TV series, using the past continuous, the past simple and *when*, e.g. *Alex was sleeping when Marty escaped from the zoo.*

8 My hero

1 Reading

a 1.26 Read Sara's project about Aimee Mullins. Why is Aimee famous?

Aimee is also a model.

Aimee has special legs for running. She says, 'My brother calls them 'RoboCop legs'!

My hero
by Sara Chester

My hero is Aimee Mullins. Aimee was born in 1976 in Pennsylvania, USA. She's famous now as an athlete, an actress and a model but the beginning of her life was very difficult.

When she was born, Aimee had a problem with her legs. When she was one, she had a double amputation. This means that doctors cut off both her legs below her knees. However, Aimee got some artificial legs and she learnt to walk and then to run and jump!

Aimee loved sports at school. She skied and she played American football, softball and volleyball. She also studied hard. In 1995 she went to Georgetown University in Washington DC.

At university Aimee was a very good student and she trained hard at sports as well. She enjoyed athletics and she ran in races against able-bodied students. She broke records for the 100-metre race and the long jump.

Now Aimee is the President of the Women's Sports Foundation. She's an inspiration for sports people around the world.

Aimee is my hero because she didn't give up. She tried hard and achieved a lot. She's an amazing person!

b Read again. Then answer these questions about Aimee.

1 What happened to her when she was one?
2 What sports did Aimee play at school?
3 When did she go to university?
4 What sports did Aimee do at university?
5 Why is she Sara's hero?

8 My hero

Photocopiable activity

- *Famous people* p109

PART 1

Introduction

Divide the class into groups of four. Ask them to make a list of popular teenage idols, e.g. film stars, musicians, athletes and discuss why people admire them. Set a time limit of four minutes. Groups read out their lists and say why these people are teenage idols.

❶ Reading

a) [1.26] Focus attention on the pictures and explain that they show Aimee Mullins. Find out if students know her. Explain that she is famous in the USA and she is a hero for many people. Students read and listen to find out why she is famous. Play the CD.

Elicit that Aimee is famous as an athlete, an actress and a model, and she has worked very hard for her career because she has no legs. Point to the descriptions under the photos and elicit or explain that *RoboCop* was a superhuman cyborg from a famous 1987 sci-fi film entitled *RoboCop*.

Tapescript

see Student's Book Activity 1a

b) Students read the text in Activity 1a again and answer the questions about Aimee. They should focus on finding the answers and ignore words which they do not know. Encourage them to mark with pencil the relevant parts of the text which contain the answers.

Students compare the answers in pairs. Check the answers with the whole class and which parts of the text justify them. Ask students if they know/can guess the meaning of the following words: *beginning, double amputation, both, below, however, artificial, softball, against, able-bodied, inspiration, give up, achieved.* Provide explanation if necessary.

Answer key

1 She had a double amputation.
2 She skied and played American football, softball and volleyball.
3 In 1995.
4 Athletics (running races and long jump).
5 Because she tried hard and didn't give up, and achieved a lot.

Teaching tip: *Improving reading comprehension*

Encourage students to read the comprehension questions before they read the text in detail so that they can focus on the information they need. They should look at the title and any headings and pictures, as they usually help with understanding the text. While reading students can pause to summarise each paragraph as this will help them find particular information. When students find the answers to the questions in the text, they can underline them and write the number of the corresponding question at the side. They can then refer to these notes to justify the answers.

Extra activity

Ask students if they can think of other famous people who manage(d) to have successful careers despite their disabilities. You can mention the following people and elicit what students know about them: Christopher Reeve (an actor, paralysed in an accident), Michael J.Fox (an actor, he suffers from Parkinson's disease), Stephen Hawking (a physicist, paralysed by motor neurone disease), Lance Armstrong (a cyclist, cancer survivor) and Stevie Wonder (a musician, blind from birth).

Dyslexia tip: *Reading longer texts*

Dyslexic students have difficulties reading longer blocks of text. Use the following techniques to help them deal with this task:

- Play the recording of the text as students may have a large auditory vocabulary and only struggle with recognising the words in print. Reading texts in *Hot Spot* have an accompanying recording on the CD
- When preparing your own materials, avoid fully justified text as the resulting spacing between words can confuse students
- Break the text into short paragraphs and ask students to focus on one paragraph at a time, covering the remaining paragraphs with a notebook or a sheet of paper.

❷ Speaking

Work in pairs. Look at the information below. Choose one person and tell your classmate about him/her.

Orlando Bloom was born in …

Orlando Bloom

- born in 1977 in Kent, England
- had a lot of problems at school because he was dyslexic
- left home at 16 to study drama
- broke his back in 1998 but recovered quickly
- became famous as Legolas in 'The Lord of the Rings' trilogy

Bethany Hamilton

- born in 1990 in Hawaii
- loved swimming and surfing
- won first surfing competition at the age of 8
- a shark attacked her in October 2003 and bit off her left arm
- went surfing again just three weeks after the shark attack
- won the NSSA surfing championships in 2005

❸ Listening

a 1.27 Listen to Adam talk about Bethany Hamilton. He makes three mistakes. Can you spot the mistakes? Use the information in Activity 2 to help you.

b 1.28 Listen and check.

❹ Writing

a Who is your hero? Think of a person you admire. It can be a famous person, a friend or someone in your family.

b Make some notes about your hero.

- Where and when was your hero born?
- What did your hero do?
- What did your hero achieve?
- Why is this person a hero for you?

c Now write about your hero.

My hero is my father. He was born in …

Writing tip

Try to use these words to link sentences together:

however	*The doctors cut off her legs.* ***However,*** *she got some artificial legs…*
but	*She's famous now as an athlete* ***but*** *the beginning of her life was very difficult.*
as well	*At university, Aimee was a very good student and she trained hard at sports* ***as well.***
because	*Aimee is my hero* ***because*** *she didn't give up.*

Past simple bingo

a Choose six verbs from this list. Write the past simple form in the grid.

run win swim get throw break do read buy go fly blow see put hear have learn study cut enjoy leave

b Listen to your teacher. When you hear a verb in your grid, put a cross through it. Shout 'Bingo!' when all six verbs are crossed through. The first person to shout 'Bingo!' is the winner.

❷ Speaking

Ask if students know the people in the photos. Divide students into pairs. They should choose one celebrity from the photos each. Explain that they are going to read some information about this person's life and then re-tell it to their classmate in their own words. Pre-teach the following words: *dyslexic, drama, recover, trilogy, bite/bit, competition, championships.* Explain that the *NSSA* (National Scholastic Surfing Association) is the most important surfing association for amateurs in the USA.

Set a time limit of twelve minutes for reading, preparation and speaking. Ask students to listen attentively and remember as much as possible. When they have finished the task, they repeat to each other everything they remember from the biography their partner has told them about.

Teaching tip: *Signalling the end of a time limit*

To get students' attention when the time limit for a given task is up, establish an easily recognisable signal. Here are some ideas:

- turn off the lights for two seconds
- clap your hands
- Put your hands in the air and ask each student who notices to copy your gesture to make the signal more visible for others
- call out: *Freeze!* and in the same second everyone should freeze like a statue. When everyone is 'frozen', say: *Melt!* and move to the next stage of the lesson.

Mixed-ability classes

In pairs, fast finishers say why they admire the famous people in the task.

Homework suggestions

1 Activity Book page 18, Activity 1
2 Students find information about a famous person they admire and they write it in note form as in Activity 2.

PART 2

Introduction

Write *Hero* on the board. Elicit what makes someone a hero. Write students' ideas on the board, e.g. *A hero is brave, does not give up, helps people.* Ask students to give some examples of heroes from real life or fiction.

❸ Listening

a) [1.27] Elicit from students everything they remember about Bethany Hamilton. Then ask them to listen to Adam talk about her. Explain that he makes three mistakes. Ask students to try to find the mistakes. They can look at Activity 2. Play the CD.

In pairs, students discuss the answers. Elicit students' ideas in full sentences, but do not reveal the answers yet.

Tapescript

Bethany Hamilton was born in 1990 in Hawaii. She loved swimming and surfing and she won her first swimming competition at the age of 8. However, in October 2003, a shark attacked her and bit off her left leg. Bethany went surfing again just three months after the shark attack, and she won the NSSA surfing championships in 2005.

b) [1.28] Play the CD for students to check their answers.

Tapescript and Answer key

1 Bethany didn't win a swimming competition. She won a surfing competition.
2 A shark didn't bite off her left leg. It bit off her left arm.
3 Bethany didn't go surfing three months after the attack. She went surfing again three weeks after the attack.

Extra activity

In pairs, students write down a short biography of Orlando Bloom on the basis of the information in Activity 2 and make three factual mistakes. Pairs exchange their texts with another pair and try to find and circle the mistakes as quickly as possible. The winner is the pair who finds the mistakes first.

❹ Writing

a) Ask students to think of their own hero: a famous person, a friend or a relative.

b) Students read the prompts and make notes about their hero, using Activity 2 as a model. If you assigned the second homework activity in the previous lesson, ask students to use their notes to write the answers.

c) Students write a text about their hero based on their notes and using Activity 1 as a model. Before they begin writing, refer them to the **Writing tip** to introduce words that link sentences together. Explain, using L1 if necessary, that we use *however* and *but* to introduce information contrasting with the information in the previous sentence or phrase, *as well* means the same as *too* and *in addition,* and *because* gives the reason for something. Point out the position of the words in the sentence and explain the punctuation rules. Encourage students to use the words in their texts.

Encourage students to make a draft copy first and rewrite it after editing. Monitor their work, providing help. Then they should exchange their texts in pairs. If they notice any mistakes in their classmate's text, they should point these out orally.

Photocopiable activity

Famous people p109; instructions p94

Past simple bingo

a) Students complete the grid with the past simple form of six verbs chosen from the box.

b) Read out the verbs in the box slowly in random order. Tick the words you have read to keep track. If students hear a verb which is in its past form in their grid, they cross it out. When they have crossed out all the six verbs, they shout: *Bingo!* Check that you have indeed read all their words. The first person to shout: *Bingo!* is the winner.

Homework suggestions

1 Activity Book page 18, Activity 2
2 Students write a few sentences about their own life with the words from Activity 4 and the **Writing tip**.

Module 2 Review

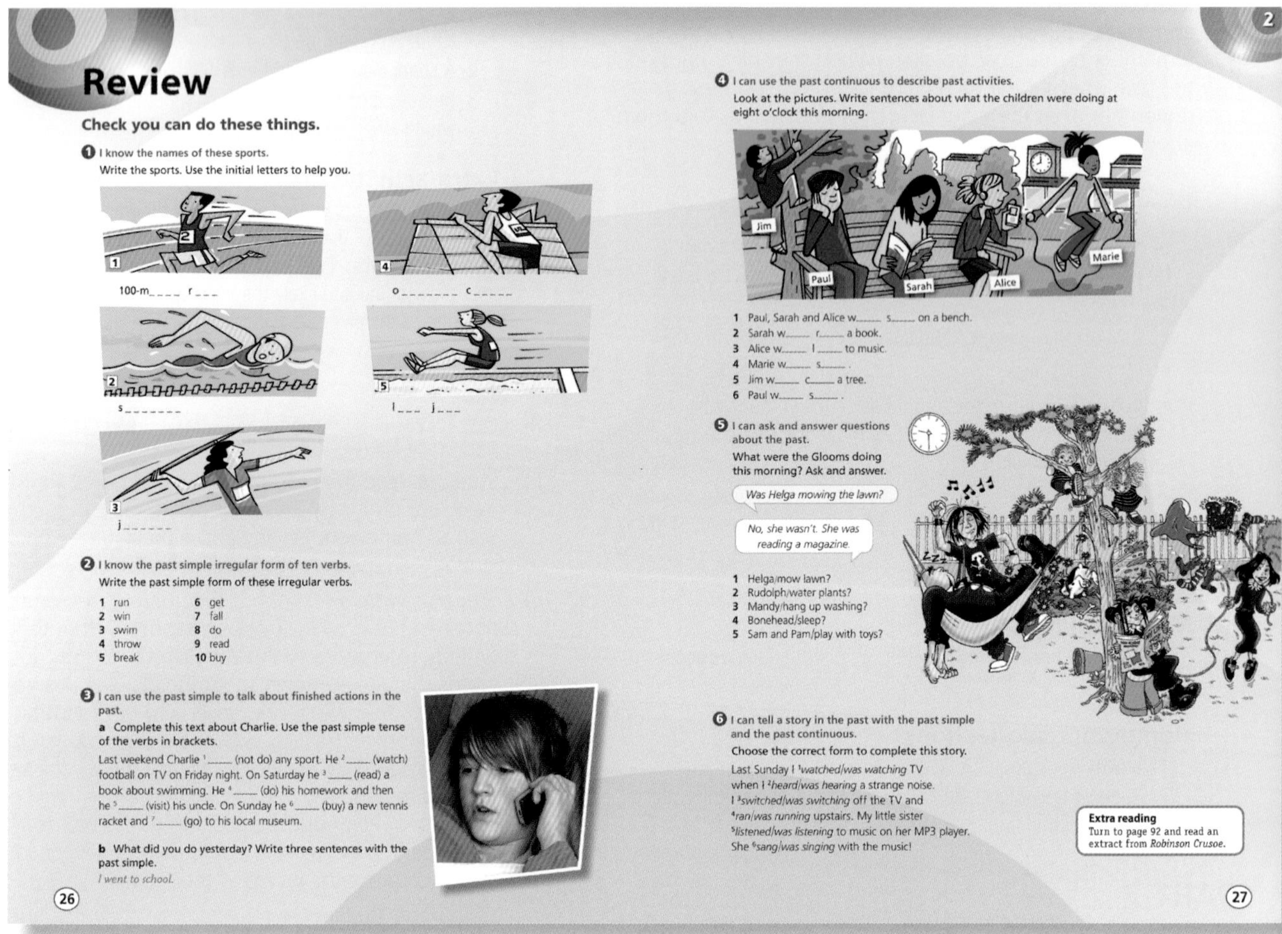

Review

Check you can do these things.

1 I know the names of these sports.
Write the sports. Use the initial letters to help you.

1 100-m_ _ _ _ r_ _ _
2 s_ _ _ _ _ _ _
3 j_ _ _ _ _
4 o_ _ _ _ _ _ _ c_ _ _ _ _
5 l_ _ _ j_ _ _

2 I know the past simple irregular form of ten verbs.
Write the past simple form of these irregular verbs.

1 run
2 win
3 swim
4 throw
5 break
6 get
7 fall
8 do
9 read
10 buy

3 I can use the past simple to talk about finished actions in the past.

a Complete this text about Charlie. Use the past simple tense of the verbs in brackets.

Last weekend Charlie 1 ____ (not do) any sport. He 2 ____ (watch) football on TV on Friday night. On Saturday he 3 ____ (read) a book about swimming. He 4 ____ (do) his homework and then he 5 ____ (visit) his uncle. On Sunday he 6 ____ (buy) a new tennis racket and 7 ____ (go) to his local museum.

b What did you do yesterday? Write three sentences with the past simple.
I went to school.

26

4 I can use the past continuous to describe past activities.
Look at the pictures. Write sentences about what the children were doing at eight o'clock this morning.

1 Paul, Sarah and Alice w____ s____ on a bench.
2 Sarah w____ r____ a book.
3 Alice w____ l____ to music.
4 Marie w____ s____ .
5 Jim w____ c____ a tree.
6 Paul w____ s____ .

5 I can ask and answer questions about the past.
What were the Glooms doing this morning? Ask and answer.

Was Helga mowing the lawn?

No, she wasn't. She was reading a magazine.

1 Helga/mow lawn?
2 Rudolph/water plants?
3 Mandy/hang up washing?
4 Bonehead/sleep?
5 Sam and Pam/play with toys?

6 I can tell a story in the past with the past simple and the past continuous.
Choose the correct form to complete this story.

Last Sunday I 1 *watched/was watching* TV when I 2 *heard/was hearing* a strange noise. I 3 *switched/was switching* off the TV and 4 *ran/was running* upstairs. My little sister 5 *listened/was listening* to music on her MP3 player. She 6 *sang/was singing* with the music!

Extra reading
Turn to page 92 and read an extract from *Robinson Crusoe*.

27

Optional materials:

- four slips of paper per group of four students

Optional revision

Before your students start this Review, you may want to direct them to the Grammar summary at the back of their coursebooks and to the Lexical sets at the back of their Activity Books. This will remind them of the main grammar and vocabulary in the module. Give them ten minutes to read through those in small groups and ask you any questions they may have.

- Activity Book: Refer your students to pages 85–86: *Sports and achievements*; *In the garden*; *Emergencies*; *Home*
- Grammar summary: Refer your students to pages 99–100, sections 5–7

Module 2 Review

The purpose of this section is revision and consolidation of the material studied in Module 2.

Completing the activities

Go over all the activities with the class, explaining rubrics and giving examples to make sure students know what to do. There are written and oral tasks, but you may decide yourself how they should be completed by students. Generally students should do the writing tasks individually and the oral tasks in pairs, testing each other's knowledge. Make sure they do not treat the *Review* as a formal test, but complete the activities in a friendly, stress-free atmosphere. Fast finishers can write down the answers to the oral tasks.

Checking answers

When students have finished, check the answers with the whole class by asking volunteers to copy their answers onto the board or to say them aloud. If necessary, explain the more difficult issues, ask additional questions about the activities and solve any problems that arise.

Self-evaluation

Tell students to evaluate themselves. They should tick the activities where at least half of their answers were correct.

Feedback

Ask students which activities were difficult, which were easy and if there is anything they would like to review. Make a note of common language problems to go over in future lessons.

Answer key

❶
1 100-metre race
2 swimming
3 javelin
4 obstacle course
5 long jump

❷
1 ran
2 won
3 swam
4 threw
5 broke
6 got
7 fell
8 did
9 read
10 bought

❸ **a)**
1 didn't do
2 watched
3 read
4 did
5 visited
6 bought
7 went

b) Students write three past simple sentences about what they did the previous day.

❹ Students study the picture showing a scene at eight o'clock in the morning and write sentences about what the characters were doing.

1 were sitting
2 was reading
3 was listening
4 was skipping
5 was climbing
6 was sleeping

❺ Students ask and answer the questions about the picture in pairs as in the example. Alternatively, they can write the questions and the answers individually.

1 Was Helga mowing the lawn? No, she wasn't. She was reading a magazine.
2 Was Rudolph watering the plants? No, he wasn't. He was listening to music.
3 Was Mandy hanging up the washing? No, she wasn't. She was skipping.
4 Was Bonehead sleeping? No, he wasn't. He was burying a bone.
5 Were Sam and Pam playing with toys? No, they weren't. They were climbing a tree.

❻
1 was watching
2 heard
3 switched
4 ran
5 was listening
6 was singing

Extra activity

Divide students into groups of four. They should write on slips of paper four past continuous sentences in the second person describing unusual activities and a specific time, e.g. *You were dancing outside your house at 5 o'clock in the morning.* Groups exchange their sentences with another group. One person picks a sentence and tells the group that they were doing this activity at the specific time yesterday. Group members ask three questions to find out more details about the activity, e.g. *Why were you dancing outside your house?* The student makes up the answers. Then it is the next student's turn to pick a sentence and so on until there are no sentences left.

Dyslexia tip: *Oral tests*

If possible, test dyslexic students in the way they perform best, i.e. with an oral test instead of writing. Read out the instructions to them and make it clear what the purpose of each activity is. Allow students some time to prepare and then listen to and evaluate their oral answers.

Extra reading

Refer students to pages 92 and 93 of their books to find an extract from *Robinson Crusoe*.

❶ Students read the background information about the book and its author and say if they know any other famous books about ships and the sea.

❷ Students read the extract from the book and answer the questions.

a three hats, a cap and two odd shoes
b a knife, a pipe and some tobacco
c a creek
d He didn't want wild animals to eat him

❸ Students discuss the questions in groups of four. Groups share the results of their discussion with the whole class.

Homework suggestions

If students enjoyed the extract, they may want to read the whole story. There is a Macmillan Reader of *Robinson Crusoe*. Visit macmillanenglish.com/readers for details.

Module 2 Tests (A and B) are on the Tests CD

Learning diary

You can refer students to page 19 of the Activity Book for further review, more study tips and self-assessment activities.

Extra special

Extra special

Mini-play

Look at the picture. What do you think the children are doing?

a 1.29 **Listen and read the first part of the play. What do you think happens at the end?**

Danny Great. The tents are up! One tent for the boys and one tent for the girls.
Maria Yes, this is brilliant! The fire is burning and the food is cooking. Our first camping trip! Now where are the others?
Sandra Hi guys! Sorry we're late. It's all Ben's fault.
Ben No, it isn't my fault; it's yours. You forgot the torch!
Sandra Yes, and you forgot the blankets!
Maria OK, OK, guys! We're all here now.
Ben Actually the real problem was Lucy.
Maria Your little sister?
Sandra Yes. She really wanted to come too. But she's too young for camping.
Ben She's at home with Mum and Dad.
Danny Anyway … I'm hungry! Let's have some food.
Sandra Great idea.
Maria Right, sausages and beans for everyone. Mmm, delicious.
Sandra Wow. Look at the stars. They're beautiful!
Danny Yes. And it's so quiet.
Ben It's quite dark here.
Maria Yes. No electric lights. This is the real natural world!
Sandra Well, Maria, it's not actually the real natural world. It's your garden!
Maria OK, OK. But it's still exciting!
Sandra Did you hear that?
Danny What?
Maria I think I heard something.
Ben What did you hear?
Maria I don't know. A strange sound.
Sandra I didn't hear anything.
Danny Did you hear that?
Sandra Yes, I did.
Ben Oh, don't be silly. It was nothing. Just a … sound.
Danny I'm not scared.
Sandra No, I'm not scared. I'm definitely not scared.
All Aaagggh!
Ben OK everyone. Calm down, calm down. It's probably a bird.
Sandra Or a fox.
Danny I've got a really good idea.
Maria What?
Danny Let's go and get Mum and Dad.
Maria No way!
Sandra That sound's coming from your tent, boys!
Ben Right! That's it! Come on, Danny, we're going in!

b 1.30 **Now listen to the last part. Did you guess the ending?**

c 1.31 **Listen again to the whole dialogue. Then read with your classmates.**

Memory challenge
Learn your lines by heart.

28

Mini-project

1 Read Jack's fact sheet. Does your school have any similar after-school sports clubs?

Sports at my school

We do lots of sports at my school. In the summer, we do cricket, rounders and athletics. In the winter we do football, rugby and gymnastics. My favourite sport is gymnastics.
We also have after-school sports clubs.

I do karate and netball after school.
Every summer we have a sports day at our school. The students take part in lots of different sports competitions and the winners get medals.

Jack

2 Write about sports at your school. Draw pictures or use photos from magazines to illustrate your fact sheet.

29

Optional materials

- a selection of items connected with camping, such as a torch, matches, a blanket or a sleeping bag, a camping mat

Extra activity

Bring a selection of items connected with camping, e.g. a torch, matches, a blanket or a sleeping bag, a camping mat, etc. Alternatively draw the items on the board. Elicit or teach the names of the objects and ask students what we use them for. Ask students to rank the items in the order of importance as camping equipment.

Mini-play

Focus students' attention on the picture. Elicit that the characters are camping.

Extra activity

In pairs, students make a list of all the things in the picture they can name in English. Set a time limit of three minutes. Ask the pair with the longest list to read it out to the whole class. Other students listen and cross out the words which repeat on their own lists, and then read out any words which have not been mentioned.

a) [1.29] Students listen and read the first part of the play about a camping adventure. Encourage them to make guesses about what happens at the end. Play the CD through.

Ask comprehension questions, e.g. *How many tents are there? Who are they for? Why are Sandra and Ben late? Who is Lucy and where is she? What are the characters cooking? Where are they? What did they hear? What do they think made the sound? Where is the sound coming from again?* Explain any vocabulary students do not understand. Elicit different endings to the story.

Tapescript

see Student's Book Activity a

b) [1.30] Play the CD for students to check their guesses. Find out who guessed the real ending in Activity b.

Divide students into groups of four and ask them to choose the parts from the play. Play the CD for students to listen carefully to their lines. Get students to read out the play in their groups. Then go over the **Memory challenge** and encourage students to learn their lines by heart. Give them five minutes to practise and memorise their lines. Then ask groups to act out the play to the rest of the class, saying as many lines from memory as possible. Get the class to vote for the best performance.

Extra activity

Students talk about their own camping experiences with the whole class.

Tapescript

Sophie: That sound's coming from your tent, boys!
Ben: Right! That's it! Come on, Danny. We're going in!
Danny and Ben: Look what we've found.
Everyone: Lucy!

c) [1.31] The whole story is recorded for you to play to students or use as you wish.

Mini-project

1. Explain to students that a boy called Jack has written a fact sheet about sports at his school. Ask students to read his project and answer if their school has similar after-school sports clubs. Clarify any vocabulary if necessary.
2. Students work individually and make a project about sports at their school. They should write at least four sentences. Encourage them to make a draft copy first. Ask students to illustrate their fact sheet. Monitor their work and provide help where necessary.

   In pairs, students exchange and read each other's fact sheets and offer feedback to each other.

Extra activity

Students write names of two school sports they like and two they dislike in mixed order. In pairs, they try to guess which activities their classmate likes and which he/she does not.

Lesson objective

Talking about experiences

9 In my life

1 Presentation

a 1.32 Listen and read. Find the things Eva talks about in the pictures.

b 1.32 Listen again. Practise saying the poem.

9 In my life

Grammar
- present perfect: *ever, never*

Vocabulary
- experiences

Optional materials
- sheets of A4 paper, one fewer than there are students in class

Optional Activity Book activities
- Fast finishers p64, Extra practice p65

Photocopiable activity
- *Experiences …* p110

PART 1

Introduction

Copy the following table onto the board:

Places we visit on holiday	*Forms of transport*	*Unusual food*	*Kinds of music*

Put students into groups of four and ask them to write as many words in each category as possible. Set a time limit of four minutes. Elicit the words from different groups onto the board and then compare how many of them appear in Activity 1 on page 30.

❶ Presentation

a) [1.32] Focus students' attention on the picture. Introduce Eva, the girl holding the poster with a poem. Ask students to listen and read Eva's poem about her experiences. They should find the things she talks about in the pictures around the text. Play the CD.

In pairs, students say which words from the poem the pictures illustrate. They should make guesses about new vocabulary. Point to the pictures in turn and elicit the words from the class. Make sure everybody understands all the words now. Explain any other vocabulary students may not understand.

Refer students to the **Grammar spot** at the top of the next page to introduce the present perfect. Go over the example sentences and elicit or explain that we use the tense to talk about experiences without giving the specific time of the events. You can draw a timeline to illustrate this point (see the teaching tip below). Explain the structure of the present perfect and use the **Remember!** box to point out the full and short forms. Point out that regular verbs take the same form as in the past simple, but irregular verbs have a different form called the past participle. Demonstrate the past participle, using the list of irregular verbs on page 106. Refer students to the **Grammar summary** on page 101 for more information on the present perfect.

Teaching tip: *Timelines*

Timelines illustrate how tenses place events in time, and in relation to other events. They show complex rules in a simple visual way. The use of the present perfect is often a difficult concept for students. To clarify it, you can draw the following timeline:

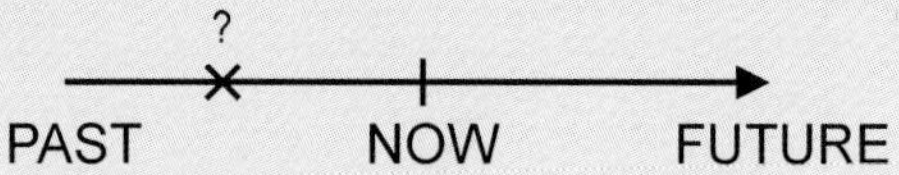

Explain that the cross marks a past event and the question mark shows that we do not know exactly when it happened.

Mixed-ability classes

Fast finishers label the pictures in writing.

Extra activity

Check understanding of the poem by asking students to mark the pictures illustrating the things Eva has done in her life with a tick (✔) and those she has not done with a cross (✘).

Tapescript

see Student's Book Activity 1a

b) [1.32] Play the CD again. Ask students to practise saying the poem aloud in chorus, then in pairs, helping each other with any pronunciation problems.

Extra activity

Encourage students to learn the poem by heart. They can use the following techniques: repetition/reading the poem several times, using the pictures to recall the complete lines, or cover every second or third word of the poem with blu-tack and then keep covering more words as they memorise the whole lines. Ask volunteers to recite the poem to the class.

Teaching tip: *Using poems in class*

Poems can serve a variety of purposes in the classroom. Primarily they are great tools to learn about the pronunciation of individual sounds and word stress. A lot of them follow a rhyming pattern. As students are listening to the poem, ask them to identify rhyming words. Before you ask students to work on the poem creatively, make sure they can read it well and hopefully memorise it, using different techniques. Ask students to first repeat the poem after you or the recording and then to practise reading it independently with fluency and expression, making use of the punctuation. Then they should read it to a classmate or in a group. Once students know the poem well, you can ask them to replace rhyming words with other rhyming words or write their own stanza following the pattern of the poem. This way students are encouraged to work on pronunciation and vocabulary, looking for words that rhyme with each other, as well as grammar, particularly tenses and sentence structure.

Tapescript

see Activity 1a

Grammar spot
Present perfect: *ever, never*

Have you **ever visited** a castle?
Yes, I **have.**/No, I **haven't**.
I've eaten spinach leaves.
I **haven't climbed** Mount Everest.
I've never been on an aeroplane.

Grammar page 101

Remember!

Full form	*Short form*
I **have**	**I've**
I **have not**	I **haven't**

2 Grammar practice

a Complete three of these phrases to make true sentences about yourself.

I've never eaten …	I've travelled on a …
I haven't tasted …	I've been to …
I've listened to …	I haven't lived in …
I've visited …	I've never danced to …

1 I've never eaten spinach.
2 I've been to Italy.
3 I've never danced to hip hop.

b Read your sentences to your classmates. Try to find someone with one or two sentences like yours.

Study tip
Remembering past participles

Write down verbs in lists of regular and irregular verbs

Regular	*Irregular*
visit – visited	*be – been*
listen – listened	*eat – eaten*
taste – tasted	*take – taken*

3 Pronunciation

1.33 Listen and practise saying these verbs.

/ɪd/ visited shouted started ended
/d/ travelled listened climbed played
/t/ danced worked helped watched

4 Speaking

a 1.34 Listen and read these questions.

Experiences Have you ever …

1 played tennis?

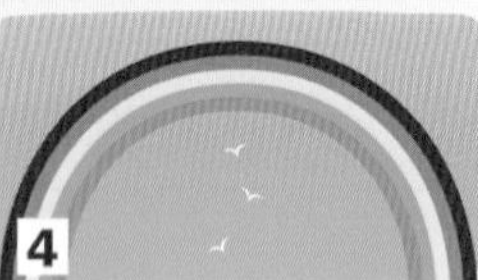
4 seen a rainbow?

2 been to London?

5 eaten Chinese food?

3 swum in the sea?

6 won a prize?

b Now ask and answer the questions with a classmate.

Have you ever played tennis?

No, I haven't. or *Yes, I have.*

5 Class poll

1.35 Listen to the questions in Activity 4 again. Put your hand up for all the things you have done. Write the results on the board.

	Yes, I have	No, I haven't
1 Tennis	9	11
2 London	…	

6 Check your English

Complete with *have, haven't, ever, never.*

A: Have you [1]_____ eaten Mexican food?
B: No, I've [2]_____ eaten Mexican food, but I [3]_____ eaten Spanish food. Have you [4]_____ eaten Spanish food?
A: No, I [5]_____.

❷ Grammar practice

a) Go over the phrases in the box and point out that some are positive and some negative. Explain that we say *been* to + a place or an event. Students choose three phrases and complete them with their own ideas to make true sentences about themselves. Demonstrate the task by reading out the example.

Mixed-ability classes

For less confident students write on the board categories of words which go with each verb, e.g. *eaten* + type of food.

b) Students read their sentences to their classmates. If anyone has the same sentence/s, they should raise their hand. If you have a large class, do this activity in groups.

Extra activity

Place chairs or sheets of A4 paper in a circle, one chair/sheet of paper less than there are students in class. Copy the phrases from Activity 2a onto the board. Students sit on the chairs/stand on the sheets of paper. A volunteer goes to the middle of the circle and makes a true sentence about their experience with one of the phrases on the board, e.g. *I've never eaten sushi.* Students who share the same experience change seats/stand on a different sheet of paper. As they are moving, the person in the middle tries to grab a vacated chair/stand on a vacated sheet of paper. If they succeed, another person is left in the middle and they repeat the activity with another sentence. Set a time limit of five minutes for the game.

Homework suggestions

1. Activity Book pages 20–21, Activities 1–3
2. Students write true sentences for themselves about the activities in the pictures in Activity 1, e.g. *I have never visited a castle.*

PART 2

Introduction

Write the following verbs from Activity 1 on the board: *travel, take, climb, eat, dance, visit, live, be.* In pairs, students decide which verbs are regular and which irregular and write down their past participle form. Check the answers with the whole class.

> **Dyslexia tip:** *Notes on the board*
>
> Make sure that the notes on the board are large and clear and that dyslexic students can see them well from where they are sitting. Use different colours for different types of words or different sentences. Leave the notes on the board as long as possible so that dyslexic students have time to copy them.

Study tip

Go over the example lists of verbs. Encourage students to add verbs in the infinitive and the past participle to the correct category as they come across them.

❸ Pronunciation

[1.33] Explain that there are three ways of pronouncing the regular verb *-ed* ending, depending on the final sound of the infinitive form of the verb: if it is /t/ or /d/, then we pronounce the ending /ɪd/, if it is a vowel or a voiced sound, we pronounce the ending /d/ and if it is a voiceless consonant, the ending is /t/.

You can ask students to place their finger gently on their throat and say different consonants; if the vocal cords vibrate, the consonants are voiced. Play the CD with the three types of pronunciation of the *-ed* ending and ask students to repeat the verbs. Then encourage them to practise pronunciation of the verbs independently.

Tapescript

see Student's Book Activity 3

❹ Speaking

a) [1.34] Students listen and read the questions and think about their own true answers. Play the CD. Ask students to use the pictures to help them understand the questions.

Tapescript

see Student's Book Activity 4a

b) In pairs, students ask and answer the questions from Activity 4a to find out about each other's experiences. Demonstrate the task by reading out the example with a confident student.

Extra activity

Before students begin asking questions, encourage them to predict their classmate's answers. They should put a cross (**✘**) for *no* and a tick (**✔**) for *yes* beside each question and then interview their classmate. They get one point for each correct guess.

Photocopiable activity

Experiences p110; instructions p94

❺ Class poll

[1.35] Play the CD again, pausing after each question. Students put their hands up if their answer is *Yes, I have.* Two volunteers count how many students have and have not had each experience and write the results on the board as in the example. Find out which experience is the most common and ask students to justify it, e.g. *Most students have swum in the sea because our town is near the sea.*

Tapescript

see Activity 4a

❻ Check your English

Students complete the dialogue with ***have, haven't, ever,*** or ***never*** and compare their answers in pairs. Ask one pair to read out the dialogue to the whole class.

Extra activity

A volunteer stands with their back to the board. Write one of the verbs from the lesson on the board, e.g. *played.* Students make present perfect sentences with the verb, but replacing the verb with beep, e.g. *I've never* beep *the piano.* The volunteer tries to guess the mystery verb.

Answer key

1 ever **2** never **3** have **4** ever **5** haven't

Homework suggestions

1. Activity Book page 21, Activities 4–6
2. Students write three questions with *Have you ever ...?* to add to the survey in Activity 4a. They can illustrate the questions. At the beginning of the next lesson they can use the questions to interview their classmates.

10 An amazing life

1 Presentation

a 1.36 Listen and read. Find the things Mandy talks about in the picture.

Sam Wow. Look at these!
Mandy Yes, Grandpa's been all over the world. Look. He's ridden an elephant in India.
Pam Cool. Has he ever climbed Mount Everest?
Mandy No, he's never climbed Mount Everest. But he's climbed Mount Kilimanjaro and that's the highest mountain in Africa.
Pam Wow! What else has he done?
Mandy Well, he's written lots of books and he's made films.
Sam Has he written any children's books?
Mandy No, he hasn't written any children's books. But he's written lots of travel books. And he's met a king and a queen and he's broken …
Sam His leg!
Mandy No, he hasn't broken his leg. He's broken world records. Look. He's sailed around the world in 80 days and he's skied down Mont Blanc. Yes, Grandpa has had a really amazing life.
Pam Umm. No wonder he's tired.

b 1.36 Listen again. Then read the dialogue with your classmates.

Real English

Cool
No wonder …

2 Class poll

What do you think is the most amazing thing Gordon Gloom has done in his life? Vote and write the results on the board.

ridden an elephant – 2
climbed Mount Kilimanjaro – 5

Grammar spot
Present perfect

Has he ever **climbed** Mount Everest?
Yes, he **has.**/No, he **hasn't.**

He**'s ridden** an elephant in India.
He **hasn't written** any children's books.

Grammar page 101

10 An amazing life

Grammar
- present perfect and past simple

Vocabulary
- travel; geography; experiences

Optional materials
- one slip of paper per student

Optional Activity Book activities
- Fast finishers p64, Extra practice p65

Photocopiable activity
- *Do you know anybody who ...?* p111

PART 1

Introduction

Individually, students write sentences on paper about three experiences they have had e.g. *I've played rugby*. One sentence should be false. Provide help with new vocabulary. In pairs, students exchange their sentences and guess which one is false about their classmate. Ask students to keep their sentences for a later stage of the lesson.

❶ Presentation

a) [1.36] Focus attention on the pictures and ask students to identify the members of the Gloom family: Mandy, Sam, Pam and Gordon. Elicit that they are in Gordon's bedroom where there are a lot of souvenirs, books and photos connected with travelling.

Ask students to listen and read and find the things Mandy talks about in the first picture. Play the CD twice, the second time getting students to point to the relevant fragments of the picture.

Clarify any vocabulary students do not understand. Refer them to **Real English** and demonstrate the meaning of the phrase, by telling students *I slept two hours last night* and then *The last meal I had was breakfast yesterday morning* to elicit *No wonder you're sleepy* and *No wonder you're hungry* respectively.

Refer students to the **Grammar spot** to elicit or explain the present perfect for the third person singular. Go over the different types of sentences in the example and encourage students to find more present perfect third person singular sentences in the dialogue. Use the **Remember!** box on the next page to point out the full and short forms of *has*. Remind students that we use the present perfect to talk about events which happened in the past but we do not know when or it is not important. Give a few examples of your family members' or friends' experiences, e.g. *My cousin has dived in the Red Sea.* Encourage volunteers to talk about some experiences of their family or friends. Refer students to the **Grammar summary** on page 101 for more information on the present perfect.

Teaching tip: *Using pictures from the Student's book*

You can use pictures from the Student's book in more ways than the Student's book tasks directly related to them, e.g.:
- ask students *who, what, where, when, why* and *how* questions about the pictures
- revise parts of speech by asking students to write adjectives, nouns and verbs from the pictures
- practise spelling or pronunciation by getting students to find words beginning with or ending in given letters or containing given sounds
- elicit ideas about what happened before and after the situation in the pictures
- use the pictures as a beginning of a story students need to continue in writing or orally as a one sentence game
- ask students to write captions for the pictures.

Tapescript
see Student's Book Activity 1a

b) [1.36] In groups of three, each student takes a role from the dialogue in Activity 1a. Play the CD again for students to pay attention to pronunciation and intonation. Then students read the dialogue within their groups. You can ask them to repeat the activity, changing roles.

Tapescript
see Activity 1a

Extra activity

If you did the introduction activity, ask students to work in the same pairs and read through each other's sentences, correcting the false sentence. Then put students in different pairs and ask them to report the experiences of the classmate they worked with before. They should make the present perfect third person singular sentences.

❷ Class poll

Ask students to choose individually the most amazing thing Gordon Gloom has done in his life. Individual students share their choice with the whole class. Students with the same answer raise their hands. Ask a volunteer to count the votes and write the results on the board as in the example.

Extra activity

Students think of the most amazing experiences of two of their family members or people they know well. In groups of four, students tell their classmates about the experiences, using the present perfect, e.g. *My cousin has ridden a camel.* Make sure they do not mention the time of the event. Groups report the most interesting experiences to the whole class.

3 Grammar practice

Look at the picture in Activity 1. Make sentences with *He has* or *He hasn't* and these words:

sailed written ridden skied
broken made met been

children's books
an elephant
to lots of countries
kings and queens
down Mont Blanc
films
around the world
his leg

He's sailed around the world.

He hasn't written children's books.

Remember!

Full form	*Short form*
He/She **has**	He/She**'s**
He/She **has not**	He/She **hasn't**

4 Listening

a 1.37 Listen and then fill in the missing words.

sailed been rode flew sailed
been flown took ridden

Sam Is it true? Have you ______ an elephant?
Gordon Yes, I ______ an elephant in India in 1948.
Pam And have you ______ around the world?
Gordon Yes, I ______ around the world in 1952. It ______ me eighty days.
Sam Have you ever ______ to the moon?
Gordon No, I haven't ______ to the moon. But I have ______ across the Pacific. Look, I ______ across the Pacific Ocean in this plane in 1937.
Pam, Sam Wow. You are brave, Grandpa.

b 1.37 Listen again and check your answers.

Grammar spot
Present perfect and past simple

Have you **ridden** an elephant?
Yes, I **rode** an elephant in India **in 1948**.

Have you **sailed** around the world?
Yes, I **sailed** around the world **in 1952**.

Grammar page 101

5 Grammar practice

a Complete the dialogue with the correct form the verb in brackets.

1 ridden, rode

1 (ride) **Sam** Have you ______ an elephant?
Gordon Yes, I ______ an elephant in 1948
2 (broke) **Pam** Have you ______ a world record?
Gordon Yes, I ______ a world record in 19
3 (meet) **Sam** Have you ______ a king and que
Gordon Yes, I ______ a king and queen ir 1960.
4 (fly) **Pam** Have you ______ across the Pacifi
Gordon Yes, I ______ across the Pacific in 1937.
5 (ski) **Sam** Have you ______ down Mont Bla
Gordon Yes, I ______ down Mont Blanc i 1977.
6 (climb) **Pam** Have you ______ Mount Kilimanj
Gordon Yes, I ______ Mount Kilimanjaro 1982.

b 1.38 Listen and check.

6 Song

1.39 Find the song *Have You Ever Seen the Rair* on page 90.

7 Check your English

a Ask and answer questions about your classmate's experiences.

1 (travel) on a plane
2 (be) to England
3 (ride) a horse
4 (break) a leg

Have you travelled on a plane?

Yes, I have. I travelled on a plane last year.

b Now write sentences about you and your classmate's experiences.

I haven't travelled on a plane.
Monica has travelled on a plane.
She travelled on a plane last year.

❸ Grammar practice

Students study the objects in Gordon Gloom's bedroom in Activity 1 and write sentences about what he has and has not done, using the verbs and the phrases in the boxes. They should first match the verbs to the correct phrases. Check the answers with the whole class.

Answer key

He's sailed around the world. He hasn't written children's books. He has ridden an elephant. He's skied down Mont Blanc. He hasn't broken his leg. He's made films. He's met kings and queens. He's been to lots of countries.

Homework suggestions

1 Activity Book page 22, Activities 1–2
2 Students choose three celebrities and write about their amazing achievements or experiences, using the present perfect.

PART 2

Introduction

Students write their own true amazing experience on a slip of paper, e.g. *I've won some money on a lottery.* Collect the sentences, mix them up and distribute randomly. To find the author of the sentence they received students mingle and ask questions about the experience, e.g. *Have you won any money on a lottery?* Set a time limit of four minutes.

❹ Listening

a) [1.37] Focus attention on the verbs in the box and point out that some are past simple verbs and some are past participles. Ask students to listen and read the conversation and fill in the gaps.

Tapescript

see Activity 4a

b) [1.37] Play the CD again for students to check their answers. Elicit or explain that we use the present perfect to talk about experiences in general, but when we say exactly when they happened and when we give details, we use the past simple. Refer students to the **Grammar spot** to illustrate the rule and point out the time references. Refer students to the **Grammar summary** on page 101 for more information.

Dyslexia tip: *Being an active learner*

Encourage dyslexic students to be active when learning new grammar and vocabulary. They can draw diagrams, pictures, use highlighter pens and different colours to help them memorise new concepts and meanings. In the case of the present perfect vs the past simple, students can use different colours for each tense, draw calendar pages to illustrate the time references and use arrows to show movement from one tense to the other.

Tapescript and Answer key

Sam: Is it true? Have you ridden an elephant?
Gordon: Yes, I rode an elephant in India in 1948.
Pam: And have you sailed around the world?
Gordon: Yes, I sailed around the world in 1952. It took me eighty days.
Sam: Have you ever been to the moon?
Gordon: No, I haven't been to the moon. But I have flown across the Pacific. Look, I flew across the Pacific Ocean in this plane in 1937.
Pam, Sam: Wow. You are brave, Grandpa.

❺ Grammar practice

a) Students complete the short dialogues with the verbs in brackets in the correct form: the present perfect or the past simple. Then they compare their answers in pairs.

Mixed-ability classes

Ask less confident students to circle the year references to remind them to use the past simple form in these sentences.

b) [1.38] Play the CD for students to check their answers.

Extra activity

Students write a sentence about an amazing experience they have had or use the sentence from the introduction activity. In pairs, students read their sentence to each other and make a dialogue based on their experience, using Activity 5 as a model and adding more details in the past simple, e.g. why, where, how it happened.

Tapescript and Answer key

1 **Sam:** Have you ridden an elephant?
Gordon: Yes, I rode an elephant in1948.
2 **Pam:** Have you broken a world record?
Gordon: Yes, I broke a world record in 1952.
3 **Sam:** Have you met a king and queen?
Gordon: Yes, I met a king and queen in 1960.
4 **Pam:** Have you flown across the Pacific?
Gordon: Yes, I flew across the Pacific in 1937.
5 **Sam:** Have you skied down Mont Blanc?
Gordon: Yes, I skied down Mont Blanc in 1977.
6 **Pam:** Have you climbed Mount Kilimanjaro?
Gordon: Yes, I climbed Mount Kilimanjaro in 1982.

Photocopiable activity

Do you know anybody who …? p111; instructions p95

❻ Song

[1.39] Refer students to page 90. Ask them to look briefly at the lyrics and play a few seconds of the recording. Find out if students recognise the song and play the CD through.

Explain any words students do not understand. Play the song again, encouraging students to join in singing. Elicit what the song is about and ask students to read the background information.

Tapescript

see lyrics on page 90 of the Student's Book

❼ Check your English

a) Students make present perfect questions, using the prompts, and then ask and answer them in pairs.

Answer key

1 Have you travelled …?
2 Have you been …?
3 Have you ridden …?
4 Have you broken …?

b) Students write sentences about their own and their classmate's experiences from Activity 7a. Go through the example before students begin the task.

Homework suggestions

1 Activity Book page 23, Activities 3–5
2 Students imagine three more amazing experiences Gordon Gloom has had. They write sentences about them in the present perfect and the past simple as in Activity 7b.

Lesson objective

Announcing news

11 My latest news

1 Guessing

Phoebe is writing about things that have happened to her recently. Look at the picture. Can you guess her news?

2 Presentation

1.40 Listen and read. How many pieces of news does Phoebe tell her cousin in Australia?

Hi Sandra,

I hope things are good for you in Australia. I've got a lot of news for you! I've just started my new school and the uniform is cool. It's purple! And guess what? I've changed my hairstyle. Now my hair is really short. But my best news is that our cat Bonny has just had three kittens. They're really gorgeous!

Oscar is fine. He's really happy at the moment because he's just bought an MP3 player with his birthday money. He listens to it all the time and he can't hear anything I say. Annoying!

Mum and Dad are fine too. They've been really busy with DIY. They've just painted the kitchen. Dad isn't very happy because he's hurt his back. Mum has found a new job at a vet's. She's very happy because she really loves animals!

I have to go now – my best pal, Julie, has just invited me to a sleepover and I have to get ready and pack my bag!

Please write with all your news!

Phoebe

Do u fancy a sleepover tonite at mine ???
Julie

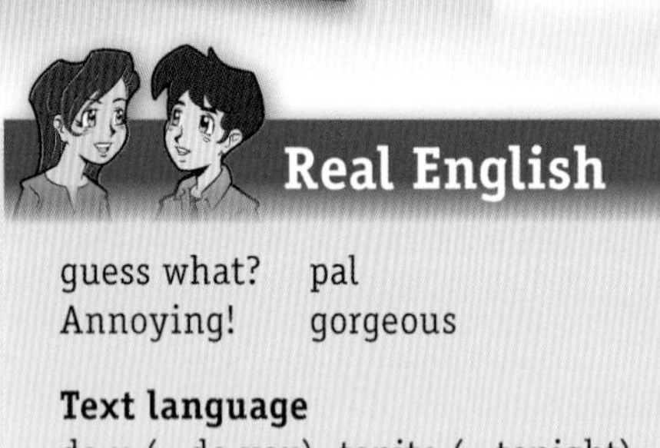

Real English

guess what? pal
Annoying! gorgeous

Text language
do u (= do you) tonite (= tonight)

Grammar spot
Present perfect: *just*

I've *just* **started** my new school.
Bonnie **has** *just* **had** three kittens.

Grammar page 101

11 My latest news

Grammar
- present perfect: *just*; present perfect and past simple

Vocabulary
- everyday activities; shopping

Optional Activity Book activities
- Fast finishers p64, Extra practice p65

Photocopiable activity:
- *What's just happened?* p112

PART 1

Introduction

On the board write the following heading: *MIELSA* and three questions:
Who do you usually write them to?
What do you usually write about?
What was the last one you wrote about?

Ask students to read the questions and guess what topic they refer to. Then they rearrange the letters in the heading to check their answer (answer: EMAILS) Divide students into groups of four and ask them to discuss the questions. Groups report the results of their discussion to the whole class.

❶ Guessing

Focus students' attention on the picture of Phoebe typing on her computer. Point to her thought bubble and explain that she is thinking about things that have happened to her and her family recently. Ask students to identify the people in the thought bubble: Phoebe's mum, dad and her brother, Oscar. Point to the message in the bottom left-hand corner and elicit it is an instant message (IM). Students should then try to guess Phoebe's news on the basis of the pictures. In pairs, students compare their ideas.

❷ Presentation

[1.40] Point to Phoebe's computer and explain that she is writing an email to her cousin, Sandra, who lives in Australia. Elicit that she is writing about her news. Explain that we say: *a piece of news* when we want to count it as *news* is singular and uncountable in English. Students listen and read the email to count the pieces of news Phoebe tells her cousin and check their guesses from Activity 1. Play the CD.

Elicit the answers. Refer students to **Real English** and demonstrate the meaning of the words and phrases by asking questions to different students, e.g. *What do we say before we give exciting news? Who are Harry Potter's best pals? What animals do you think are gorgeous?* Scratch the board with your fingernails to elicit *Annoying!*

Point to the **Text language** section and elicit or explain in L1 that text language is a type of slang where words are abbreviated or simplified so that typing is faster and we need fewer characters. Make sure students understand it is used between young people in text messages or instant messages.

Students read the instant message in the picture again. Ask them to explain what it says in their own words. Provide help if necessary. Find out if students use any abbreviations in their own text or instant messages.

Check if students know or can guess the meaning of the following words and phrases from the email: *uniform, hairstyle, had kittens, birthday money, at a vet's, get ready.* Explain any words students still find difficult.

Refer students to the **Grammar spot** to elicit or explain the use of the present perfect to report news. Explain that we often use *just* with the present perfect, which refers to a short time ago. When we use the present perfect, it means that we can still see the results of the event, e.g. *I've changed my hairstyle* – Phoebe's hair is now different to what it looked like before. Refer students to the **Grammar summary** on page 101 for more information on the present perfect with *just.*

Cultural information

Text language is the English language slang used mainly in SMSs (Short Message Service, a form of text messaging on mobile phones) and IMs (Instant Messages, text-based communication between people over the Internet). It cannot usually be found in standard dictionaries. To use the fewest number of characters and speed up typing common words are abbreviated, replaced by numbers, or their spelling is simplified. You can introduce some common abbreviations your students may want to use in their own text or instant messages, e.g. plz=please, sry=sorry, thx=thanks, bf=boyfriend, gf=girlfriend, love=luv, np=no problem, cu l8r=see you later, 4=for, u=you.

Tapescript

see Student's Book Activity 2

Answer key

1. Phoebe has just started her new school.
2. She has changed her hairstyle.
3. Her cat has just had three kittens.
4. Oscar has just bought an MP3 player.
5. Her mum and dad have been busy with DIY.
6. They have just painted the kitchen.
7. Her dad has hurt his back.
8. Her mum has found a new job at a vet's.
9. Her pal Julie has just invited her for a sleepover.

Extra activity

Write the following exclamations on the board: *Oops! Ouch! Wow! Sorry! Phew! How nice! Help!* Elicit when we use them. In pairs, students make short dialogues orally, using the exclamations and the present perfect with *just.* Write a sample dialogue on the board:

A: Oops!
B: What's happened?
A: I've just dropped my glasses.

Set a time limit of eight minutes. Elicit one or two dialogues for each exclamation.

3 Grammar practice

a Match the words in A with the words in B to make sentences using the present perfect.

I've just started my new school.

	A		B
1	I just (start)	**a**	an MP3 player.
2	I (change)	**b**	his back.
3	Bonny just (have)	**c**	really busy.
4	Oscar just (buy)	**d**	my hairstyle.
5	Mum and Dad (be)	**e**	kittens.
6	They just (paint)	**f**	a new job at a vet's.
7	My dad (hurt)	**g**	me to a sleepover.
8	Mum (find)	**h**	the kitchen.
9	Julie just (invite)	**i**	my new school.

b 1.41 Listen and check.

4 Listening

a 1.42 Listen. What news is Oscar telling his friend?

b 1.42 Listen again. Answer these questions.

1. What has Oscar just spent?
2. What did he buy?
3. Was it expensive?
4. Where did he buy it?
5. How many songs can it hold?
6. How many songs has Oscar put on it?

Grammar spot
Present perfect and past simple

I**'ve just spent** my birthday money.
What **did** you **buy**?
I **bought** an MP3 player.

5 Speaking

Work with a classmate. Make a dialogue with the words in the boxes. Complete it with your own answer.

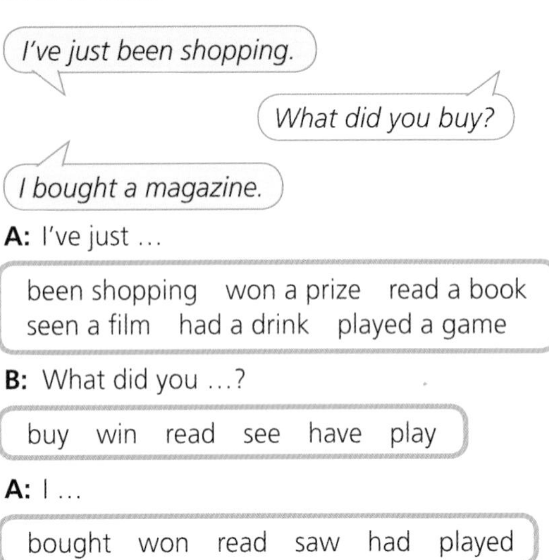

I've just been shopping.

What did you buy?

I bought a magazine.

A: I've just …

been shopping won a prize read a book seen a film had a drink played a game

B: What did you …?

buy win read see have play

A: I …

bought won read saw had played

My English file
My latest news

Write a dialogue between you and your friend.

My latest news

Me: Guess what! I've just been to a restaurant.
Karl: Cool. What did you eat?
Me: I had pizza.
Karl: Was it good?
Me: It was great.
Karl: What did you have for dessert?
Me: I had ice cream.

6 Check your English

a Complete with the present perfect of the verb in brackets.

1. I _____ just _____ a T-shirt. (buy)
2. My cat _____ just _____ kittens. (have)
3. My friend _____ just _____ a new school. (start)
4. We _____ our house. (paint)
5. My dad _____ a new job. (find)

b Now write questions about the above with the past simple.

1 Where did you buy it?

❸ Grammar practice

a) Students match the words in column A with words in column B. Check the answers. Then students make sentences about Phoebe's news, using the joint phrases and the present perfect. They should pay special attention to the position of *just* in the sentence and whether the subject is singular or plural as they require different forms of ***have***. Students compare their answers in pairs and then check with the email in Activity 2.

Mixed-ability classes

Fast finishers imagine that Julie has made some preparations for the sleepover at her house. They write three sentences about what she has done, using the present perfect, e.g. *Julie's just made pancakes for the evening.*

b) [1.41] Play the CD for students to check their answers.

Tapescript and Answer key

1 (i) I've just started my new school.
2 (d) I've changed my hairstyle.
3 (e) Bonny's just had kittens.
4 (a) Oscar's just bought an MP3 player.
5 (c) Mum and Dad have been really busy.
6 (h) They've just painted the kitchen.
7 (b) My dad's hurt his back.
8 (f) Mum's found a new job at a vet's.
9 (g) Julie's just invited me to a sleepover.

Homework suggestions

1. Activity Book pages 24–25, Activities 1–3
2. Students write four sentences in the present perfect with the news from their town or country.

PART 2

Introduction

Write the following words on the board: *busy, kitchen, back, job at a vet's, kittens, hairstyle, sleepover, school, MP3 player.* Divide students into four groups and ask them to recall from memory Phoebe's news in Activity 2 on the basis of these words. Set a time limit of five minutes. Then groups take it in turns to choose a word and make a sentence with it in ten seconds. If it is grammatically and factually correct, give them one point and erase the word. If it is not, leave the word on the board for other groups to choose.

❹ Listening

a) [1.42] Elicit that the photo shows Oscar talking on the phone. Ask students to guess what news he is telling his friend. Play the CD for students to check their guesses. Elicit that Oscar is telling his friend about the MP3 player he has just bought.

b) [1.42] Play the CD again and ask students to answer the questions about the conversation. Students compare their answers in pairs before you check them with the whole class. Refer students to the **Grammar spot** to point out we tell the news using the present perfect, but then we give details about it in the past simple.

Extra activity

Ask students if they or their family members do some of their shopping on-line. Find out what they usually buy and which websites are the most popular for shopping on-line.

Tapescript

Oscar: Guess what! I've just spent my birthday money.
Harry: What did you buy?
Oscar: I bought an MP3 player!
Harry: Fantastic. Was it expensive?
Oscar: No, it wasn't. I bought it on-line.
Harry: Cool. How many songs can it hold?
Oscar: 2000.
Harry: Wow. How many songs have you put on it?
Oscar: Er…16.
Harry: Only 16!
Oscar: Well, I've just bought it!

Answer key

1 His birthday money	**4** On-line
2 An MP3 player	**5** 2000
3 No, it wasn't	**6** 16

❺ Speaking

In pairs, students make short dialogues with the words in the boxes. They should use the first phrase in a present perfect sentence to introduce a piece of news, and then ask and answer about details, using the verbs in the second and third box in the past simple. They should complete the answers using their own ideas. The phrases and the verbs are in the same order. Read out the example with a confident student before students begin the task. Explain that the dialogues do not have to be true.

Set a time limit of five minutes. Ask different pairs to repeat their dialogues to the whole class.

Mixed-ability classes

For less confident students write ideas for the answers on the board in mixed order, e.g. *a milkshake, a comedy, an English dictionary, basketball, a present for my brother, £20.*

My English file

Explain that students are going to write a dialogue between themselves and their friend about their news. The dialogue must have at least seven lines. They do not have to write about true events. They should use the present perfect to introduce the news and then the past simple to talk about details. Go through the example before students begin the task.

When students have finished writing, they exchange their notebooks in pairs. They read each other's dialogues and point out orally any mistakes they notice.

Photocopiable activity

What's just happened? p112; instructions p95

❻ Check your English

a) Students complete the sentences with the present perfect form of the verbs in brackets. In pairs, students compare their answers. Check the answers with the whole class.

Answer key

1. have … bought
2. has … had
3. has … started
4. have painted
5. has found

b) Students write their own past simple questions to find out more about the news in Activity 6a.

Homework suggestions

1. Activity Book page 25, Activities 4–5
2. Students write an email to a friend with their own true news, using Activity 2 as a model.

12 Sumeo's story

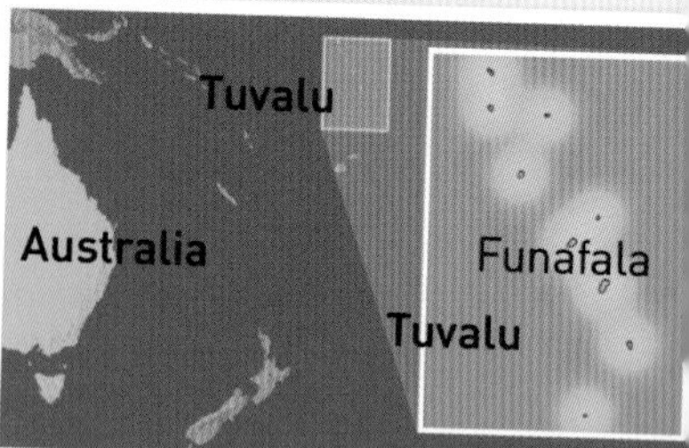

1 Reading

a 1.43 Listen and read about the Tuvaluan island of Funafala. Why do you think people on the island are afraid for its future?

Tuvalu fears for its future

My name is Sumeo and I live on the tiny island of Funafala in the South Pacific. This is my house. As you can see our house is very close to the sea. It isn't good to live close to the sea on Funafala because the land is very low. Sometimes the sea floods our island.

Two families have just left our island to live in New Zealand. One of these was my aunt and uncle's family. I am very sad because my cousins live so far away from Funafala. Now there are only five families on the island.

All the men on my island are fishermen. We have just brought a big net of fish back to the island. We share everything on my island and now we are going to share the fish between the five families. Fish is our main food on Funafala. We also eat chicken, pork and vegetables.

We have our own language in Tuvalu and we have our own songs and dances too. We are happy tonight but we are often sad when we think of the future.

b Read again. Are these sentences true or false?

1 True

1 Funafala is a tiny island.
2 The land on Funafala is very high.
3 All the men are farmers.
4 Sumeo's uncle and aunt live in New Zealand.
5 There are only two families on Funafala.
6 They are sad tonight.

12 Sumeo's story

Optional materials	Photocopiable activity
• a CD with music	• *Interesting stories*, p113

PART 1

Introduction

Write the word *island* on the board. Divide students into groups of four and ask them to brainstorm all the words they associate with the topic. Set a time limit of two minutes and elicit all the groups' words onto the board. Students open their books, look at the pictures in Activity 1a and check how many of their words appear there.

❶ Reading

a) [1.43] Focus attention on the first picture and introduce the boy named Sumeo. Then point to the map and explain that he lives on the island of Funafala which is in Tuvalu, a small country in the South Pacific. Ask students to listen and read about Funafala and say why they think people living there are afraid for the island's future. Play the CD.

Check if students know/can guess the meaning of the following words and phrases: *tiny, low, floods, net, share, main, one of these, so far away.* Provide explanation if necessary. Point out that *fish* is uncountable in English.

Elicit that people are afraid for Funafala's future because the sea sometimes floods the island and families leave.

Tapescript

see Student's Book Activity 1a

b) Students read the text in Activity 1a again and decide if the sentences are true or false about Funafala. Encourage them to mark with pencil the relevant parts of the text which contain the answers. Set a time limit of five minutes. If your students like it, you can play music in the background for the duration of the activity.

Students compare the answers in pairs. Check the answers with the whole class and elicit which parts of the text prove that the sentences are true or false.

Mixed ability classes

Fast finishers correct the false statements in writing.

Extra activity

Divide students into pairs. Ask Student A to study pictures 1 and 2 in Activity 1a for thirty seconds. Then they should close their books and describe the pictures from memory to Student B. Student B checks if the description is correct and asks Student A at least one question about each picture, e.g. *How many people are standing in the water?* Then students repeat the procedure with Student B studying, describing and answering questions about pictures 3 and 4.

Teaching tip: *Music in the classroom*

Music in the classroom can enhance concentration; it stimulates the brain, relaxes students and makes learning more enjoyable. You can find music related to the story in the textbook, e.g. Polynesian music (in the case of the reading activity above), and play it to help students make associations with a given place or topic. You can play music in the background for the duration of the activity, so when you pause it, students know that the time is up. To help students concentrate on grammar tasks use harmonic music with repeated patterns, e.g. Mozart, and to stimulate ideas in brainstorming activities use music with irregular patterns.

Answer key

1 true **2** false (It is very low) **3** false (All the men are fishermen) **4** true **5** false (There are five families) **6** false (They are happy)

Cultural information

Tuvalu is the fourth smallest country in the world. It is located between Hawaii and Australia in the Pacific Ocean. Tuvalu's Independence Day is on October 1st. Tuvalu comprises islands and atolls. Funafala is one of Tuvalu's islets. The land on the islands is very low, the highest elevation is 5 metres above sea level. Because of the climate change and the resulting rise of the sea level, Tuvaluan islands can be partially or completely flooded and food crops may be destroyed by salt water in the future. Tuvaluan people are Polynesian people who settled on the islands 2000 years ago. Due to the environmental threats they have now begun moving away to New Zealand.

❷ Listening

a 1.44 Listen to the interview with Sumeo. Then answer these questions.

1. Why is Sumeo's house on stilts?
2. Why have Sumeo's uncle and aunt left the island?
3. What food do they eat on Funafala?
4. Why are they happy tonight?

b 1.44 Listen again and check.

❸ Speaking

a 1.45 Look at the pictures in Activity 1 and listen. Think about the answers.

b Now play a quiz game. Get into small teams and write five questions to ask another team.

c Then close your books and ask and answer your questions. You get one point for every correct answer.

Why is Sumeo's house on stilts?

Because it's very close to the sea.

❹ Writing

Write a paragraph about the island of Funafala. Try to use as many of these words as you can.

tiny South Pacific houses close to the sea
land low stilts afraid of two families
floods New Zealand afraid for the future
five fishermen net fish share
main food chicken pork vegetables

Funafala

Funafala is a tiny island in the South Pacific. The island is ...

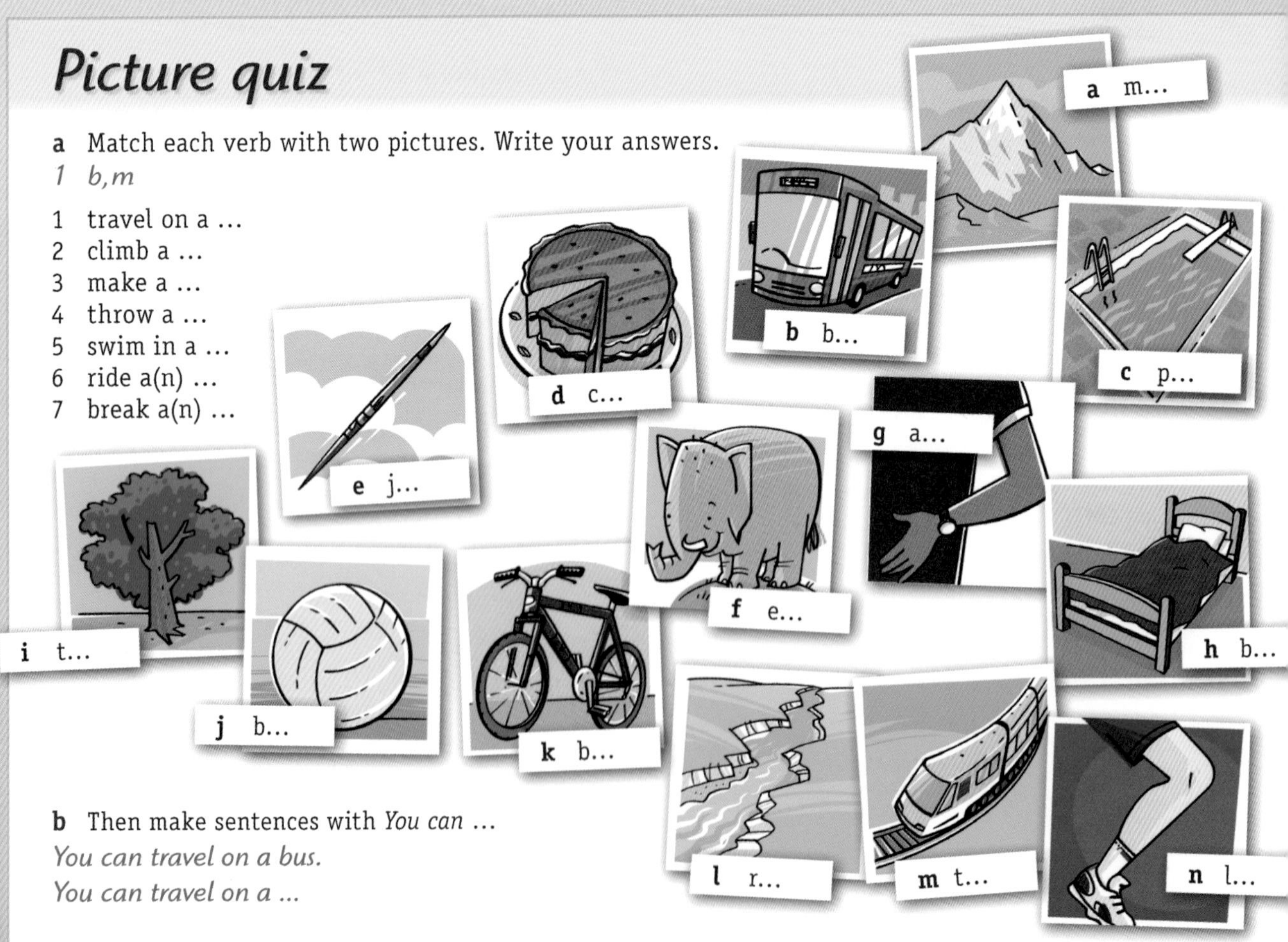

Picture quiz

a Match each verb with two pictures. Write your answers.

1 b,m

1. travel on a ...
2. climb a ...
3. make a ...
4. throw a ...
5. swim in a ...
6. ride a(n) ...
7. break a(n) ...

b Then make sentences with *You can ...*

You can travel on a bus.
You can travel on a ...

❷ Listening

a) [1.44] Pre-teach the word *stilts*. Students listen to the interview with Sumeo and answer the questions. Play the CD.

Tapescript

Interviewer: Hello Sumeo, can I ask you some questions about your island?
Sumeo: Yes, sure. Go ahead.
Interviewer: OK. Tell me, why is your house on stilts?
Sumeo: My house is on stilts because we are afraid of the sea. Sometimes the sea floods our island and it can be very dangerous.
Interviewer: Ah, right, I see. So, your aunt and uncle have left Funafala to live in New Zealand, is that right?
Sumeo: Yes, it is.
Interviewer: Why have they left the island?
Sumeo: They are afraid for the island's future.
Interviewer: They are afraid?
Sumeo: Yes, because of the sea.
Interviewer: You have caught a lot of fish today. What other food do you eat on the island?
Sumeo: Well, fish is our main food. But we also eat chicken, pork and vegetables.
Interviewer: Why are you happy tonight?
Sumeo: We are happy tonight because we are having a celebration.

b) [1.44] Play the CD again for students to check their answers. Individual students read the questions and the answers for the whole class to check.

Tapescript

see Activity 2a

Answer key

1 Because sometimes the sea floods the island. **2** Because they are afraid for the island's future. **3** Fish, chicken, pork and vegetables. **4** Because they are having a celebration.

Homework suggestions

1 Activity Book page 26, Activity 1
2 Students write three more questions they would like to ask Sumeo about his life on the island.

PART 2

Introduction

Divide the class into two teams. Ask Team A to write as many good points about living on Funafala as they can think of. Team B writes all the bad points about living on the island. Set a time limit of four minutes. Group representatives read out their lists. The team with the longer list wins the game.

❸ Speaking

a) [1.45] Students look at the pictures in Activity 1a again and listen to the questions. They should think about the answers.

Tapescript

Where is Sumeo's island?
Where is Sumeo's house?
Why is the house on stilts?
Why isn't it good to live close to the sea?
How many families have left the island?
Where do Sumeo's uncle and aunt live?
How many families now live on the island?
What have the fishermen brought back to the island?
What food do they eat on the island?
Why are they happy tonight?

b) Put students into groups of three or four to have an even number of groups in the class. They should write five questions about Funafala to ask to another team. They can use some of the example questions they heard in Activity 3a. They need to make sure they know the answers. Set a time limit of eight minutes.

c) Ask each group to work with another team. With their books closed, they take turns to ask and answer the questions. The whole team has to agree on the same answer within 30 seconds. They get one point for each correct answer. The team with more points wins the game.

❹ Writing

Review the words in the box. Individually, students write a paragraph describing the island of Funafala. They should use as many words from the box as possible. Ask them to write the text from memory without looking at Activity 1. They should cover page 36 with a sheet of paper. Set a time limit of 20 minutes.

Encourage students to make a draft copy first and rewrite it after editing. Monitor their work, providing help. Then they exchange their texts in pairs. If they notice any mistakes in their classmate's text, they should point these out orally. Find out how many words students have managed to use and if there is anyone who has used all the words.

Mixed-ability classes

Allow less confident students to check information in Activity 1, but ask them not to copy the sentences from there.

Picture quiz

a) Students match each verb with two pictures and write their answers.

Answer key

1 b, m (bus, train)
2 a, i (mountain, tree)
3 d, h (cake, bed)
4 e, j (javelin, ball)
5 c, l (pool, river)
6 f, k (elephant, bike)
7 g, n (arm, leg)

b) In pairs, students make sentences with *You can* and the verb and noun collocations.

Extra activity

In pairs, students guess which activities in the **Picture quiz** their classmate has done and ask questions to check their guesses, e.g. *Have you made a cake?* They get one point for each correct guess.

Photocopiable activity

Interesting stories p113; instructions p95

Homework suggestions

1 Activity Book page 26, Activity 2
2 Students write true sentences about their own country, using any relevant words from the box in Activity 4.

Dyslexia tip: *Organising homework*

Make sure that dyslexic students write down homework instructions correctly. You can also type and hand out instructions or make them accessible online, e.g. on the school website. Encourage students to use different colours to separate homework and lesson notes. If they write their homework on separate sheets of paper, they should clip these to their notebook to find them easily.

Module 3 Review

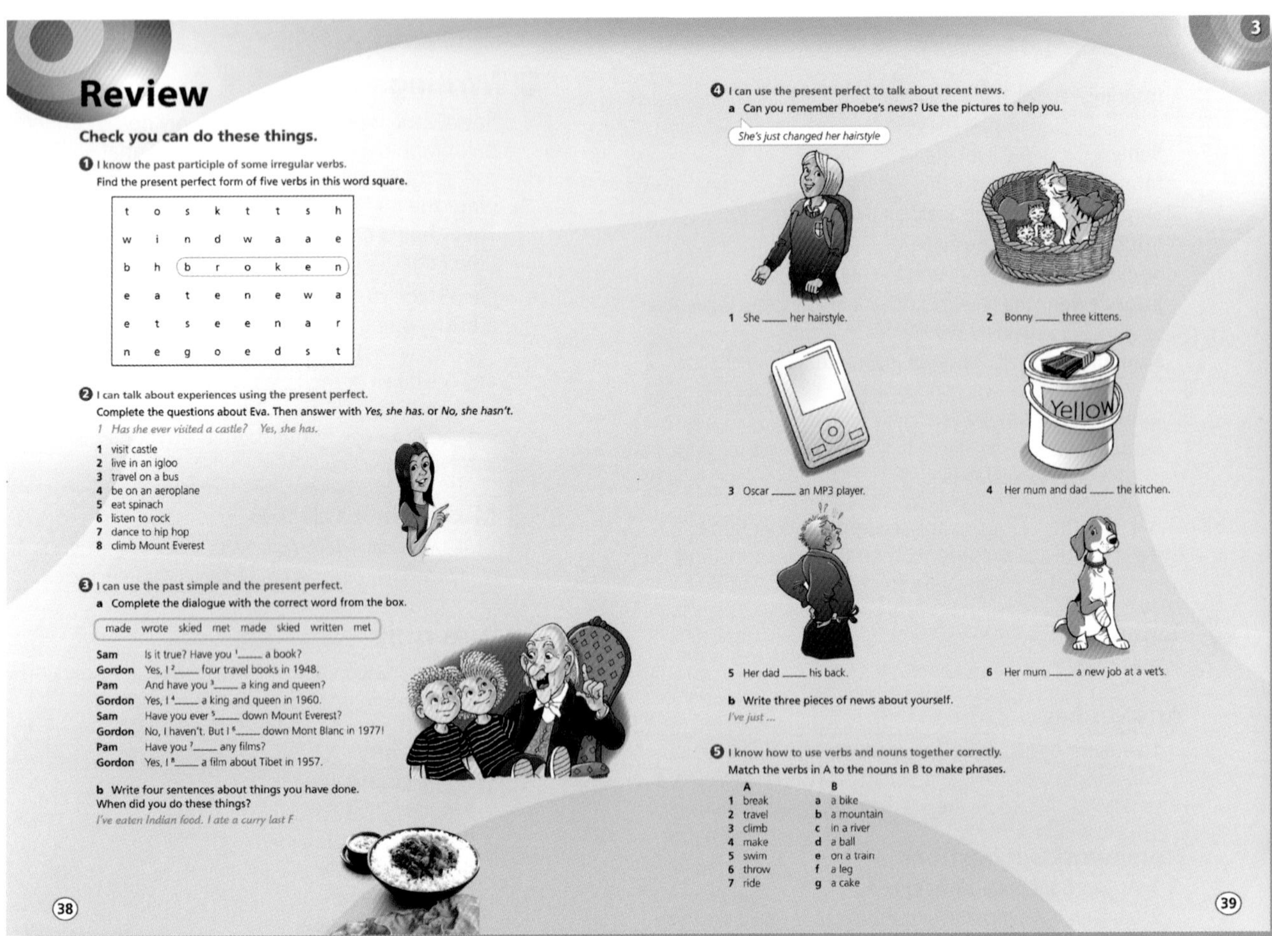

Review

Check you can do these things.

1 I know the past participle of some irregular verbs.
Find the present perfect form of five verbs in this word square.

t	o	s	k	t	t	s	h
w	i	n	d	w	a	a	e
b	h	b	r	o	k	e	n
e	a	t	e	n	e	w	a
e	t	s	e	e	n	a	r
n	e	g	o	e	d	s	t

2 I can talk about experiences using the present perfect.
Complete the questions about Eva. Then answer with *Yes, she has.* or *No, she hasn't.*

1 Has she ever visited a castle? Yes, she has.

1 visit castle
2 live in an igloo
3 travel on a bus
4 be on an aeroplane
5 eat spinach
6 listen to rock
7 dance to hip hop
8 climb Mount Everest

3 I can use the past simple and the present perfect.
a Complete the dialogue with the correct word from the box.

made wrote skied met made skied written met

Sam Is it true? Have you [1]___ a book?
Gordon Yes, I [2]___ four travel books in 1948.
Pam And have you [3]___ a king and queen?
Gordon Yes, I [4]___ a king and queen in 1960.
Sam Have you ever [5]___ down Mount Everest?
Gordon No, I haven't. But I [6]___ down Mont Blanc in 1977!
Pam Have you [7]___ any films?
Gordon Yes, I [8]___ a film about Tibet in 1957.

b Write four sentences about things you have done. When did you do these things?
I've eaten Indian food. I ate a curry last F

4 I can use the present perfect to talk about recent news.
a Can you remember Phoebe's news? Use the pictures to help you.

She's just changed her hairstyle

1 She ___ her hairstyle.
2 Bonny ___ three kittens.
3 Oscar ___ an MP3 player.
4 Her mum and dad ___ the kitchen.
5 Her dad ___ his back.
6 Her mum ___ a new job at a vet's.

b Write three pieces of news about yourself.
I've just ...

5 I know how to use verbs and nouns together correctly.
Match the verbs in A to the nouns in B to make phrases.

A	B
1 break	a a bike
2 travel	b a mountain
3 climb	c in a river
4 make	d a ball
5 swim	e on a train
6 throw	f a leg
7 ride	g a cake

38 39

Optional materials

- one Post-it™ note per student

Optional revision

Before your students start this Review, you may want to direct them to the **Grammar summary** at the back of their coursebooks and to the **Word lists** at the back of their Activity Books. This will remind them of the main grammar and vocabulary in the module. Give them ten minutes to read through those in small groups and ask you any questions they may have.

- Activity Book: Refer your students to pages 85–86: *Adverbs*; *Food*
- **Grammar summary**: Refer your students to Page 101 section 8

Module 3 Review

The purpose of this section is revision and consolidation of the material studied in Module 3.

Completing the activities

Go over all the activities with the class, explaining rubrics and giving examples to make sure students know what to do. There are written and oral tasks, but you may decide yourself how they should be completed by students. Generally students should do the writing tasks individually and the oral tasks in pairs, testing each other's knowledge. Make sure they do not treat the *Review* as a formal test, but complete the activities in a friendly, stress-free atmosphere. Fast finishers can write down the answers to the oral tasks.

Checking answers

When students have finished, check the answers with the whole class by asking volunteers to copy their answers onto the board or to say them aloud. If necessary, explain the more difficult issues, ask additional questions about the activities and solve any problems that arise.

Self-evaluation

Tell students to evaluate themselves. They should tick the activities where at least half of their answers were correct.

Feedback

Ask students which activities were difficult, which were easy and if there is anything they would like to review. Make a note of common language problems to go over in future lessons.

Answer key

1 Students look for five past participles in the word square. The words are hidden horizontally and vertically.

vertically: ***been, won, taken***; horizontally: ***broken, seen***

2 Students complete the questions about Eva from Lesson 9 and answer them from memory.

1 Has she ever visited a castle? Yes, she has.
2 Has she ever lived in an igloo? No, she hasn't.
3 Has she ever travelled on a bus? Yes, she has.
4 Has she ever been on an aeroplane? No, she hasn't.
5 Has she ever eaten spinach? Yes, she has.
6 Has she ever listened to rock? Yes, she has.
7 Has she ever danced to hip hop? No, she hasn't.
8 Has she ever climbed Mount Everest? No, she hasn't.

3 **Sam:** Is it true? Have you written a book?
Gordon: Yes, I wrote four travel books in 1948.
Pam: And have you met a king and queen?
Gordon: Yes, I met a king and queen in 1960.
Sam: Have you ever skied down Mount Everest?
Gordon: No, I haven't. But I skied down Mont Blanc in 1977!
Pam: Have you made any films?
Gordon: Yes, I made a film about Tibet in 1957.

b) Students write about four true things they have done. They should use the present perfect in the first sentence and the past simple in the second as they are explaining when.

4 **a)** **1** She's just changed her hairstyle.
2 Bonnie's just had three kittens.
3 Oscar's just bought an MP3 player.
4 Her mum and dad have just painted the kitchen.
5 Her dad's just hurt his back.
6 Her mum's just found a new job at the vet's.

b) Students write three pieces of news about themselves using *just* and the present perfect.

5 **1** f **2** e **3** b **4** g **5** c **6** d **7** a

Extra activity

Give each student a Post-it™ note and ask them to draw a symbol of a special experience they have had, e.g. if they have climbed a high mountain, they can draw a mountain. Students stick the Post-it™ notes to their fronts and mingle. If somebody's drawing attracts their attention, they stop and try to guess their experience, e.g. *Have you climbed a mountain?* The person asked confirms or explains their experience, using the present perfect and adds additional information about it in the past simple, e.g. *Yes, I have. I climbed Mount Dumbier in Slovakia in 2009.* Then students find a new classmate to talk to. Set a time limit of five minutes and encourage students to share the most interesting facts they found out about their classmates.

Module 3 Tests (A and B) are on the Tests CD

Learning diary

You can refer students to page 27 of the Activity Book for further review, more study tips and self-assessment activities.

Extra special

Extra special

What's just happened?

a Work in a small team. Look at the picture. Find the twelve people who have just done these things. The first team to write the 12 correct letters is the winner.

1 j

1 He has just thrown a ball.
2 He has just scored a goal.
3 She has just jumped into the water.
4 He has just hurt his leg.
5 She has just bought an ice cream.
6 She has just fallen off her bike.
7 He has just got out of the pool.
8 He has just come into the park.
9 She has just dropped the ball.
10 He has just sat down.
11 She has just dived into the water.
12 She has just taken a photo.

b 1.46 Listen and check your answers.

40

3

Mini-project

1 Read Helen's poster. Have you done anything similar?

My latest news ...

These are some things I've done:

1 I've played netball for my school team. We won 11–6.

2 I've just passed my Maths test. I got a very good mark!

3 I've made some biscuits. They were delicious!

4 I've just started piano lessons. I had my first lesson last week.

5 I've been to the dentist. I went yesterday.

Helen

2 Make a poster about your news. Write at least five sentences.

3 Show your poster to your classmates. Answer questions about your news.

41

What's just happened?

a) Ask students to keep their books closed. Divide the class into groups of four. Explain that they are going to read 12 sentences referring to people who have just done something. Their task is to find those 12 people in a picture in their books. The people are labelled with letters, so students have to write the correct letter beside each sentence. When you say *Start,* the teams open their books and try to complete the task as quickly as possible. When they are ready, they raise their hands. Remember the order in which teams have finished.

b) [1.46] Play the CD for students to check their answers. Students are not allowed to change them. Check the answers of the team that finished the task first. If their answers are correct, they win the game. If not, check the answers of the team that finished second and so on until you find the winner.

Extra activity

Invite two students to the front of the classroom. They should look at the room and their classmates carefully for one minute and then they leave the classroom. Make eight major changes in the classroom, using the remaining students' suggestions, e.g. ask some students to change seats, rearrange the books on your desk, put the pot plants on the floor. Students return to the classroom and say what has changed, e.g. *Alex has changed his seat; You have put the plants on the floor.* Make sure it is clear who has made the changes, so that students are not forced to use the passive voice.

Tapescript and Answer key

1 He has just thrown a ball. **j**
2 He has just scored a goal. **a**
3 She has just jumped into the water. **d**
4 He has just hurt his leg. **h**
5 She has just bought an ice cream. **f**
6 She has just fallen off her bike. **g**
7 He has just got out of the pool. **e**
8 He has just come into the park. **l**
9 She has just dropped the ball. **b**
10 He has just sat down. **i**
11 She has just dived into the water. **c**
12 She has just taken a photo. **k**

Mini-project

1. Explain to students that a girl called Helen has made a poster about her news. Elicit or explain what the title *My latest news* means. Ask students to read Helen's project and check if they have done anything similar recently. If they have, they should share their stories with the whole class. Clarify any vocabulary in the project if necessary.
2. Students make a poster about their own news. They should write at least five pieces of news, using the present perfect with *just* and the past simple as in Helen's project. Encourage them to make a draft copy first. Ask them to illustrate their fact sheet. Monitor their work and provide help where necessary.
3. In groups of six, students present their posters. Encourage them to ask and answer questions about each other's news. Each group can then choose the person with the most exciting news and report their choice to the whole class.

Extra activity

Write the following categories on the board: *Our town, Our country, The world, Celebrities, Our school, Our class.* Divide students into groups of four. Ask them to imagine that you have just spent a month on Funafala and did not watch TV or use the Internet. Now you have returned home and you are interested in the news. Groups try to write at least one piece of news in each category to report to you, e.g. *Our president has just visited the USA.* Set a time limit of eight minutes and elicit the answers.

Lesson objective
Making predictions

13 The talent show

1 Vocabulary

2.01 Find these words in the picture.

costume d

costume judge
microphone
audience
stage guitar

2 Presentation

2.02 Listen and read Phoebe's and Oscar's diaries. What do they think will happen at the talent show?

15th February

It's the School talent show tomorrow and I'm dreading it. Will I remember the words to my song? Will the audience fall asleep? I think it'll be a disaster. I'll fall off the stage and I'll drop my guitar. The microphone won't work and my friends will laugh at me.

15th February

I can't wait for the show tomorrow! I think it'll be great! I'll dance brilliantly and I won't make any mistakes. My costume will look amazing. My friends will all cheer for me.

The judges will love me and I'll win the first prize. Then my picture will be in the local newspaper and I'll be famous.

3 Comprehension

What are Oscar and Phoebe's predictions? Read again then answer the questions.

1 The microphone.

1 What won't work?
2 Who will fall off the stage?
3 Who will have an amazing costume?
4 Who won't make any mistakes?
5 Who will laugh at Oscar?
6 Who will love Phoebe?

Real English

I can't wait for …
I'm dreading it.

13 The talent show

Grammar
- future predictions with *will*

Vocabulary
- performing arts; contests; future life events

Optional materials
- large selection of magazine photos showing different objects, places, people, colours

Optional Activity Book activities
- Fast finishers p66, Extra practice p67

Photocopiable activity
- *The future* p114

PART 1

Introduction

Write *talent show* on the board and ask students if they know the rules of talent shows and any examples of such shows on TV. Find out if students have ever taken part in talent shows at their school or elsewhere, or if they know someone who has. Brainstorm all the words they associate with talent shows and write them on the board. Then ask students to look at Activity 1 in their books to check if they came up with the same words.

❶ Vocabulary

[2.01] Students look at the words in the box and listen as you play the CD. Then they find the words in the picture in Activity 2. They should make guesses about new vocabulary.

Students work individually on the task and then compare their answers in pairs. Play the CD again and get students to point to the right part of the picture. Make sure everybody understands all the words now and drill the pronunciation.

Mixed-ability classes

Fast finishers check what other things related to a talent show they can name in the picture. Elicit their ideas when everyone has finished working on Activity 1.

Tapescript

see Student's Book Activity 1

Answer key

costume – **d**	judge – **e**	microphone – **a**
audience – **b**	stage – **c**	guitar – **f**

❷ Presentation

[2.02] Ask students to read the information on the poster of the school talent show. Check understanding by asking questions, e.g. *When is the talent show? What are the prizes? What can you do at the show?* Then point to the pictures of Oscar and Phoebe. Explain that they are going to take part in the school talent show. On the basis of the pictures students predict what the characters think will happen at the show. Then students listen and read Oscar's and Phoebe's diaries and check their predictions. Play the CD.

Ask students if they guessed correctly, that Oscar thinks bad things will happen and Phoebe thinks good things will happen at the show. Refer students to the **Grammar spot** on the next page to elicit or explain *will* for future predictions. Go over the different types of sentences and point out that *'ll* is a short form of *will* and *won't* is a short form of *will not.* Refer students to the **Grammar summary** on page 102 for more information on *will* for future predictions.

Refer students to **Real English** and demonstrate the meaning of the phrases by writing, e.g. *a maths test, the next episode of my favourite TV series, a dentist's appointment, my birthday party* on the board and getting students to say which of these things they are dreading and which they can't wait for. Check if students know/can guess what the following words mean: *fall asleep, disaster, cheer, local.* Provide explanation if necessary.

Tapescript

see Student's Book Activity 2

Extra activity

Explain that Oscar is a pessimist and Phoebe is an optimist. Ask students to decide if they usually think like Oscar or like Phoebe. Then count how many pessimists and optimists there are in your classroom. Write the results on the board. Find out if students are surprised by the results and why.

❸ Comprehension

Students read the diary entries in Activity 2 again and answer the questions about Oscar and Phoebe's predictions. They should underline the parts of the text which contain the answers. Students check their answers in pairs. Individual students read out the questions and their answers. Encourage them to justify the answers by reading the right part of the text.

Extra activity

Put students into groups of four. Ask them to imagine that Oscar and Phoebe are going on a two-day school trip to London next week and write at least three predictions each character makes about the trip. Oscar's predictions should be bad, e.g. *I'll get lost* and Phoebe's good, e.g. *The weather will be great.* Set a time limit of five minutes and ask groups to report the predictions to the whole class. Get students to vote which prediction is the worst and which is the best.

Answer key

1 the microphone
2 Oscar
3 Phoebe
4 Phoebe
5 Oscar's friends
6 the judges

Homework suggestions

1 Activity Book pages 28–29, Activities 1–3
2 Students think of a real future event in their personal life, e.g. school trip, party, family dinner and make at least four predictions about it, using *will* or *won't.*

Grammar spot
Future predictions with *will*

I**'ll** fall off the stage.
My friends **will** laugh at me.
I **won't** make any mistakes.
Will I remember the words to the song?
Yes, I **will**./No, I **won't**.

Grammar page 102

4 Grammar practice

a Phoebe and Oscar are talking about the talent show. Use *will, 'll* or *won't* to complete the dialogue.

1 it'll be
2 won't remember

Oscar Oh Phoebe, I'm really worried about the talent show. I'm sure it [1]_____ (be) a disaster. I [2]_____ (not remember) the words to my song and the judges [3]_____ (hate) me.

Phoebe Don't be silly, Oscar! You [4]_____ (sing) really well and you [5]_____ (play) your guitar brilliantly. You [6]_____ (not forget) the words to your song, and the judges [7] _____ (give) you the silver medal.

Oscar The silver medal! Who [8]_____ (get) the gold medal?

Phoebe I will, of course!

b 2.03 Listen and check your answers.

5 Speaking

a Write three predictions about your future. Use the ideas in the box.

I think I'll be a teacher. I'll travel to another country and I'll speak six languages.

be a pop star
be a pilot
be a teacher
live in a big house
marry a famous person
have ten children
meet an important stranger
travel to another country
win an amazing prize
speak six languages
help other people
design an amazing invention

b Work in pairs. Can you guess your partner's predictions?

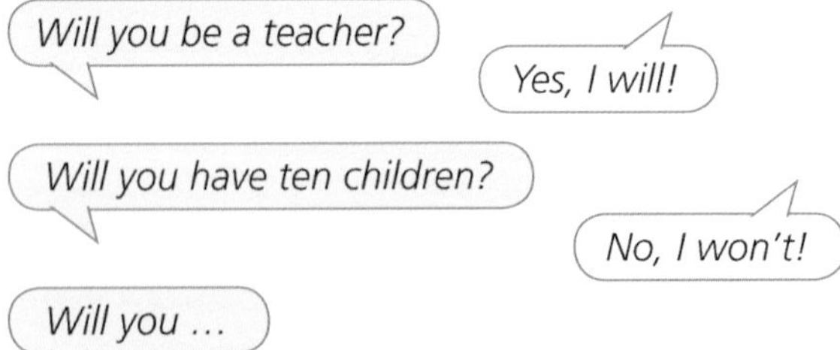

My English file

Write four true predictions about your future. Use your own ideas.

I think I will learn to drive a train and …

6 Check your English

Choose the correct verb from the box with *will* or *won't* to complete these predictions.

become cheer not forget
dance give not fall over

1 Phoebe _____ well at the Talent Show.
2 The judges _____ Phoebe a gold medal.
3 Phoebe _____ a famous dancer.
4 Oscar _____ at the Talent Show.
5 He _____ the words to his song.
6 The audience _____ loudly.

PART 2

Introduction

Draw a noughts and crosses grid with the following words in the squares: *newspaper, disaster, stage, microphone, mistakes, costume, guitar, first prize, friends.* Divide students into two teams: A and B. Assign the symbol of nought to one team and the cross to the other. With their books closed, teams take it in turns to choose a word and use it to reconstruct Oscar's or Phoebe's prediction about the Talent Show from Activity 1a, e.g. *Phoebe will be in the local newspaper.* If their prediction is correct, they can put their symbol in the square. The winner is the first team to put three of their symbols in one line, horizontally, vertically or diagonally.

4 Grammar practice

a) Focus students' attention on the picture and explain that Phoebe and Oscar are talking about the talent show. Remind students that Phoebe is an optimist and Oscar is a pessimist. Students use *will* or *won't* and the verbs in the brackets to complete the conversation. Encourage them to use the short form of *will* when possible.

b) [2.03] Play the CD for students to check their answers.

Tapescript and Answer key

Oscar: Oh, Phoebe, I'm really worried about the talent show. I'm sure it'll be a disaster. I won't remember the words to my song and the judges will hate me.
Phoebe: Don't be silly, Oscar! You'll sing really well and you'll play your guitar brilliantly. You won't forget the words to your song, and the judges will give you the silver medal.
Oscar: The silver medal! Who'll get the gold medal?
Phoebe: I will, of course!

Extra activity

Put students into groups of four. Find out which TV series all of your students watch. If there is not one TV series everybody watches, students form groups with classmates who watch the same TV series as them. Elicit what happened in the most recent episode. Then groups make predictions about the next episode. They should use *I think … will/won't.* Allow four minutes for the activity and elicit ideas from different groups. You can ask them to take notes and check their ideas when the next episode is on.

5 Speaking

a) Go through the phrases in the box and clarify any vocabulary students may not understand. Ask them to predict three things about their future and make predictions with them, using *will.* Go over the example before students begin the task.

b) Divide students into pairs. They try to guess which predictions in Activity 5a their classmate chose. They should ask questions to find out. If they ask about one of the predictions their classmate wrote about, the classmate answers *Yes, I will.* If they ask about a prediction their classmate did not write about, the classmate answers *No, I won't.* The winner in each pair is the person who guessed all three predictions, using fewer questions. Read out the example with a confident student before pairs begin the task.

Extra activity

Write the following categories on the board: *transport, schools, ecology, technology.* Elicit what was different in these categories 50 years ago, e.g. *People didn't have computers.* In groups of four, students predict at least two changes that they think will happen in each of these categories in the next 50 years. Allow five minutes for discussion and elicit the predictions from different groups.

My English file

Students write four predictions they think are true about their own future. They should use their own ideas, other than in Activity 5. Go through the example before they begin the task.

When students have finished writing, they exchange their notebooks in pairs. They read each other's dialogues and point out orally any mistakes they notice.

Mixed-ability classes

Fast finishers write two more predictions. For less confident students you can write the following categories on the board to help them come up with ideas for predictions: *job, money, family, travel, house, hobbies.*

Extra activity

Spread on the floor a large selection of magazine photos showing different objects, places, people, colours, etc. There should be more pictures than students in class. Students stand around the pictures and find one that represents a prediction about their future, e.g. a blue piece of paper for *I will have blue walls in my house.* Students then mingle, show each other their pictures and explain their predictions.

Photocopiable activity

The future p114; instructions p96

6 Check your English

Students match the verbs in the box to the correct sentences and use *will* or *won't* to complete Phoebe's predictions about Oscar and herself. Students compare their answers in pairs. Ask one pair to read out the dialogue to the whole class.

Answer key

1 will dance
2 will give
3 will become
4 won't fall over
5 won't forget
6 will cheer

Dyslexia tip: *Summary of the lesson*

Encourage dyslexic students to write short summaries and notes about the most important points after each lesson. They can do it at home in note form and illustrate the notes with drawings or pictures. This way they will find revision much easier and will remember the objectives of each lesson.

Homework suggestions

1 Activity Book page 29, Activities 4–6
2 Students choose a friend or a relative and write five predictions about their future, e.g. *I think Marcus will become a photographer. He will live in South America.*

14 Helpful Herbert

Lesson objective
Making offers and requests

1 Vocabulary

2.04 Look at the pictures and find these words.

violin d

violin drums keyboards recorder
double bass accordion flute amp

2 Presentation

2.05 Listen and read. Who asks Herbert to:

1 close the window?
2 get some food?
3 fix the amp?

Real English

Sure.
No problem.
Oh, dear.
Of course.

14 Helpful Herbert

Grammar • *can* and *could* for requests; *will* for offers **Vocabulary** • instruments; music; everyday objects; verb and noun collocations	**Optional Activity Book activities** • Fast finishers p66, Extra practice p67 **Photocopiable activity** • *Problems and solutions* p115

PART 1

Introduction

Write the following questions on the board for students to discuss in pairs:

What's your favourite type of music?
Who is your favourite musician or music band?
Have you ever been to a concert?
How many instruments can you name in English?
What was the last song or album you listened to?

Set a time limit of five minutes. Individual students report any surprising information they found out about their classmate.

1 Vocabulary

[2.04] Students look at the words in the box and listen as you play the CD. Then they match the words to the objects in picture 1 in Activity 2. They should make guesses about new vocabulary.

Students work individually on the task and then compare their answers in pairs. Play the CD again and get students to call out the letter labelling the corresponding object. Make sure everybody understands all the words now and drill the pronunciation.

Extra activity

Divide the class into two teams. Give three clues about each instrument in Activity 1 in random order, e.g. *black and white keys, electric, piano* (answer: *keyboards*). Make sure you use words which students know. The team to call out the correct instrument gets one point. The winner is the team with most points at the end. To avoid chaos, you can assign team captains to call out the answers.

Tapescript

see Student's Book Activity 1

Answer key

violin – **d**	drums – **c**	keyboards – **g**
recorder – **e**	double bass – **h**	accordion – **f**
flute – **a**	amp – **b**	

2 Presentation

[2.05] Point to the pictures and introduce the musicians. Explain that Herbert is an assistant to the musicians. Ask students to listen and read and find out who asks Herbert to close the window, get some food and fix the amp respectively. Play the CD.

Elicit the answers. Point to the title of the lesson and ask if students think that Herbert is really helpful. Find out if students know/can guess the meaning of the following words and phrases: *so cold, crisps, turn up the volume.* Provide explanation if necessary. Make sure students understand that *drinks* can refer to cold drinks like juice or cola or hot drinks like tea.

Refer students to the **Grammar spot** on the next page to explain *can* and *could* for requests. Go over the example sentences. Explain that *could* is a little more polite than *can.* It is also very polite to use ***please*** at the end of the request. Point out we say *Could/Can* ***I*** to ask permission and *Could/Can* ***you*** to ask someone to do a favour for us. To practise that you can write *I'm tired and I don't understand this word* on the board and get students to make two requests for each problem, one starting with *Could/Can I* and the other *Could/Can you, e.g. Can I lie down on your sofa? Can you help me with the housework?*

Refer students to **Real English** to find three ways of responding to requests. Practise the phrases by asking students to use them to respond to the following requests and statements: *Can you open the window? Could you lend me your book? Could I borrow your pen, please? You're going to do a test tomorrow.*

Teaching tip: *Explaining new vocabulary*

When students are unable to guess the meaning of new words from the context, there are several ways in which you can convey the meaning without using L1 translation:

- mime and sound
- pictures
- real objects, which are especially useful for tactile learners
- graphs to show degree, e.g. for adverbs of frequency
- synonyms and antonyms
- definitions based on words students already know
- monolingual dictionaries designed especially for lower level students and containing simple definitions.

The above techniques require more planning, but they help students understand new words within the framework of the target language independently of their L1.

Extra activity

Find out how many students in your class can play musical instruments. Divide the class into as many groups as there are 'musicians' in the class. Put one musician in each group. Write the following question words on the board: *What instrument do you play? Why do you play this instrument? Where do you practise? Who teaches you?* Ask group members to interview their classmate with the questions on the board and then to report the answers to the whole class.

Tapescript

see Student's Book Activity 2

Answer key

1 Gabby
2 Bob and Art
3 Dan

❸ Comprehension

Read the story again. What three things does Herbert offer to do?

1 find some gloves for Gabby

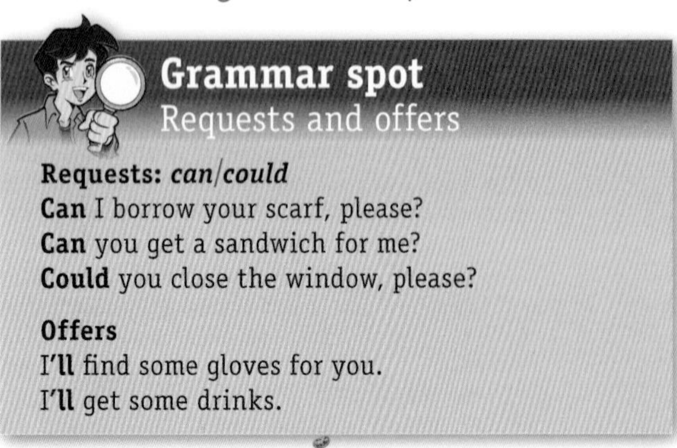

Grammar spot
Requests and offers

Requests: *can/could*
Can I borrow your scarf, please?
Can you get a sandwich for me?
Could you close the window, please?

Offers
I'll find some gloves for you.
I'll get some drinks.

Grammar page 102

❹ Grammar practice

a Put the words in order to make requests.

1 I'm hot. Could you open the window, please?

1 I'm hot.
open | Could | the window | please | you | ?

2 I'm thirsty.
a drink | you | Could | for | me | get | please | ?

3 I'm bored.
please | your magazine | I | Could | borrow | ?

4 I can't find the library.

Could | please | I | your map | look at | ?

5 My head hurts.

you | Could | please | quiet | be | ?

b Now make offers from these prompts.

1 I'll buy an ice cream for you.

1 I/buy/an ice cream for you.
2 I/make/a cup of tea for you.
3 I/switch on/the TV.
4 I/walk there/with you.
5 I/get/some medicine for you.

Study tip
Record verbs and nouns that go together.
open + window   switch on + TV

❺ Listening

a 2.06 Listen to these four people. What are the problems? Complete the sentences.

I want to go to the ____, but my ____ is broken.

I can't find my ____.

I want to phone my ____, but I haven't got a ____.

I don't ____ the ____.

b Think of an offer for each problem.

I'll lend you my bike.

❻ Pronunciation

2.07 Listen and practise saying these requests. Notice the intonation.

1 Could you fix my computer?
2 Can I borrow your calculator?
3 Could I look at your book?
4 Could you fetch my coat?
5 Can you close the door?
6 Can I use your MP3 player?

❼ Check your English

a Choose the correct words and make requests

1 Could *I/you* open the door for me, please?
2 Can *I/you* use your phone, please?
3 Could *I/you* borrow your DVD, please?
4 Could *I/you* switch on the light for me, please?

b Put these words into the correct order to mal offers.

1 your | for | fix | bike | you | I'll
2 you | snack | I'll | a | get | for
3 some | I'll | lend | money | you

❸ Comprehension

Students read the story again and find three things Herbert offers to do. Check the answers with the whole class and elicit Herbert's actual words. Then refer students to the **Grammar spot** to explain that we use *will* for offers. Ask three students to think of a problem they are having in the class and get the others to call out offers of help. Refer students to the **Grammar summary** on page 102 for more information on requests and offers.

Answer key

1 find some gloves for Gabby **2** get some drinks
3 turn up the volume

Teaching tip: *Feedback from the class*

In the final three minutes of each lesson you can ask students to write on sheets of paper answers to the following questions: *What is the most important thing you have learnt today? Is there anything you still do not understand from today's lesson?* A strong class can write their responses in English, otherwise accept the answers in L1. Collect the answers and use them as feedback. Find out what students still do not understand and review the material in your next lesson, asking volunteers for help with explanations.

Homework suggestions

1 Activity Book page 30, Activities 1–2
2 Students add one more scene to the story in Activity 2. They write a dialogue with a request and an offer. They can illustrate the dialogue.

PART 2

Introduction

Put students into groups of four to discuss requests they usually make when they are visiting a friend's house, using *Could/Can I/ you*. Write the following nouns on the board to help them come up with ideas: *bathroom, computer, music, phone, food/drink*. Elicit the most common requests from all the groups.

❹ Grammar practice

a) Students put the words in order to make requests. Point out that we need a comma before *please* at the end of the sentence. In pairs, students compare their answers. Individual students read out the requests to the whole class.

Answer key

1 Could you open the window, please?
2 Could you get a drink for me, please?
3 Could I borrow your magazine, please?
4 Could I look at your map, please?
5 Could you be quiet, please?

b) Students make offers from the prompts to solve the problems in Activity 4a. Offer 1 refers to problem 1 in Activity 4a, offer 2 to problem 2 and so on. Students should use *will* as in the example. Check the answers with the whole class.

Answer key

1 I'll buy an ice cream for you.
2 I'll make a cup of tea for you.
3 I'll switch on the TV.
4 I'll walk there with you.
5 I'll get some medicine for you.

Study tip

Encourage students to note verbs and nouns that often go together as they come across them in their books. Point to the examples in the box and elicit more noun and verb collocations by naming different verbs students know and asking them to provide nouns that go with them, *e.g. turn up (the volume), mow (the lawn), water (the plants).*

Teaching tip: *Collocations*

Collocations are words which frequently occur together. Students tend to learn individual words and then often make wrong combinations, e.g. *make homework*. Use texts and dialogues in the book to point out collocations and when introducing a new word without a context, teach words that usually accompany it. Encourage students to use dictionaries of collocations for their written tasks. Make cards with collocations written separately for students to play pelmanism, i.e. matching up pairs from cards laid face down, or to do mingling activities in which they have to find someone with a matching card.

❺ Listening

a) [2.06] Students guess on the basis of the pictures the problems the four people have. Play the CD for students to check their guesses. They should then complete the sentences. Play the CD once again for students to check their answers.

Mixed-ability classes

For less confident students write the missing words in mixed order on the board.

Tapescript and Answer key

1: I want to go the cinema, but my bike is broken.
2: I can't find my dictionary.
3: I want to phone my dad but I haven't got a mobile phone.
4: I don't understand the homework.

b) In pairs, students make an offer for each of the problems in Activity 5a, using *will*. Elicit all possible offers for each problem. You can ask the class to vote for the best solutions by raising their hands.

Photocopiable activity

Problems and solutions p115; instructions p96

❻ Pronunciation

[2.07] Students listen to the requests and repeat them. Then encourage students to practise saying the requests independently.

Tapescript

see Student's Book Activity 6

Extra activity

Tell students that they can make five requests about the lesson and the classroom within reason and if they are correct and polite, you will respond positively. Try to fulfil students' requests.

❼ Check your English

a) Students choose the correct words to make logical requests. Check the answers with the whole class.

Answer key

1 you **2** I **3** I **4** you

b) Students put the words in the correct order to make offers. Check the answers with the whole class.

Answer key

1 I'll fix your bike for you. **2** I'll get a snack for you.
3 I'll lend you some money.

Homework suggestions

1 Activity Book page 31, Activities 3–6
2 Students write a dialogue between two students who are decorating their classroom for a school play and make at least two requests each.

15 The festival

Lesson objective
Making and responding to suggestions

1 Presentation

2.08 Listen. Mel, Sophie and Charlie are at the Edinburgh Festival with Sophie's dad. What do they want to see? Complete the speech bubbles.

I want to see the New York Street Dancers.

How about going to this ______.

I want to see ______.

Let's listen to ______.

Venue	Show
Queen's Hall	Shakespeare's classic play: Romeo & Juliet
The Music Box	River Roots Band: modern folk music
New Theatre	Puppet Show: Sleeping Beauty
The Assembly Rooms	Comedy Show
Festival Tent	Peppo's Circus
The Bongo Club	The New York Street Dancers
Cabaret Club	The Modern Mime Men

Saturday afternoon, 25th August at the Edinburgh Festival.

2 Comprehension

2.08 Listen again. Are these sentences true or false?

1 Mel saw the New York Street Dancers on TV last year.
2 Charlie says dance is boring.
3 The River Roots Band is Mel's favourite band.
4 Charlie hates folk music.
5 Mel, Charlie and Sophie think that Sophie's dad's decision is a good idea.

No way!
It's so lame!
They're wicked!

15 The festival

Grammar
- *how about …ing; let's; would like to; want to* for suggestions

Vocabulary
- performing arts

Optional materials
- a map of Europe

Optional Activity Book activities
- Fast finishers p66, Extra practice p67

Photocopiable activity
- *Youth club* p116

PART 1

Introduction

Write *festival* on the board. Divide students into five groups and ask them to brainstorm all the words they associate with festivals. Set a time limit of four minutes. Elicit their ideas onto the board. Keep the words on the board for a later stage of the lesson.

1 Presentation

[2.08] Write *Edinburgh* on the board and elicit that it is the capital city of Scotland. If you have a map of Europe, show students the location of the city. Explain that each August there is a famous festival in Edinburgh. Ask students to read the festival programme for Saturday afternoon. Explain what a *venue* is and make sure students do not try to translate the names of the venues, but study the details of the shows.

Point to the picture and explain that Mel, Sophie and Charlie are at the Edinburgh Festival with Sophie's dad. Students listen to their conversation and find out what each of them wants to see. Play the CD and ask students to complete the speech bubbles.

Elicit the answers. Then refer students to **Real English** and demonstrate the meaning of the phrases by suggesting seeing a concert of an old-fashioned local singer or band to elicit *No way!* and by naming different types of music and bands to elicit students' opinion of them, either *It's so lame!* or *They're wicked!*

Refer students to the **Grammar spot** on the next page to elicit or explain the language used for making and responding to suggestions. Point out the different verb forms used after each phrase. Explain that *I'd like to* is polite while *I want to* can be used between friends. Refer students to the **Grammar summary** on page 103 for more information on the language of suggestions.

Cultural information

The Edinburgh International Festival presents three weeks of arts and cultural shows every August in Edinburgh, Scotland, making it the largest arts festival in the world. It started in 1947 and continues every year to focus on performing arts: music, theatre, opera, dance and visual art. The shows are presented at a number of venues in Edinburgh, including major theatres and concert halls.

Tapescript

Dad: OK guys. This is our last day at the Festival. Let's choose something we all want to see this afternoon. Mel, what would you like to see?

Mel: I want to see the New York Street Dancers. I saw them on TV last week. They're wicked!

Dad: New York Street Dancers. OK. What about you, Charlie?

Charlie: I don't want to see dance! No way! Boring! How about going to this comedy show at the Queen's Hall?

Dad: So, Charlie, you want to see the comedy show. Hmm. And Sophie, would you like to see The New York Street Dancers or the comedy show?

Sophie: Neither! Let's listen to the River Roots Band at the Music Box. They're my favourite band!

Charlie: Folk music! Aaagggh! I hate folk music! It's so lame!

Dad: OK, OK. Well, it's the last day, so I'm going to decide. I want to see Shakespeare's Romeo & Juliet at the …

Mel, Sophie, Charlie: Oh no! / No way! / Not Shakespeare!

Answer key

Charlie – comedy show
Sophie – the River Roots Band
Dad – Shakespeare's Romeo & Juliet

2 Comprehension

[2.08] Students listen to the recording again and decide if the sentences are true or false. Then they discuss their answers in pairs. Check the answers with the whole class and ask volunteers to correct the false statements.

Tapescript

see Activity 1

Answer key

1 false (She saw them on TV last week)
2 true
3 false (It's Sophie's favourite band)
4 true
5 false (They don't like Shakespeare)

Extra activity

Find out if students have ever been to any festivals. Ask them to share their experiences with the whole class. They should describe the show, the performers, the venue and give their opinion. If you did the introduction activity, ask students to use as many words from the board as possible.

❸ Vocabulary

Match the word in A to its definition in B.

1 c

	A		B
1	mime	a	a doll with strings
2	comedy	b	traditional music from a country
3	circus	c	acting with no talking
4	puppet	d	a travelling group of performers
5	folk music	e	a funny play or film

Grammar spot
Making and responding to suggestions

How about going to this show?
Let's listen to the River Roots Band.
Would you like to see the comedy show?

I'd like to see this Shakespeare play.
I **don't want to** see dance.
No way.
Good idea.

Grammar page 103

❹ Grammar practice

a Use the correct form of the verb in brackets to complete this conversation.

1 to go

Saturday night, 25th August at the Edinburgh Festival.

Venue	Show
Edinburgh Castle	Fireworks
Cabaret club	Mime and Modern Dance
New Theatre	Puppet Show: Robin Hood
Ross Open Air Theatre	Mozart's classic opera: The Magic Flute
Festival Tent	Peppo's Circus
The Bongo Club	Comedy Club Night
The Music Box	Jazz and Blues Band

Dad Would you like [1] ______ (go) to the festival tonight?
Charlie Let's [2] ______ (walk) to the Castle and [3] ______ (watch) the fireworks.
Mel No, I don't like fireworks.
Sophie How about [4] ______ (go) to the Opera in the Park?
Charlie Oh no! Boring!
Dad Let's [5] ______ (go) back to the hotel and [6] ______ (watch) TV.
Mel, Sophie, Charlie No way!

b 2.09 Listen and check.

❺ Speaking

a Work with two or three classmates. Design your own festival programme.

b Exchange programmes with another group. Choose a show. Make suggestions and reach a group decision.

What would you like to see, Mika?

How about …

❻ Check your English

Put these sentences into the correct order.

1 What would you like to do tonight?

1 you | what | to | tonight | would | do | like | ?
2 about | cinema | going | how | to | the | ?
3 don't | watch | I | a | to | film | want
4 listen | the | band | let's | to | jazz
5 walk | you | would | to | park | the | afternoon | like | to | this | ?

❸ Vocabulary

Students match the words to their definitions. Check the answers with the whole class after students have compared them in pairs. Drill the pronunciation of the words.

Dyslexia tip: *Memorising spelling*

You can teach dyslexic students to memorise spelling of words by using visual and kinaesthetic memory, e.g. to remember that the word *puppet* has double *p*, draw a pair of jeans with two puppets in the pockets and below write: *Puppets in pockets*. Ask students to repeat the words and touch their pockets with both hands at the same time. Then students copy the drawing and words into their notebooks, which should remind them in the future about the double *p* in *puppet*.

Answer key

1 c **2** e **3** d **4** a **5** b

Extra activity

In pairs, students tell each other which show from the programme in Activity 1 they would like to see and why. Find out which show most of the class would like to see.

Homework suggestions

1. Activity Book page 32, Activities 1–2
2. Students choose one of the types of entertainment in Activity 3 they have seen and write a short paragraph about the experience, saying what they saw, where they saw it and what they thought of it.

PART 2

Introduction

Write the following phrases on the board: *How about ...?, Let's ..., Would you like ...?* Explain you would like to have a fun lesson with your students today, but cannot think of any nice games or activities. Ask students to make suggestions, using the phrases on the board and the correct verb form. When you have heard a few suggestions, say that you cannot use them all, but you will try to include some of them towards the end of the lesson or over the course of the next few lessons.

❹ Grammar practice

a) Focus students' attention on the festival programme for Saturday evening. Clarify any vocabulary students do not understand. Students read the conversation about the programme and complete it with the correct form of the verb in brackets: infinitive with or without *to* or gerund. If necessary, refer students to the **Grammar spot** to review the verb forms different phrases require. Ask students to compare their answers in pairs.

Mixed-ability classes

Fast finishers continue the dialogue by adding one or two lines.

b) [2.09] Play the CD for students to check their answers.

Tapescript and Answer key

Dad: Would you like to go to the Festival tonight?
Charlie: Let's walk to the Castle and watch the fireworks.
Mel: No, I don't like fireworks.
Sophie: How about going to the Opera in the Park?
Charlie: Oh no! Boring!
Dad: Let's go back to the hotel and watch TV.
Mel, Sophie, Charlie: No way!

❺ Speaking

Divide students into groups of three or four. Ask them to study the programme in Activity 4 and choose one show to watch together. They should use the language of making and responding to suggestions from the **Grammar spot.** They should justify why they want or do not want to see a given show. Read out the example with a confident student before groups begin the task. Monitor the activity.

Set a time limit of four minutes. Groups report which show they have decided to watch.

Extra activity

Divide students into groups of four and ask them to plan a great two-day school trip for their class. They should plan the destination, transport, accommodation, places to eat and any tourist attractions and activities. Encourage them to use the language of suggestions. Set a time limit of ten minutes for discussion. Group representatives present their projects to the whole class. Get students to vote for the best project. They can vote only once and not for their own project.

Photocopiable activity

Youth club p116; instructions p96

❻ Check your English

Students put the words in order to make sentences. In pairs, they compare their answers. Check the answers with the whole class.

Answer key

1. What would you like to do tonight?
2. How about going to the cinema?
3. I don't want to watch a film.
4. Let's listen to the jazz band.
5. Would you like to walk to the park this afternoon?

Dyslexia tip: *Handwriting*

Handwriting can be very difficult for some students, but you need to make them aware that legibility must be their priority. Dyslexic students may write neatly when they copy words from the board or the textbook, but their handwriting tends to deteriorate when they write their own sentences or compositions. Make it clear that you need to be able to read their work to evaluate it. However, be flexible about students' handwriting as long as it is legible, allow them to use printed writing and accept typed homework. In collaboration with their L1 teacher, you can encourage students to change the style of the most confusing letters in their handwriting, e.g. putting a loop across *e* so that it cannot be confused with *c* or *l*.

Homework suggestions

1. Activity Book pages 32–33, Activities 3–6
2. Students find a current local cinema guide or newspaper and write a six-line dialogue between three friends who want to choose a film to watch together. They should use the phrases from the **Grammar spot**. If they mention English language films, encourage them to use the original titles, which they can find on the Internet.

16 The Brit School

1 Reading

a 2.10 Read the article. What do students learn at the Brit School?

Would you like to learn how to dance?

How about learning to play the drums?

Lunch break has just started at The Brit School, in South East London, and there's an hour before lessons begin again. However, at this school, the students want to study during their lunch break. Outside, three students are playing the guitar together and are writing a song. In the corridor inside, another student is stretching and practising some dance exercises. And in the library, some friends are doing their homework and talking about their dreams and plans for the future. Freya thinks that she will be a singer and star in famous musicals in the West End of London. Bill thinks he'll be a soap star and Tania hopes she'll be a successful actress.

The Brit School is a special performing arts school for 14-19 year olds who want to work in music, theatre, dance or design. The school is state-funded. This means that the students don't pay any money to go to the school. The students have to work very hard at The Brit School. 'People think that we have a lot of fun here and sing and dance all day,' says 16-year-old Tania, 'but there are a lot of things to learn. We also study the normal school subjects: History, Science, English, Maths and IT. By Friday afternoon, I'm always exhausted!'

The Brit School opened in 1991 and it now has some very famous old students. Adele, Katie Melua, The Kooks and Athlete, all went to The Brit School.

b Find these words in the article. Can you guess what they mean?

corridor stretching musicals successful state-funded exhausted

c Read the article again and answer the questions.

1 Where is The Brit School?
2 How long is the lunch break?
3 How old are the students at the school?
4 What subjects do students study?
5 When did the school open?

16 The Brit School

Photocopiable activity
- *Two schools* p117

PART 1

Introduction

Draw a spidergram with the word *school* as the topic and *places, classroom, subjects, activities* as sub-categories. Divide students into groups of four and ask them to brainstorm all the words to add to each category. Set a time limit of four minutes. Ask group representatives to come to the board and add their words to the spidergram. They should not repeat any words that are already there.

Teaching tip: *Spidergrams*

A spidergram is a spider-shaped diagram in which information relating to a topic is written in boxes or circles joined by lines from the central box which contains the topic. Spidergrams are an excellent tool for organizing information in a brainstorming activity; they help recall vocabulary, develop awareness of connections between words and join different topics, e.g. the topic of *school* can relate to the topic of *furniture*. When working with spidergrams, encourage students to add more sub-categories that you may not have thought of. As students are adding words on the board, ask them to explain the words they offer. When the spidergram is complete, students should copy it into their notebooks.

1 Reading

a) [2.10] Explain that the photos relate to an unusual school called the Brit School. Ask the class to study the photos and make guesses about what students learn at the school. Then ask students to listen and read the article to check their guesses. Play the CD. Make sure that students understand that the article does not describe the pictures directly.

Elicit that students of the Brit School learn performing arts, e.g. dancing and singing as well as normal school subjects, e.g. *History, Science,* etc.

Tapescript

see Student's Book Activity 1a

b) Students look at the words in the box and find them in the article in Activity 1a. Encourage them to guess their meaning from the context. In pairs, students compare their ideas. Elicit the meaning of the words and provide further explanation if necessary.

Check if students know/can guess the meaning of the following words and phrases from the article: *star in famous musicals, soap star, design, by Friday afternoon.* Provide explanation if necessary.

c) Ask students to read the article in Activity 1a again and answer the questions. Encourage them to mark with pencil the relevant parts of the text which contain the answers. Set a time limit of five minutes.

Students compare the answers in pairs. Check the answers with the whole class and elicit the parts of the text which justify them.

Find out if students know the famous people who studied at the Brit School. If you have access to the Internet in the classroom, ask students to find information on the celebrities on the Internet or explain who they are yourself, using the cultural information note below.

Mixed-ability classes

Fast finishers write more questions about the article. They can ask their questions to the whole class when everyone has completed the task in Activity 1c.

Extra activity

Have a class discussion about their dream school. Ask students how they imagine its building, classrooms, rules and subjects. You can ask them for ideas on how to improve their own school, but make sure these are constructive rather than a series of complaints.

Cultural information

Adele (Adele Laurie Blue Adkins), born in 1988, is an English singer and songwriter. She has won a number of music awards, including two Grammy Awards in 2009.

Katie Melua, born in 1984, is a Georgian/British singer and songwriter. She is one of the most popular female singers in Europe. Her albums sell millions of copies worldwide.

The Kooks are an English rock band, formed in Brighton in 2004. Their albums have reached the top of the UK Albums Chart.

Athlete are an English rock band, formed in London in 1999. The musicians are childhood friends. Their songs have appeared in many films and TV series.

Answer key

1 in South East London
2 an hour
3 14–19
4 History, Science, English, Maths, IT
5 in 1991

2 Listening

a 2.11 Tim wants to go to the Brit School. Listen to his interview. What does he want to study at the Brit School?

b 2.11 Listen again and complete the dialogue.

Teacher So, Tim, why do you want to come to this school?

Tim Well, I really love [1]_____ and I think that this school is a great place to learn. I want to study [2]_____ here.

Teacher Hmm. I see. What job do you think you'll have in the future?

Tim I hope I'll [3]_____ a professional singer. I think I'll be in a band and we'll [4]_____ and [5]_____ our own songs.

Teacher Do you [6]_____ your music at home?

Tim Yes, I do. I sing every day, even in the holidays. And I'm also [7]_____ to play the guitar.

Teacher Who is your favourite singer?

Tim I really love Justin Timberlake. I think he's got an amazing voice and he's a great [8]_____ too.

3 Speaking

Act out the interview. Work in pairs.

Student A: You are a teacher at the Brit School. Student B wants to join your school. Ask the questions below. Think of two more questions for Student B.

Student B: You want to go to the Brit School. Prepare your answers to the questions below.

- What do you want to study at the school?
- What job do you think you'll have in the future?
- Do you practise at home?
- Who is your favourite singer/actor/dancer?

So Michelle, what do you want to study at the school?

I want to study dancing …

4 Writing

Write a paragraph to explain why you want to go to the Brit School. Use your ideas from Activity 3.

I want to go to the Brit School because I really like …

Writing tip

Use different ways of writing about what you like and what you want:

I **really like** theatre and dance.
I **really love** singing.
I **want to** study music.
I **hope** I'll be a professional singer.
I **enjoy** acting.
I **think** I'll be an actress.

Let's go swimming

Work in groups of three or four.

Student A: Make a suggestion about what to do today. Use *Let's go*.

Student B: Repeat Student A's suggestion and add your own idea.

Student C: Repeat Student A's and B's suggestions and add your own idea.

If you forget a suggestion, you're out of the game.

❷ Listening

a) [2.11] Point to the photo and introduce Tim. Explain that he wants to go to the Brit School. Ask students to listen to Tim's interview and find out what he wants to study. Play the CD. Elicit that Tim wants to study music at the school.

Tapescript

see Activity 2b

b) [2.11] Play the CD again and ask students to complete the dialogue. Students compare their answers in pairs. Check the answers with the whole class. Explain that the interview is part of admissions procedure at the Brit School. Students are selected based on their artistic abilities and determination to study.

Tapescript and Answer key

Teacher: So, Tim, why do you want to come to this school?
Tim: Well, I really love singing and I think that this school is a great place to learn. I want to study music here.
Teacher: Hmm. I see. What job do you think you'll have in the future?
Tim: I hope I'll be a professional singer. I think I'll be in a band and we'll write and perform our own songs.
Teacher: Do you practise your music at home?
Tim: Yes, I do. I sing every day, even in the holidays. And I'm also learning to play the guitar.
Teacher: Who is your favourite singer?
Tim: I really love Justin Timberlake. I think he's got an amazing voice and he's a great dancer too.

Mixed-ability classes

For less confident students write the missing words on the board in mixed order.

Extra activity

Divide students into pairs and ask them to write three questions about the interview, e.g. *Who is Tim's favourite singer?* Set a time limit of three minutes. Students close their books and work with another pair. Pairs take turns to ask each other their questions and answer them from memory.

Homework suggestions

1. Activity Book page 34, Activity 1
2. Students write their own sentences with the words in Activity 1b.

PART 2

Introduction

Elicit from students what admissions procedures there are in different schools in their own country, e.g. interviews, final exam results, entrance exams, etc. Help them with any new vocabulary. Ask them which procedures they think are the best.

❸ Speaking

Divide students into pairs. Explain that they are going to role-play an interview at the Brit School. Students A and B in each pair should read their respective role instructions. Student A reads the questions and prepares two more for Student B. Student B prepares his/her answers to the questions. Allow five minutes for preparation. You can demonstrate the task by playing the interview from Activity 2 as an example.

When the time is up, students act out the interview within their pairs. Monitor the activity. When everybody has finished, ask Student As in different pairs if they think their classmate should get to the school based on their answers. Then ask one or two pairs to act out their interview for the whole class.

Teaching tip: *Successful role-plays*

Students need sufficient preparation for a role-play to be successful. The most common problems they encounter are not being able to think of anything to say, or digressions and mistakes as they focus on what they want to say without thinking of how they are going to say it. To avoid these problems allow enough time for preparation, ask students to make notes of what they want to say and add phrases they should use in the conversation. Point out that role-plays in the textbook are related to the general material of the lesson, so students should look for ideas and the target language in earlier activities. You can ask students to do the same role-play twice with different classmates. After the first role-play they can ask you to help them with any problems they encountered, so that they will feel confident acting out the second time.

❹ Writing

Students imagine they want to study at the Brit School. They can invent skills and abilities they have in performing arts. Then they should write a paragraph to explain why they want to go to the Brit School, mentioning at least three reasons. Encourage them to use the ideas from Activity 3. Go over the **Writing tip** and point out different ways to express the same idea. Encourage students to use different expressions and grammar structures in their text to make it more interesting. Ask students to read the example before they begin the task.

Photocopiable activity

Two schools p117; instructions p97

Let's go swimming

Divide students into groups of three or four and ask them to play the long sentence game. They should repeat their classmates' suggestions starting with *Let's …* and add their own as in the instructions. If they cannot remember the sequence, they are out of the game. The winner in each group is the last person to stay in the game.

Homework suggestions

1. Activity Book page 34, Activity 2
2. Students write a paragraph, explaining why they would or wouldn't like to study at the Brit School.

Module 4 Review

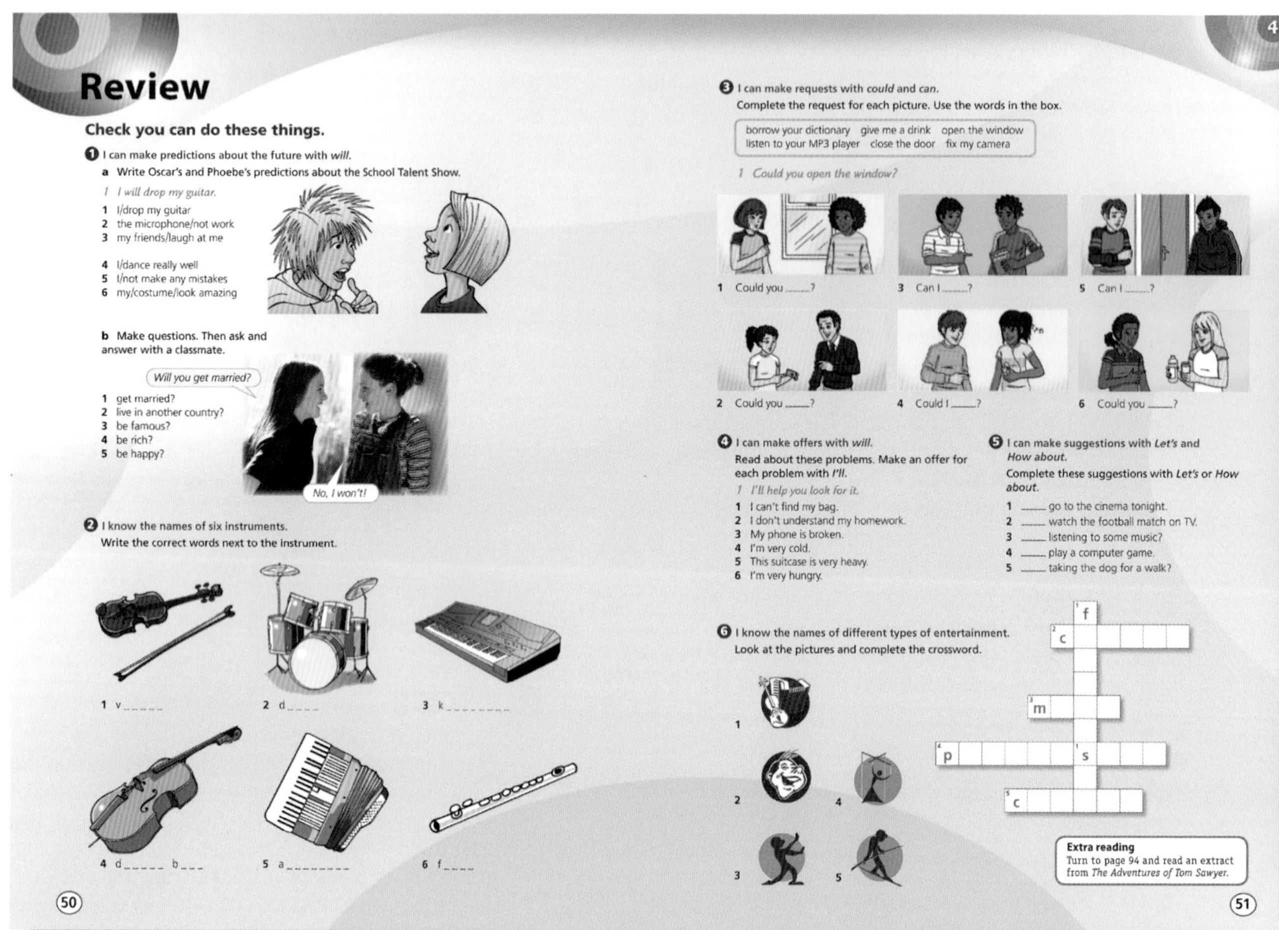

Review

Check you can do these things.

1 I can make predictions about the future with *will*.

a Write Oscar's and Phoebe's predictions about the School Talent Show.

1 I will drop my guitar.
1 I/drop my guitar
2 the microphone/not work
3 my friends/laugh at me
4 I/dance really well
5 I/not make any mistakes
6 my/costume/look amazing

b Make questions. Then ask and answer with a classmate.

Will you get married?
1 get married?
2 live in another country?
3 be famous?
4 be rich?
5 be happy?

No, I won't!

2 I know the names of six instruments.
Write the correct words next to the instrument.

1 v_ _ _ _ _
2 d_ _ _ _
3 k_ _ _ _ _ _ _ _
4 d_ _ _ _ _ b_ _ _
5 a_ _ _ _ _ _ _ _
6 f_ _ _ _

3 I can make requests with *could* and *can*.
Complete the request for each picture. Use the words in the box.

borrow your dictionary   give me a drink   open the window
listen to your MP3 player   close the door   fix my camera

1 Could you open the window?
1 Could you ____?
2 Could you ____?
3 Can I ____?
4 Could I ____?
5 Can I ____?
6 Could you ____?

4 I can make offers with *will*.
Read about these problems. Make an offer for each problem with *I'll*.

1 I'll help you look for it.
1 I can't find my bag.
2 I don't understand my homework.
3 My phone is broken.
4 I'm very cold.
5 This suitcase is very heavy.
6 I'm very hungry.

5 I can make suggestions with *Let's* and *How about*.
Complete these suggestions with *Let's* or *How about*.

1 ____ go to the cinema tonight.
2 ____ watch the football match on TV.
3 ____ listening to some music?
4 ____ play a computer game.
5 ____ taking the dog for a walk?

6 I know the names of different types of entertainment.
Look at the pictures and complete the crossword.

1 f
2 c
3 m
4 p
5 c
s

Extra reading
Turn to page 94 and read an extract from *The Adventures of Tom Sawyer*.

50 51

Optional materials

- five pieces of paper per student

Optional revision

Before your students start this Review, you may want to direct them to the **Grammar summary** at the back of their coursebooks and to the **Word lists** at the back of their Activity Books. This will remind them of the main grammar and vocabulary in the module. Give them ten minutes to read through those in small groups and ask you any questions they may have.

- Activity Book: Refer your students to pages 85–86: *Musical Instruments*; *Performance and shows*; *Modals*
- **Grammar summary**: Refer your students to pages 102–103 sections 9–11

Module 4 Review

The purpose of this section is revision and consolidation of the material studied in Module 4.

Completing the activities

Go over all the activities with the class, explaining rubrics and giving examples to make sure students know what to do. There are written and oral tasks, but you may decide yourself how they should be completed by students. Generally students should do the writing tasks individually and the oral tasks in pairs, testing each other's knowledge. Make sure they do not treat the *Review* as a formal test, but complete the activities in a friendly, stress-free atmosphere. Fast finishers can write down the answers to the oral tasks.

Checking answers

When students have finished, check the answers with the whole class by asking volunteers to copy their answers onto the board or to say them aloud. If necessary, explain the more difficult issues, ask additional questions about the activities and solve any problems that arise.

Self-evaluation

Tell students to evaluate themselves. They should tick the activities where at least half of their answers were correct.

Feedback

Ask students which activities were difficult, which were easy and if there is anything they would like to review. Make a note of common language problems to go over in future lessons.

Answer key

1 **a)** Students complete Oscar's and Phoebe's predictions about the talent show with *will* or *won't*. They can use short and full forms.

1 I will drop my guitar.
2 The microphone won't work.
3 My friends will laugh at me.
4 I will dance really well.
5 I won't make any mistakes.
6 My costume will look amazing.

b) Individually, students make questions with the prompts and *will*. Then in pairs, they take turns to ask the questions and answer with *Yes, I will or No, I won't.*

1 Will you get married?
2 Will you live in another country?
3 Will you be famous?
4 Will you be rich?
5 Will you be happy?

2 **1** violin
2 drums
3 keyboards
4 double bass
5 accordion
6 flute

3 **1** Could you open the window?
2 Could you fix my camera?
3 Can I borrow your dictionary?
4 Could I listen to your MP3 player?
5 Can I close the door?
6 Could you give me a drink?

4 Students make their own offers with ***will*** to solve the problems.

5 **1** Let's
2 Let's
3 How about
4 Let's
5 How about

6 **1** folk music
2 comedy
3 mime
4 puppet show
5 circus

Extra activity

Ask students to choose five words they have learnt in the module. They should write them on separate pieces of paper. Set a time limit of three minutes. Then ask students to mingle and give their words to five students. They have to elicit the meaning of the word from the person they want to give the word to. If the classmate does not remember the word, they should explain the meaning themselves. Individual students say which words they have received and explain their meaning to the whole class.

Extra reading

Refer students to pages 94 and 95 of their books to find an extract from *The Adventures of Tom Sawyer.*

1 Students read the background information about the book and its author and say if they know any other famous books with children as the main characters.

2 Students read the extract from the book and decide if the statements are true or false. They should correct the false statements.

Answer key

a false (He wants to go swimming, fishing and play with his friends)
b true
c false (He gave him all of his apple)
d false (He wants to paint the fence)

3 Students discuss the questions in groups of four. Pre-teach: *clever, naughty* if necessary. Groups share the results of their discussion with the whole class.

Homework suggestions

If students enjoyed the extract, they may want to read the whole story. There is a Macmillan Reader available of *The Adventures of Tom Sawyer*. Visit macmillanenglish.com/readers for details.

Module 4 Tests (A and B) are on the Tests CD

Learning diary

You can refer students to page 35 of the Activity Book for further review, more study tips and self-assessment activities.

Extra special

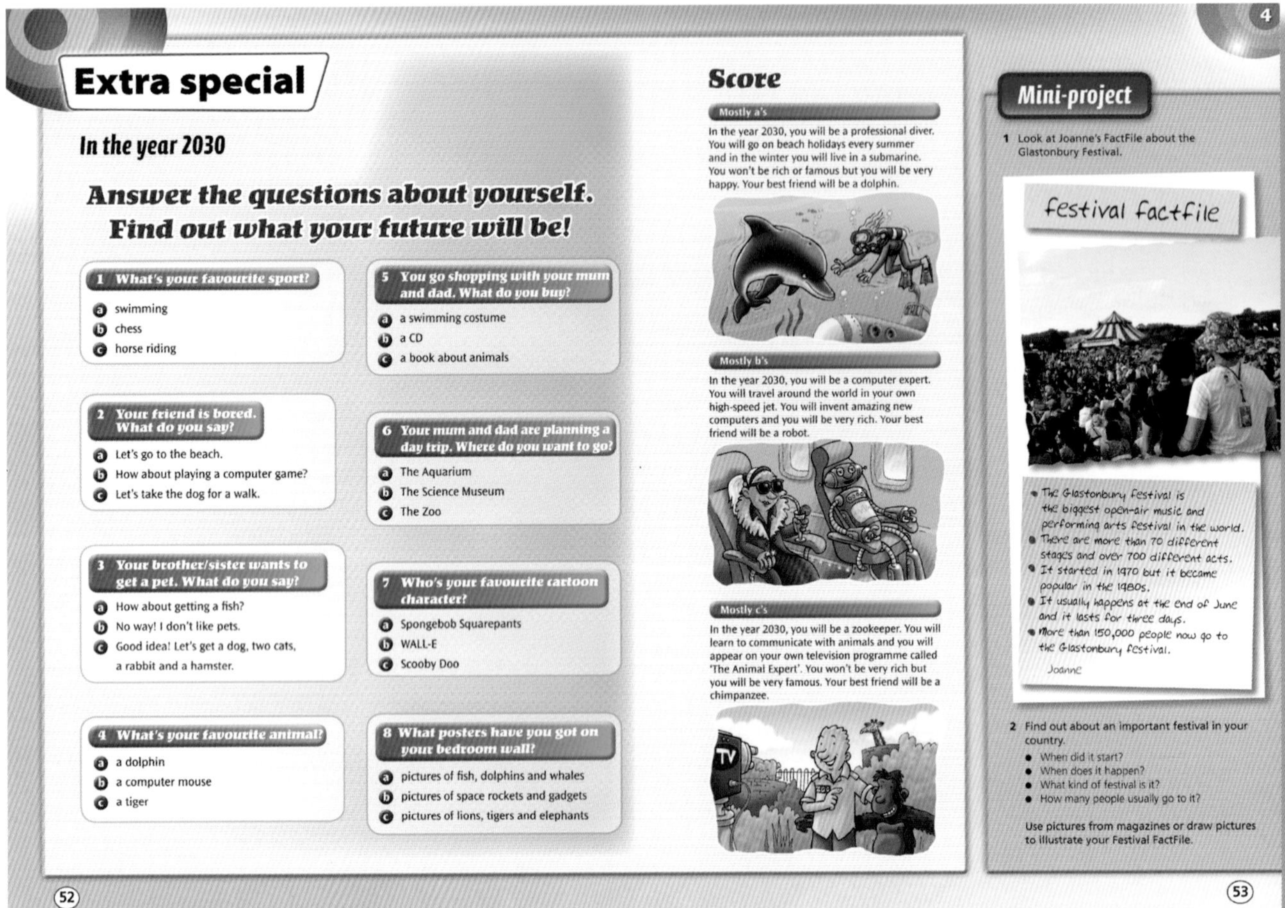

4

Extra special

In the year 2030

Answer the questions about yourself. Find out what your future will be!

1 What's your favourite sport?
- a swimming
- b chess
- c horse riding

2 Your friend is bored. What do you say?
- a Let's go to the beach.
- b How about playing a computer game?
- c Let's take the dog for a walk.

3 Your brother/sister wants to get a pet. What do you say?
- a How about getting a fish?
- b No way! I don't like pets.
- c Good idea! Let's get a dog, two cats, a rabbit and a hamster.

4 What's your favourite animal?
- a a dolphin
- b a computer mouse
- c a tiger

5 You go shopping with your mum and dad. What do you buy?
- a a swimming costume
- b a CD
- c a book about animals

6 Your mum and dad are planning a day trip. Where do you want to go?
- a The Aquarium
- b The Science Museum
- c The Zoo

7 Who's your favourite cartoon character?
- a Spongebob Squarepants
- b WALL-E
- c Scooby Doo

8 What posters have you got on your bedroom wall?
- a pictures of fish, dolphins and whales
- b pictures of space rockets and gadgets
- c pictures of lions, tigers and elephants

Score

Mostly a's

In the year 2030, you will be a professional diver. You will go on beach holidays every summer and in the winter you will live in a submarine. You won't be rich or famous but you will be very happy. Your best friend will be a dolphin.

Mostly b's

In the year 2030, you will be a computer expert. You will travel around the world in your own high-speed jet. You will invent amazing new computers and you will be very rich. Your best friend will be a robot.

Mostly c's

In the year 2030, you will be a zookeeper. You will learn to communicate with animals and you will appear on your own television programme called 'The Animal Expert'. You won't be very rich but you will be very famous. Your best friend will be a chimpanzee.

Mini-project

1 Look at Joanne's FactFile about the Glastonbury Festival.

festival factfile

- The Glastonbury Festival is the biggest open-air music and performing arts festival in the world.
- There are more than 70 different stages and over 700 different acts.
- It started in 1970 but it became popular in the 1980s.
- It usually happens at the end of June and it lasts for three days.
- More than 150,000 people now go to the Glastonbury festival.

Joanne

2 Find out about an important festival in your country.
- When did it start?
- When does it happen?
- What kind of festival is it?
- How many people usually go to it?

Use pictures from magazines or draw pictures to illustrate your Festival FactFile.

52 53

Extra activity

Ask students to brainstorm all the ways people think they can tell the future and write their ideas on the board. Advise students to treat predictions as a fun activity rather than take them seriously.

In the year 2030

Find out how old students will be in 2030. Explain that students are going to answer a questionnaire and the results will tell them about their future. Make sure students understand it is only a fun game.

Students read the questions and circle their answers. They can choose only one answer per question. When they have finished, they count how many **a** answers they have got, how many **b***s* and **c***s*. They should read the result for the type they have got most of. Explain difficult vocabulary.

Ask students to discuss their results in groups of four. They should say if they think the predictions are true about them or not, giving their reasons.

Extra activity

Divide the class into two teams. Members of Team A imagine they are fortune tellers and think how to make optimistic predictions referring to money, job, family and travel, e.g. *You will be rich, You will become a National Geographic reporter*, etc. Students in Team B think of an unusual dream they had and do not mind sharing with their classmates, or invent a dream where unusual things happened. Allow four minutes for preparation and help with any vocabulary problems. When the time is up, each Student B visits a fortune teller from Team A to talk about their dream. Fortune tellers have to make optimistic predictions based on the dreams. Student Bs repeat the task twice, each time with a different Student A. Elicit whose predictions each Student B liked the most.

Mini-project

1. Explain to students that a girl called Joanne has made a FactFile about a festival in England. Ask students to read her FactFile and decide if they would like to go to the Glastonbury Festival or not. Clarify any vocabulary in the project if necessary.
2. Elicit names of different festivals in your students' countries. Ask students to choose one festival each and to find the answers to the questions about the festival and any other interesting facts. You can ask students to do research for homework in a previous lesson, use the Internet in class, or set the project as a homework activity.

   Students make their own Festival FactFile based on their research and illustrate it with pictures from magazines or their own drawings. They should write at least four sentences about the festival, using Joanna's project as a model. Encourage them to make a draft copy first. Monitor their work and provide help where necessary. When they have finished, they can present their projects to the whole class.

Lesson objectives
- Talking about illne
- Talking about future possibilities

17 How are you feeling?

1 Vocabulary

2.12 Listen. Match the words with the pictures.

flu e

flu medicine a temperature a sore throat
a cold a headache a cough a stomach ache

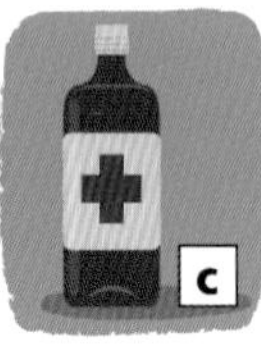

2 Presentation

a 2.13 Listen and read. Does Phoebe think Oscar is really ill?

Phoebe Hello Oscar. How are you feeling?
Oscar Terrible. I'm really ill. I've got a headache and I've got a sore throat. And I've got a cough.
Phoebe Umm. Have you been to the doctor?
Oscar Yes, I have. I think I've got flu.
Phoebe Have you got a temperature?
Oscar Yes, I think so.
Phoebe Let's see. Umm. No, you haven't. Your temperature's normal. I think you've only got a cold.
Oscar But I feel terrible.
Phoebe Have you taken your medicine?
Oscar No, I haven't.
Phoebe Well, if you don't take your medicine, you won't get better.
Oscar But it tastes horrible.
Phoebe Go on. Take it. And what are you doing? If you watch TV, your headache will get worse. Give me the remote.
Oscar But I was watching that!
Phoebe And I think I'll take this chocolate away …
Oscar But …
Phoebe If you eat all this chocolate, you'll get a stomach ache. And if you get a stomach ache, you'll have to stay at home another day. And I know you don't want to miss school again, Oscar!

b 2.13 Listen again. Which of the health problems from Activity 1 does Oscar say he has?

How are you feeling?
I feel terrible.
Go on.

17 How are you feeling?

Grammar
- first conditional

Vocabulary
- health; illnesses

Optional materials
- pieces of paper with words from Activity 1

Optional Activity Book activities
- Fast finishers p68, Extra practice p69

Photocopiable activity
- *Telepathy* p118

PART 1

Introduction

Say to students: *I want to be healthy.* Divide students into groups of four and ask them to make a list of tips for you on how to be healthy, e.g. *Eat a lot of fruit and vegetables; Exercise.* Set a time limit of five minutes. Elicit groups' ideas onto the board. Ask students to vote for the three most important tips.

❶ Vocabulary

[2.12] Students look at the words in the box and listen as you play the CD. Then they match the words to the pictures. They should make guesses about new vocabulary.

Students work individually on the task and then compare their answers in pairs. Play the CD again and elicit the corresponding pictures. Make sure everybody understands all the words now and drill the pronunciation.

Mixed-ability classes

Fast finishers make a list of any other health problems they know in English. Elicit their ideas when everyone has finished working on Activity 1.

Teaching tip: *Fast finishers*

Students who finish activities early need to be kept busy or they will distract other students. You can give them tasks extending a textbook activity and fast finisher activities in the Activity Book. Alternatively, at the beginning of the school year you can tell the whole class what fast finishers should generally do. Here are some ideas you may wish to use:

- have age-appropriate English magazines in the corner of the classroom for fast finishers to read quietly
- keep copies of puzzles, fill-in the blank activities and crosswords in a fast finisher box for students to select and complete
- have laminated memory game cards with words and pictures. Fast finishers can choose a set and match the words to the pictures or play pelmanism in pairs
- set up an ongoing project fast finishers can contribute to, e.g. a classroom newsletter. Students can write fun facts, summaries of what they have recently studied, accounts of school trips, etc. and put the drafts in the designated folder to be edited and proofread later.

Make sure that the activities you prepare are not too attractive so that students working at a normal pace do not feel punished and do not rush through tasks to be rewarded with something more interesting.

Tapescript

see Student's Book Activity 1

Answer key

flu – **e**	medicine – **c**
a temperature – **f**	a sore throat – **b**
a cold – **g**	a headache – **a**
a cough – **d**	a stomach ache – **h**

❷ Presentation

a) [2.13] Focus students' attention on the picture. Ask volunteers to describe the situation in the picture to the whole class. Then ask students to guess whether Oscar is really ill. Play the CD for students to check their guesses. Elicit that he is not really ill.

Refer students to **Real English** and demonstrate the meaning of the phrases by miming that you are very tired and feeling unwell to elicit: *How are you feeling?* then mouth your response for students to say out loud: *I feel terrible.* Pretend that you are offering a student some food and shake your head to signal to them that they should refuse. Keep offering the imaginary food for them and elicit from the class that you could say *Go on* in this situation.

Check if students know/can guess what the following words mean: *get worse, remote, miss school.* Provide explanation if necessary.

Tapescript

see Student's Book Activity 2a

b) [2.13] Ask students to listen and read the conversation again and find which of the health problems in Activity 1 Oscar says he has. Play the CD. Elicit the answers.

Extra activity

Write the following questions on the board: *Do you eat a lot of fruit and vegetables? Do you drink a lot of water? Do you exercise every day? Do you see the dentist twice a year? Do you sleep more than 7 hours every night? Do you play outdoor sports? Do you go for long walks? Do you relax for one hour or more every day?* In pairs, students interview each other with these questions and note down their classmate's answers. Give the results of the test for students to tell their classmate: if they answered *Yes* to five questions or more, they have a very healthy lifestyle. If most of their answers are *No*, they should make some changes.

Tapescript

see Student's Book Activity 2a

Answer key

flu, temperature, cough, headache, sore throat

Grammar spot
First conditional

If you **watch** TV, your headache **will get** worse.
If you **don't take** your medicine, you **won't get** better.

Grammar page 103

Writing tip

comma

If you watch TV, your headache will get worse.

❸ Grammar practice

Match the words in A with the words in B to make sentences.

A

1 If you study hard,
2 If you don't go to bed now,
3 If you eat lots of apples,
4 If you don't get up now,
5 If you don't write notes,

B

a you'll get a stomach ache.
b you'll be late for school.
c you won't remember the answers.
d you'll pass the test.
e you'll feel tired in the morning.

❹ Pronunciation

a 2.14 Listen to this tongue twister.

/t/

Take Tony's temperature tonight and tomorrow.

b 2.15 Listen again and repeat. How fast can you say it?

❺ Speaking

a Complete these sentences with your own ideas.

1 If my friend is late, I won't wait for him.

1 If my friend is late, I'll/I won't …
2 If it rains tomorrow, I'll/I won't …
3 If you watch too much TV, you'll …
4 If …, I'll watch TV.
5 If it …, I won't go to the beach.
6 If you eat all that ice-cream, you'll …

b Now work with a classmate.
Student A: Say the first part of the sentence.
Student B: Finish the sentence. Then swap roles.

If my friend is late,

I won't wait for him.

❻ Check your English

a Find eight words connected to health in this word puzzle.

D	I	M	C	O	U	G	H	K	F	P	V	M	E
S	R	R	Y	I	T	S	E	Q	L	J	E	S	R
K	T	E	M	P	E	R	A	T	U	R	E	T	W
B	S	T	J	C	W	A	D	G	C	S	A	N	O
H	R	A	S	T	O	M	A	C	H	A	C	H	E
E	U	Q	H	B	U	U	C	V	L	Y	O	L	R
G	W	D	B	X	M	M	H	Z	H	I	L	U	E
M	E	D	I	C	I	N	E	P	O	E	D	Y	K
M	R	O	S	O	R	E	T	H	R	O	A	T	C

b Answer these questions.

1 Is your temperature normal?
2 How many of these things have you had?
  a flu
  b a sore throat
  c a cough
3 Have you got any of them now?
4 Have you been to the doctor this year?
5 Do you think these sentences are true?
  a If you watch a lot of TV, you'll get a headache.
  b If you eat a lot of chocolate, you'll get a stomach ache.
6 Do you stay away from school when you are ill?

Grammar spot

Ask students to read the sentences and elicit or explain the use and structure of the first conditional. Make sure students understand the first conditional refers to future possibilities and that they remember to use the present simple in the *if* phrase. You can write an example sentence on the board, using different colours for the present simple and *will* to point out that different tenses are used in the first conditional. Refer students to the **Writing tip** to point out we use a comma after the *if* phrase. Elicit all the examples of the first conditional in Activity 2a. Then give the class different future possibilities, e.g. *If I open the window/turn off the lights/drop this glass …* and encourage students to call out the likely results. Refer students to the **Grammar summary** on page 103 for more information on the first conditional.

Extra activity

Ask students to close their books. Copy the sentences from the **Grammar spot** onto the board, leaving gaps instead of the verbs, e.g. *If you ________ TV, your headache ________ get worse.* Ask students to complete the gaps from memory. Circle *if* and remind them that it is the first conditional and they need to use two different tenses.

Homework suggestions

1 Activity Book page 36, Activities 1–3
2 Students write three pieces of advice for one of the health problems in Activity 1, e.g. *flu – go to the doctor, take medicine, stay in bed.*

PART 2

Introduction

Before the lesson write the words from Activity 1 on pieces of paper and stick them under students' chairs in the classroom. At the beginning of the lesson, ask students to check if they have a word under their chair. If they do, they should read it in secret and mime it for their class to guess.

3 Grammar practice

a) Quickly review the first conditional with the **Grammar spot**. Ask students to match the phrases in A with the phrases in B to make first conditional sentences. Encourage them to try to memorise the sentences.

Answer key

1 d **2** e **3** a **4** b **5** c

b) Divide students into pairs. Student A should say one of the *if* phrases from part A in Activity 3b. Student B closes the book and tries to finish the sentence from memory. Then they change roles. Students repeat the task twice with different phrases.

Extra activity

In pairs, students invent and write a different ending for each of the phrases in part A of Activity 3a. Remind them it has to be logical and grammatically correct.

4 Pronunciation

a) [2.14] Point out that the tongue twister offers practice of the English sound /t/ at the beginning of words. Explain that we make the sound by putting our tongue right behind our top teeth and then moving it to release quite a big puff of air. Students can test it by putting their hand in front of their mouth and practising the sound.

b) [2.15] Play the CD again and ask students to repeat the tongue twister. Point out the collocation *take someone's temperature*. They should then practise saying the tongue twister individually as fast as they can.

Teaching tip: *Tongue twisters*

Tongue twisters are an enjoyable way of practising individual sounds. Before you ask students to repeat the whole sentence, explain which sound is being practised in it and demonstrate how it is formed. Students repeat the sound after you. Play the whole tongue twister and ask students to repeat it after the recording. Then get them to repeat it a few times, each time going faster. You can later put students into pairs to time each other on how many times they can say the tongue twister within a minute.

Tapescript

see Student's Book Activity 4a

5 Speaking

a) Students complete the sentences with their own ideas.
b) In pairs, students start and finish the sentences from 5a. Monitor the activity, providing help.

6 Check your English

a) Students find eight words connected to health in the word puzzle. Ask them to compare their answers in pairs and then check with the whole class.

Answer key

Down: flu, headache, cold
Across: cough, temperature, stomach ache, medicine, sore throat

b) Students ask and answer the questions in pairs. Remind them to use the correct tense.

Photocopiable activity

Telepathy p118; instructions p97

Homework suggestions

1 Activity Book page 37, Activities 4–5
2 Students write three first conditional sentences with warnings their family members usually give them about any bad habits, e.g. *If you surf the Internet all evening, you will get a headache.*

Lesson objective

Talking about possible events

18 I'm worried

1 Vocabulary

2.16 Find these things in the pictures.

games insect spray torch
bull tent warm clothes

2 Presentation

a 2.17 Listen and read. What do you think Nicole and her friends are doing this weekend?

Sophie I'm worried it may be cold.
Nicole Don't worry. It may not be cold, but if it is, we'll wear warm clothes.
Sophie Oh, yes, good idea.
Mel I'm worried there may be a lot of insects.
Nicole Don't worry. I'm going to take some insect spray. If there are lots of insects, we'll spray them.
Mel Ah, yes, of course.
Sophie I'm also worried it may rain all the time.
Nicole Don't worry. If it rains all the time, we'll play games in the tent.
Sophie Yes, that's a great idea.
Nicole Anyway the weather's going to be great this weekend. We can go for a walk in the countryside.
Mel But we may see some bulls.
Sophie Yes, there may be bulls.
Nicole Umm. Yes, well, if we see any bulls … we'll run!

b 2.17 Listen again. What four things are Sophie and Mel worried about? Choose from the box. Then read the dialogue with your classmates.

bulls games insect spray the tent rain
insects clothes cold the countryside

Grammar spot
may (possibility)

It **may be** cold.
It **may not be** cold.
There **may be** a lot of insects.
We **may see** some bulls.

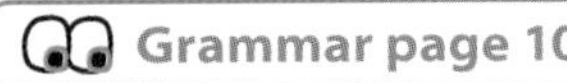
Grammar page 103

18 I'm worried

Grammar
- first conditional; *may* for possibility; *to be*; *going to*

Vocabulary
- camping equipment; camping activities; adjectives

Optional materials
- a sheet of A4 paper for each group of five

Optional Activity Book activities
- Fast finishers p68, Extra practice p69

Photocopiable activity
- *What may happen?* p119

PART 1

Introduction

Ask students to imagine that they are going on holiday and they need to pack their bags. Ask two volunteers to leave the classroom. Explain the following rules to the rest of the class: *You can only take objects that begin with the same letter as your first name, e.g. Blanca, you can take a book, Pawel, you can take paints, etc.* Invite the volunteers back to the classroom, but do not reveal the rules. Ask individual students, including the two volunteers: *What are you going to take?* Remember to ask them by their name. If the students who left the room name objects that do not begin with the first letter of their name, say: *Sorry, you can't take it/them.* Their task is to listen attentively to their classmates' answers and work out the rules.

❶ Vocabulary

[2.16] Students look at the words in the box and listen as you play the CD. Then they find the objects in the pictures on page 56. They should make guesses about new vocabulary.

Students work individually on the task and then compare their answers in pairs. Play the CD again and ask students to point to the corresponding objects in the pictures. Make sure everybody understands all the words now and drill the pronunciation.

Mixed-ability classes

Fast finishers check what else in the pictures they can name in English.

Tapescript

see Student's Book Activity 1

❷ Presentation

a) [2.17] Focus attention on the pictures and ask students to identify the characters: Sophie, Mel and Nicole. Elicit what they remember about Sophie and Mel from earlier modules in their book. Ask students to study the pictures and guess what the girls are doing this weekend. Students listen and read the dialogue to check their guesses. Play the CD.

Elicit that Nicole and her friends are going camping. Clarify any vocabulary students do not understand.

Extra activity

Find out if students have ever been camping. Ask them to share their experiences with the whole class. Write the following prompts on the board to help students decide what to talk about: *where, when, who with, good points, bad points.*

Tapescript

see Student's Book Activity 2a

b) [2.17] Students listen and read again and decide what four things Sophie and Mel are worried about. They should use the words from the box. Play the CD.

Elicit that Sophie and Mel are worried about the cold, insects, rain and bulls. Elicit that they use *may* to say that there is a possibility that something will happen. Refer students to the **Grammar spot** to elicit or explain how *may* is used in positive and negative sentences. Refer students to the **Grammar summary** on page 103 for more information on *may*. Point out that Nicole is an optimist and she shows her friends that they do not need to worry, using the first conditional.

Divide students into groups of three. Ask them to read out the dialogue. Boys can change the names of the characters to male names if they want to. You can ask groups to read out the dialogue twice, changing names.

Extra activity

Divide students into pairs. Ask them to study the pictures in Activity 2 for 30 seconds. Then they should close their books and recall from memory everything that Nicole and her friends are going to take on their camping holiday. Next they should open their books and check if they remembered everything.

Tapescript

see Activity 2a

Answer key

Sophie and Mel are worried about being cold, insects, rain and bulls.

3 Grammar practice

2.18 Sophie and Mel have some more worries. Listen then complete the dialogue with these words:

lost dark hot hungry	make some sandwiches switch on the torch look at our map go for a swim

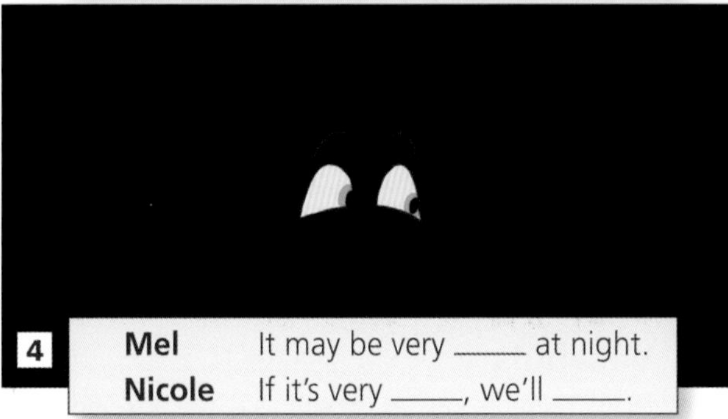

4 Speaking

a Make lists of the things you are *going to do* and the things you *may do* this weekend. Don't show your classmates.

Things I'm going to do	*Things I may do*
hang out with my friends	*play football*
go shopping	*buy some new jeans*

b Now ask your classmates about their plans for this weekend.

What are you going to do this weekend?

I'm going to hang out with my friends. We may play football. What are you going to do?

I'm going to …

My English file

Think about your plans for the next school holiday. Write about the things you are *going to do* and the things you *may do*.

My next school holiday

In my next school holiday I'm going to go camping with my family. We may go to the mountains or we may go to the beach. I'm also going to …

5 Check your English

a Choose the sentence that is true about you this weekend.

1
a I'm going to hang out with my friends.
b I may hang out with my friends.
c I'm not going to hang out with my friends.

2
a I'm going to tidy my room.
b I may tidy my room.
c I'm not going to tidy my room.

b Nicole is thinking about this weekend. Complete with:

be go play meet is rains watch

❸ Grammar practice

[2.18] Explain that Sophie and Mel have more worries and Nicole tries to find solutions.

Go over the words and phrases in the boxes. Students listen to the dialogue and complete it with the words and phrases from the boxes. Explain that some need to be used twice. Students should use the pictures to help them with the task. Play the CD.

Students compare their answers in pairs. Play the CD again for students to check their answers.

Extra activity

Divide students into groups of four and ask them to imagine that they are going camping together. Brainstorm all the objects they may need and write them on the board. Students discuss the objects and choose the six most important ones to take. They should use *may* in their discussion, e.g. *Let's take a camping stove, because we may want to cook something.* Set a time limit of six minutes. Groups report their answers to the whole class and give reasons, using *may*.

Tapescript and Answer key

Mel: It may be very hot.
Nicole: If it's very hot, we'll go for a swim.
Mel: We may be hungry.
Nicole: If we are hungry, we'll make some sandwiches.
Sophie: We may get lost.
Nicole: If we're lost, we'll look at our map.
Mel: It may be very dark at night.
Nicole: If it's very dark, we'll switch on our torch.

Photocopiable activity

What may happen? p119; instructions p97

Homework suggestions

1 Activity Book pages 38-39, Activities 1–3
2 Students write which three objects their friend should take for a holiday in the jungle and give reasons, using *may*.

PART 2

Introduction

Divide students into groups of five. Give each group a sheet of A4 paper. Ask students to think of typical weekend activities that people in their country do, e.g. *tidy the house*. In each group, one student writes down one activity and passes the sheet of paper on to the student on their left and so on. Each group member can write only one activity at a time or they can pass the paper on. Set a time limit of four minutes. The group with the longest list wins and reads out the activities. Other groups cross out the activities which repeat on their lists and read out any that have not been mentioned.

Teaching tip: *Choosing a person to start an activity*

If taking the first turn gives a student advantage, let students roll the dice to decide. The student with the highest number begins. If the order is not important, you can tell students that the winner of a given category in their group should start. You can use the following categories: the oldest/youngest student, the student with the longest/shortest surname, the student who lives the furthest from/the closest to the school, etc.

❹ Speaking

a) Students make a list of four things they are going to do and four things they may do the coming weekend. Elicit that *going to* is used to talk about definite plans and *may* for possible plans. Set a time limit of four minutes. Students should not show their lists to their classmates.

You can remind students that the present continuous is often interchangeable with *going to* when talking about actions planned before the moment of speaking, but we generally use the present continuous to refer to fixed arrangements and *going to* to talk about more general intentions.

b) In groups of four, students interview each other individually about their plans for the weekend. They should respond with *going to* and *may*. Read out the example with a confident student first. Individual students report their classmates' most interesting plans to the whole class.

My English file

Students write about their plans for the next school holiday, using *going to* for definite plans and *may* for possible plans. They should write at least six sentences. If they are not going to travel, they should write about things they are going to/may do in their own town. Go through the example first.

When students have finished, they exchange their notebooks in pairs. They read each other's texts and point out orally any mistakes they notice.

Dyslexia tip: *Marking written work*

When evaluating dyslexic students' work, separate the content from technicalities of the language such as spelling. You may wish to mark only the former, but then inform dyslexic students of your decision. Use two different colours, one for comments about the ideas and planning and one for spelling, punctuation etc. Make comments legible and useful, i.e. point out what is good, what is wrong and how it could be improved.

❺ Check your English

a) Students choose the sentence in part 1 and 2 which is true about them this weekend. Individual students report their choices to the whole class, adding extra information if they want to.

b) Students complete Nicole's sentences about this weekend with the words in the box. Check the answers with the whole class.

Answer key

1 rains **2** play **3** watch **4** be **5** is **6** meet **7** go

Homework suggestions

1 Activity Book page 39, Activity 4–5
2 Students write about two things they are going to do and two things they may do this evening.

19 You should say thank you

1 Guessing

Look at the pictures. Rachel, Sun and Lukas are talking about customs where they live. Can you guess what customs they are talking about?

2 Presentation

a 2.19 Listen and read. Check your ideas.

1

Amish people look different, but you shouldn't star
at us. We think it's rude. We like visitors, but you shouldn't come on Sundays because we go to chur
and spend time with our family then.

2

When someone gives you a present, you should say thank you. But you shouldn't open the present immediately. People think that's very rude. You can open the present when you get home.

3

Where I live, you shouldn't wear your shoes inside someone's house. There's a lot of snow in the Yukon in the winter and people don't want wet shoes in their homes. Even in the summer it is often muddy and dirty so you should always take off your shoes.

b 2.19 Listen and read again. Have you got the same customs where you live?

Grammar spot
obligation and advice
should, shouldn't

You **should say** thank you.
You **shouldn't stare** at us.

Grammar page 104

19 You should say thank you

Grammar	Optional Activity Book activities
• *should/shouldn't* for obligation and advice	• Fast finishers p68, Extra practice p69
Vocabulary	**Photocopiable activity**
• customs; special occasions; health problems	• *Dear Teen Dreams* p120

PART 1

Introduction

On the board write the names of the characters from the Student's Book: *Rachel, Sun* and *Lukas.* Divide students into three groups and assign one character to each group. Ask groups to brainstorm everything they remember about their character and where they live. Then groups should look through the earlier modules of their books to find their characters, check their ideas and review more facts. Set a time limit of five minutes. Group representatives should report everything they have found out about their character and the place where they live to the whole class.

❶ Guessing

Focus students' attention on the pictures in Activity 2. Pre-teach the word *custom.* Explain that Rachel, Sun and Lukas are talking about customs where they live and the pictures illustrate the customs. Divide students into pairs and ask them to make guesses about the customs.

❷ Presentation

a) [2.19] Students listen and read the texts to check their guesses in Activity 1. Play the CD. Elicit what the customs refer to in general. Students should answer in their own words.

Check if students know or can guess the meaning of the following words and phrases: *stare, rude, visitors, immediately, wet.* Explain any words students still find difficult.

Refer students to the **Grammar spot** to elicit or explain *should* and *shouldn't* for obligation and advice. Ask students to find more examples of the modal verb in the texts. Then encourage them to say which things they should and shouldn't do in their school. Refer students to the **Grammar summary** on page 104 for more information on *should.*

Dyslexia tip: *Teaching grammar*

It is beneficial for students to discover new grammar within a carefully designed context, but dyslexic students may take longer to process data presented within a written text. You can give dyslexic students information at the end of the previous lesson about which grammar point is going to be studied next, enabling them to study the topic independently at home, think about the rules and prepare any initial questions they may have.

Tapescript

see Student's Book Activity 2a

b) [2.19] Ask students to listen and read again to decide if they have the same customs where they live. Play the CD and elicit the answers.

Extra activity

If students do not have the same customs where they live, ask them the following questions about their country or community: *What do people think is rude? What do people do on Sundays? What do people do when they get a present? What do people do when they visit someone's house, but their shoes are muddy?*

❸ Grammar practice

a Look at the sentences. Can you guess what the missing word is: *should* or *shouldn't?*

Customs around the world

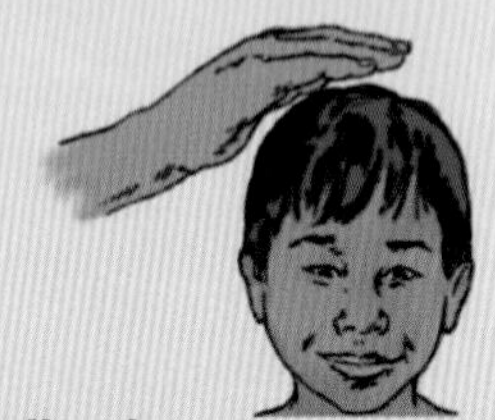

1 In Thailand …
You ______ pat anyone on the top of the head.

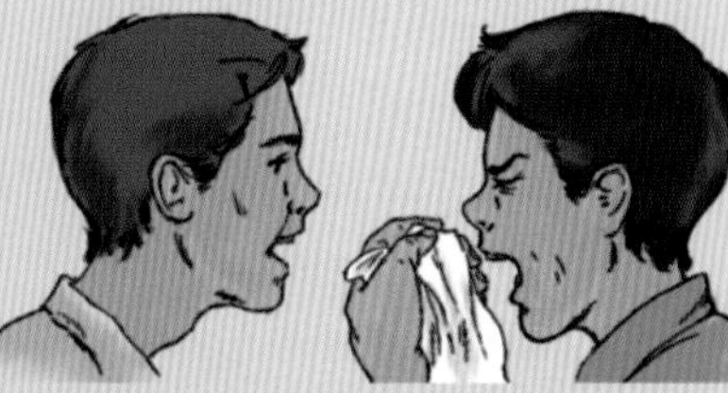

2 In the UK …
You ______ say, 'Bless you' when someone sneezes.

3 In Saudi Arabia …
You ______ say no to coffee when you visit someone's home.

4 In China …
You ______ leave some food on your plate when you eat at someone's house.

b 2.20 Listen and check. Do you have the same customs in your country?

❹ Class poll

a Brainstorm some customs where you live and write them on the board. Here are some ideas:

meals birthdays weddings presents school buses

b Now vote for the custom you think is most important.

You shouldn't talk with your mouth full of food.

You should stand up when the teacher comes in the room.

❺ Speaking

a Match the problems in A with the advice in B.

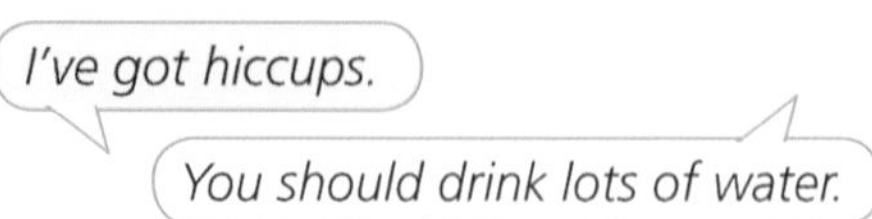

A		B	
1	I've got hiccups.	a	You should count sheep.
2	I can't sleep at night.	b	You shouldn't eat cheese at night.
3	I've got flu.	c	You should drink lots of water.
4	I have bad dreams.	d	You shouldn't sleep on your back.
5	I snore when I sleep.	e	You should stay in bed.

b Can you give some different advice for the problems?

❻ Song

2.21 Find the song *I Have a Dream* on page 90.

❼ Check your English

Write mini dialogues about three of these problems using *should/ shouldn't*.

I'm cold. I'm hungry. I'm not fit.
I've got a headache. I'm sad.
I've hurt my leg. I'm tired.
I've got a stomach ache.
I'm thirsty. I've lost my bag.

A: I'm cold.
B: You should wear warm cloth

❸ Grammar practice

a) Explain that students are going to find out about more customs around the world. Ask them to study the pictures, read the sentences and decide if the missing word is *should* or *shouldn't*. Clarify any vocabulary students do not understand. In pairs, students compare their answers.

b) [2.20] Play the CD for students to check their answers. You can explain the reasons for these customs, using the cultural information below. Find out if students have the same customs in their country. If they do not, ask them what they do when someone sneezes and if they should eat all the food on the plate when they eat at someone else's house.

Cultural information

Thai people believe that the head is the most sacred part of the body, which is why they consider it rude to pat or touch someone on the head.

In the UK it is polite to say *Bless you* when someone sneezes. There are different theories behind the origin of the custom, e.g. the old belief that souls could escape during a sneeze, or the time of the bubonic plague when sneezing was a symptom of infection.

In Saudi Arabia it is impolite to refuse coffee when visiting someone's home. This tradition comes from nomadic times when food, drink and shelter saved visitors' lives in the country's harsh desert.

In China finishing all the food on the plate shows the host that the guest is still hungry and needs more food, so it is polite to leave some food on the plate.

Tapescript and Answer key

1 In Thailand ... You *shouldn't* pat anyone on the top of the head.
2 In the UK ... You *should* say 'Bless you' when someone sneezes.
3 In Saudi Arabia ... You *shouldn't* say no to coffee when you visit someone's home.
4 In China ... You *should* leave some food on your plate when you eat at someone's house.

Homework suggestions

1 Activity Book pages 40–41, Activities 1–3
2 Students write about a custom from another country, using *should* or *shouldn't*. They can use information they know from TV or do research on the Internet.

PART 2

Introduction

Ask the class: *Have you ever met people from other cultures? What interesting customs did they have?* Let students talk about their experiences. You can write the following ideas to prompt students' answers: *meals, house, special holidays.*

❹ Class poll

a) Put students into groups of four and ask them to brainstorm customs where they live. Encourage them to use ideas from the box. They can also mention different customs. Go through the example before students begin the task. Set a time limit of four minutes. Ask group representatives to write their ideas on the board. They should not repeat anything that has already been written by another student.

b) Read out the ideas from the board and ask students to vote for the most important one by raising their hands. They can vote only once.

Extra activity

Write the following questions on the board for students to discuss in groups of four: *What are your favourite customs in your country? Which customs in your country would you like to change? Which customs from other countries would you like to have in your country?* Groups share the most interesting answers with the whole class.

❺ Speaking

a) Students match the problems in A with the advice in B. In pairs, students compare their answers. Check the answers with the whole class and ask students if they agree with the advice. Explain that this is typical advice British people give to these problems.

b) Divide students into pairs and ask them to give different advice for the problems. They can talk about typical advice that people in their country give if it is different to what British people say, or they can come up with their own ideas. They should use *should/shouldn't*. Monitor the activity, providing help with new vocabulary. Elicit the most interesting or funniest ideas from different groups.

Answer key

1 c **2** a **3** e **4** b **5** d

Photocopiable activity

Dear Teen Dreams p120; instructions p98.

❻ Song

[2.21] Refer students to page 90. Ask them to look briefly at the lyrics and play a few seconds of the recording. Find out if students recognise the song and play the CD through.

Explain any words students do not understand. Play the song again, encouraging students to join in singing. Elicit what the song is about and ask students to read the background information.

Tapescript

see lyrics on page 90 of the Student's Book

❼ Check your English

Go over the problems in the box and clarify any vocabulary students may not understand. Students choose three problems and write mini dialogues, adding advice. Go through the example before students begin the task. Individual students read out their mini dialogues.

Mixed-ability classes

Fast finishers write mini dialogues for as many problems in the box as possible.

Homework suggestions

1 Activity Book page 41, Activities 4–5
2 Students write three problems they have and suggest one or two solutions, e.g. *I am always tired. I should go to bed earlier. I shouldn't play computer games at night.*

20 Survival

1 Reading

a 2.22 Read the questionnaire. Use a dictionary to help with words you don't understand.

What should you do?

You are walking in a forest in Canada. You turn a corner and see a black bear in front of you. The bear begins to walk towards you. What should you do?

A Speak to the bear in a very quiet voice.
B Run away.
C Climb a tree.

You are lost in a jungle and are trying to find a village or a town. You are very tired and hungry. You find a river. What should you do?

A Walk along the river upstream.
B Go back into the jungle.
C Walk along the river downstream.

Your car has got a puncture. You are in the middle of a forest and you can't see any houses. There is a terrible storm and you are worried lightning will hit your car. What should you do?

A Climb under the car.
B Stand under a tree.
C Stay in the car.

You are in your room and you see there is a fire in your bin. There is a window but your bedroom is on the third floor. There is a lot of smoke and flames and the door is on the other side of the room. What should you do?

A Open the window and shout for help.
B Crawl along the floor to the door.
C Run to the door.

b Read again. Work in a small team. Agree on one answer and write it down.

c 2.23 Listen and check.

20 Survival

Optional materials
- bilingual or monolingual dictionaries

Photocopiable activity
- *Survival kit* p121

PART 1

Introduction

Write *survival* on the board. Elicit from students a definition of the word. Brainstorm the objects we should have at home to survive if there was a flood and we could not leave the house. Write them on the board. Make sure they include the following objects: *candles, matches, a torch, plasters, medicines, scissors, duct tape, a sleeping bag, rubber gloves, a tin opener.* In pairs, students tell each other if they have the objects in their home and if they know exactly where they are.

❶ Reading

a) [2.22] Ask students to study the pictures and guess what emergency situations they illustrate. Then ask students to listen and read to check their ideas. Hand out dictionaries for students to check new words. Play the CD.

Elicit a brief description of each situation. Clarify any vocabulary students still do not understand.

Mixed-ability classes

Write new words on the board: *puncture, lightning, corner, towards, third floor, smoke, flames, crawl, upstream, downstream.* Illustrate them with drawings for less confident students to use as a reference instead of a dictionary.

Extra activity

Ask students if they have ever been or know someone who has been in similar situations to the ones in the pictures, i.e. seeing a wild animal in the forest, experiencing a storm in the forest, being in a fire in a building, being lost in the wild. Encourage students to share any experiences with the class.

Tapescript

see Student's Book Activity 1a

b) Divide students into groups of four. Ask them to read the text again and discuss the answers. They should agree on one solution to each problem and write it down. Elicit the answers from different groups, but do not confirm if they are right or not.

Teaching tip: *Checking answers to multiple choice tasks*

To make checking answers more enjoyable you can ask students to signal with their bodies which answer they have chosen. They can jump, stand up and squat for A B C respectively.

c) [2.23] Play the CD for students to check their answers. Explain that each correct answer is worth one point. Groups count their points. Find out which group or groups managed to score the most points.

Tapescript and Answer key

1. You should, A: Speak to the bear in a very quiet voice.
2. You should, C: Walk along the river downstream.
3. You should, C: Stay in the car.
4. You should, B: Crawl along the floor to the door.

Extra activity

Divide the class into two teams. Ask members of Team A to imagine that they are leaders of an expedition to the jungle and they are looking for expedition members. They should discuss what skills the candidates need and what questions to ask them during an interview. Members of Team B should imagine that they want to go on an expedition to the jungle and discuss what skills they have and why they think they are good candidates. Allow five minutes for preparation. Then pair each member of Team A with a member of Team B to role-play the interview.

❷ Speaking

Can you remember? Work with a classmate. Ask and answer about the situations in Activity 1.

You see a bear. What should you do?

You should …

❸ Listening

2.24 Look at pictures 1 and 2 in Activity 1 and listen. Then write the missing words.

a [1]speak

run walk climbers dangerous running climb speak run tree

a You should [1]_____ to the bear in a very quiet voice and then [2]_____ away. This is still [3]_____ but it is better than [4]_____ away. If you [5]_____, bears will nearly always [6]_____ after you. You also shouldn't [7]_____ a [8]_____ because bears are very good [9]_____.

downstream village walk river jungle closer go back upstream

b You should [1]_____ along the river [2]_____. This is better than walking [3]_____. You have got a better chance of finding a [4]_____ or town on lower land [5]_____ to the sea. You shouldn't [6]_____ into the [7]_____ as you may not find the [8]_____ again.

❹ Writing

Work with a classmate. Write your own survival situation. Use the situations in Activity 1 as a model. Use a dictionary to help with new vocabulary.

You are swimming in the sea and see a shark. The shark is very close to you and is opening its mouth. What should you do?

A Swim away from the shark.

B Shout for help.

C Hit the shark in the eye.

Observation game

a 2.25 Look at the picture and listen. Try to find the people. Don't tell your classmates the answers.

b 2.25 Now work in a small team. Listen again. Match the people with the sentences you hear. Write your answers. The first team with all the correct answers is the winner.

❷ Speaking

Divide students into pairs. They should take turns to ask and answer questions about the situations in Activity 1. Encourage them to discuss possible explanations for the answers. Go through the example before students begin the task.

Homework suggestions

1 Activity Book page 42, Activity 1
2 Students choose one of the situations in Activity 1 and write advice about how to be prepared for this situation, e.g. *Situation 2 – You should have a map and a GPS. You should take a lot of water with you.*

PART 2

Introduction

Draw the following table on the board:

You should	*You shouldn't*

Ask students to copy the table into their notebook. Read the following advice: 1 … *move a person with a broken back* 2 … *put your burnt hand under cold water* 3 … *lie down when your nose bleeds* 4 … *touch a strange dog.* Students decide if each phrase should begin with *You should* or *You shouldn't* and they put a tick in the appropriate column. Reveal that there should be three ticks below *shouldn't* and one below *should* (answers: **1** *You shouldn't* **2** *You should* **3** *You shouldn't* **4** *You shouldn't*). Discuss the reasons for each piece of advice with the whole class.

❸ Listening and writing

[2.24] Students look at pictures 1 and 2 in Activity 1 and listen to detailed advice for the situations. Play the CD.

Ask students to read the texts and complete them with the words in the box. In pairs, students compare their answers. Check the answers with the whole class. Find out if students are surprised by the advice given and why.

Tapescript and Answer key

a You should [1] speak to the bear in a very quiet voice and then [2] walk away. This is still [3] dangerous but it is better than [4] running away. If you [5] run, bears will nearly always [6] run after you. You also shouldn't [7] climb a [8] tree because bears are very good [9] climbers.
b You should [1] walk along the river [2] downstream. This is better than walking [3] upstream. You have got a better chance of finding a [4] village or town on lower land [5] closer to the sea. You shouldn't [6] go back into the [7] jungle as you may not find the [8] river again.

Elicit explanations of the correct answers in situations 3 and 4 in Activity 1a. If students are unable to provide them, give the following explanations:

Situation 3 – You should stay in the car. If lightning hits the car, it will travel down the outside of car into the ground. You will be safe inside the car. You shouldn't climb under the car or stand under a tree, because the lightning will hit you when it travels down the car or a tree and hits the ground.

Situation 4 – You should crawl along the floor to the door. Smoke rises and there will be more oxygen close to the floor. You shouldn't run through the smoke because it will be difficult to breathe. You shouldn't open the window because more oxygen will come into the room and the fire will get bigger and more dangerous.

❹ Writing

Divide students into pairs. Ask them to write their own survival situation, using the situations in Activity 1 as a model. You can prompt them with some ideas, e.g. *being stranded on a desert island, being lost in a foreign city, deep sea diving, being injured in sports.* Give students dictionaries to look up new words. Remind them to write three answers, but only one should be correct. Go through the example first.

Set a time limit of ten minutes. Encourage students to illustrate the text. You can then ask students to exchange their texts and choose the correct answer.

Dyslexia tip: *Pair and group work*

Pairs or small groups mixing dyslexic and non-dyslexic students are beneficial for dyslexic students. All the participants bring their strengths and ideas to the task and complete it together; they can discuss any problems and ask the teacher for help together rather than individually in front of the whole class; the teacher can monitor dyslexic students without drawing attention to the fact and take notes to discuss privately after the lesson. Once the task is accomplished, volunteers can present the results to the whole class and answer any questions, sparing dyslexic students from public speaking.

Photocopiable activity

Survival kit p121; instructions p98

Observation game

a) [2.25] Students look at the picture and listen to the sentences about the people in the picture. Students try to find the people. They should not tell the answers to their classmates.

b) [2.25] Divide students into groups of four. Ask them to listen again and match the people with the sentences they hear. Groups put their hands up when they have all the answers. Remember the order in which groups finished the task. Check the answers of the group that was first. If their answers are correct, they win the game. If not, check the answers of the second team and so on.

Tapescript and Answer key

1 This person has got a sore throat. **b**
2 This person is sunburnt. **g**
3 This person has got a cut. **c**
4 This person has got a cough. **h**
5 This person has got stomach ache. **i**
6 This person has got flu. **d**
7 This person has got a headache. **f**
8 This person has hurt a foot. **a**
9 This person has got a broken arm. **e**

Extra activity

In pairs, students tell each other which problems in the **Observation game** they have had. Then read out the problems one by one and ask students to raise their hands if they have had them. Write the results on the board and find out which problem is the most common in your class.

Homework suggestions

1 Activity Book page 42, Activity 2
2 Students choose two people in the picture in the **Observation game** and write the advice they think their doctor is going to give them.

Module 5 Review

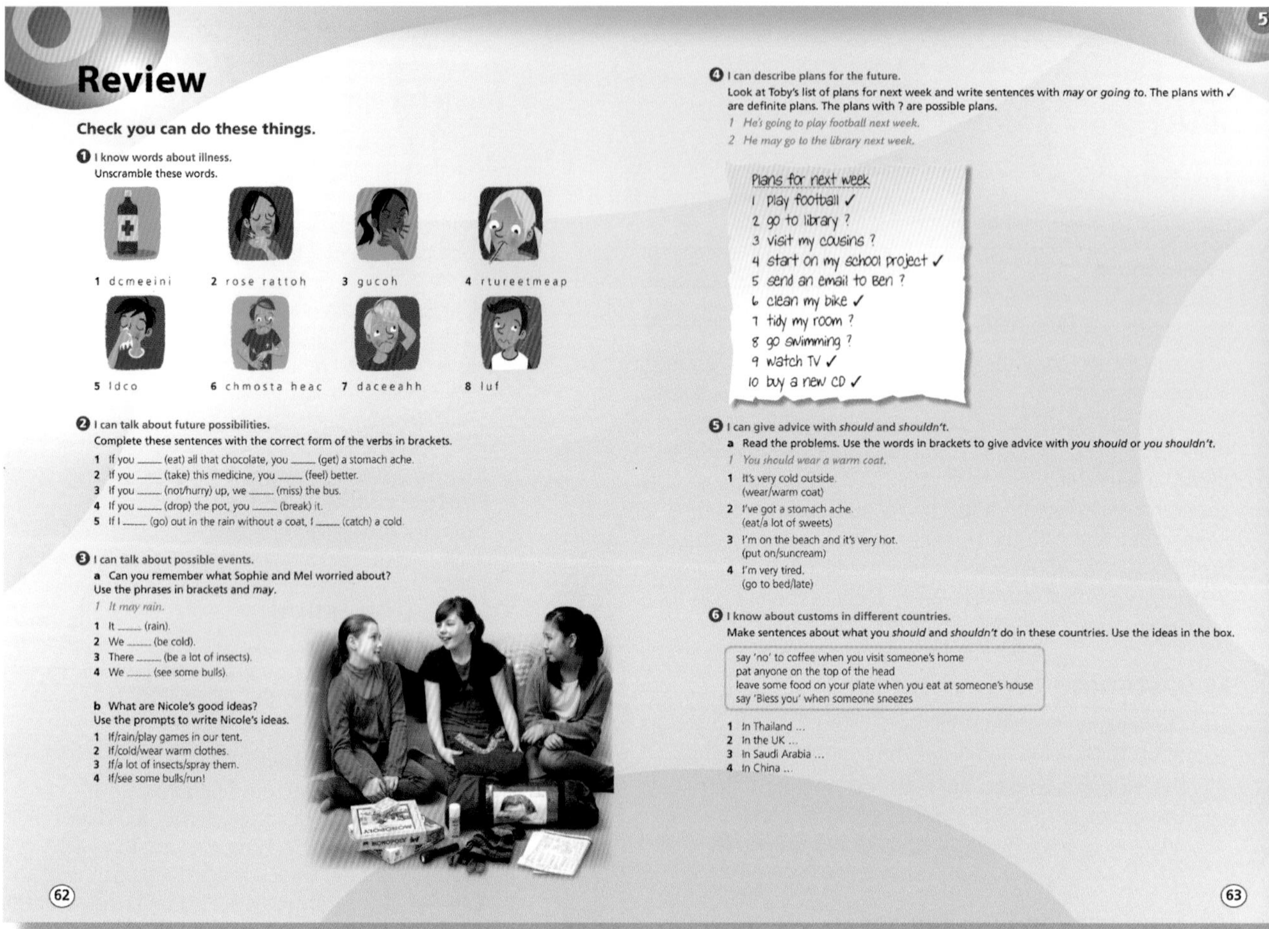

Review

Check you can do these things.

1 I know words about illness.
Unscramble these words.

1 dcmeeini
2 rose rattoh
3 gucoh
4 rtureetmeap
5 ldco
6 chmosta heac
7 daceeahh
8 luf

2 I can talk about future possibilities.
Complete these sentences with the correct form of the verbs in brackets.

1 If you ____ (eat) all that chocolate, you ____ (get) a stomach ache.
2 If you ____ (take) this medicine, you ____ (feel) better.
3 If you ____ (not/hurry) up, we ____ (miss) the bus.
4 If you ____ (drop) the pot, you ____ (break) it.
5 If I ____ (go) out in the rain without a coat, I ____ (catch) a cold.

3 I can talk about possible events.

a Can you remember what Sophie and Mel worried about?
Use the phrases in brackets and *may*.

1 It may rain.

1 It ____ (rain).
2 We ____ (be cold).
3 There ____ (be a lot of insects).
4 We ____ (see some bulls).

b What are Nicole's good ideas?
Use the prompts to write Nicole's ideas.

1 If/rain/play games in our tent.
2 If/cold/wear warm clothes.
3 If/a lot of insects/spray them.
4 If/see some bulls/run!

4 I can describe plans for the future.
Look at Toby's list of plans for next week and write sentences with *may* or *going to*. The plans with ✓ are definite plans. The plans with ? are possible plans.

1 He's going to play football next week.
2 He may go to the library next week.

Plans for next week
1 play football ✓
2 go to library ?
3 visit my cousins ?
4 start on my school project ✓
5 send an email to Ben ?
6 clean my bike ✓
7 tidy my room ?
8 go swimming ?
9 watch TV ✓
10 buy a new CD ✓

5 I can give advice with *should* and *shouldn't*.

a Read the problems. Use the words in brackets to give advice with *you should* or *you shouldn't*.

1 You should wear a warm coat.

1 It's very cold outside.
(wear/warm coat)
2 I've got a stomach ache.
(eat/a lot of sweets)
3 I'm on the beach and it's very hot.
(put on/suncream)
4 I'm very tired.
(go to bed/late)

6 I know about customs in different countries.
Make sentences about what you *should* and *shouldn't* do in these countries. Use the ideas in the box.

say 'no' to coffee when you visit someone's home
pat anyone on the top of the head
leave some food on your plate when you eat at someone's house
say 'Bless you' when someone sneezes

1 In Thailand ...
2 In the UK ...
3 In Saudi Arabia ...
4 In China ...

62 63

Optional materials

- a mirror, an umbrella, cake candles, a salt shaker

Optional revision

Before your students start this Review, you may want to direct them to the **Grammar summary** at the back of their coursebooks and to the **Word lists** at the back of their Activity Books. This will remind them of the main grammar and vocabulary in the module. Give them ten minutes to read through those in small groups and ask you any questions they may have

- Activity Book: Refer your students to pages 85–86: *Accidents and illnesses*; *Nature and the outdoors*
- **Grammar summary**: Refer your students to pages 103–104, sections 12–14

Module 5 Review

The purpose of this section is revision and consolidation of the material studied in Module 5.

Completing the activities

Go over all the activities with the class, explaining rubrics and giving examples to make sure students know what to do. There are written and oral tasks, but you may decide yourself how they should be completed by students. Generally students should do the writing tasks individually and the oral tasks in pairs, testing each other's knowledge. Make sure they do not treat the *Review* as a formal test, but complete the activities in a friendly, stress-free atmosphere. Fast finishers can write down the answers to the oral tasks.

Checking answers

When students have finished, check the answers with the whole class by asking volunteers to copy their answers onto the board or to say them aloud. If necessary, explain the more difficult issues, ask additional questions about the activities and solve any problems that arise.

Self-evaluation

Tell students to evaluate themselves. They should tick the activities where at least half of their answers were correct.

Feedback

Ask students which activities were difficult, which were easy and if there is anything they would like to review. Make a note of common language problems to go over in future lessons.

Answer key

1
1 medicine
2 sore throat
3 cough
4 temperature
5 cold
6 stomach ache
7 headache
8 flu

2
1 eat … will get
2 take … will fee
3 don't hurry … will miss
4 drop … will break
5 go … will catch

3
a) **1** It may rain.
2 We may be cold.
3 There may be a lot of insects.
4 We may see some bulls.

b) **1** If it rains, we'll play games in our tent.
2 If it's cold, we'll wear warm clothes.
3 If there are a lot of insects, we'll spray them.
4 If we see some bulls, we'll run!

4 Students write sentences about Toby's plans for next week, using *going to* for definite plans marked with a tick (✔) and *may* for possible plans marked with a question mark (?). Remind them that they should change the possessive pronoun *my* to *his*.

He's going to play football next week; He may go to the library next week; He may visit his cousins; He's going to start on his school project; He may send an email to Ben; He's going to clean his bike; He may tidy his room; He may go swimming; He's going to watch TV; He's going to buy a new CD.

5
1 You should wear a warm coat.
2 You shouldn't eat a lot of sweets.
3 You should put on suncream.
4 You shouldn't go to bed late.

6
1 In Thailand you shouldn't pat anyone on the top of the head.
2 In the UK you should say 'Bless you' when someone sneezes.
3 In Saudi Arabia you shouldn't say 'no' to coffee when you visit someone's home.
4 In China you should leave some food on your plate when you eat at someone's house.

Extra activity

Bring the following objects to the class: a mirror, an umbrella, birthday cake candles, a salt shaker. Explain that they represent English superstitions. In groups of four students guess what the superstitions may be, using the first conditional. Write an example sentence about another English superstition on the board for students to use as an example, e.g. *If you see a black cat, you will have good luck.* Set a time limit of five minutes and elicit students' ideas. Reveal the true answers: *If you break a mirror, you will have seven years of bad luck; If you open an umbrella inside the house, you will have bad luck; If you blow out all the candles on the birthday cake, your wish will come true; If you spill salt, you will have an argument.* Ask students if they have the same superstitions in their country and encourage them to make sentences about other superstitions they know.

Module 5 Tests (A and B) are on the Tests CD

Learning diary

You can refer students to page 43 of the Activity Book for further review, more study tips and self-assessment activities.

Extra special

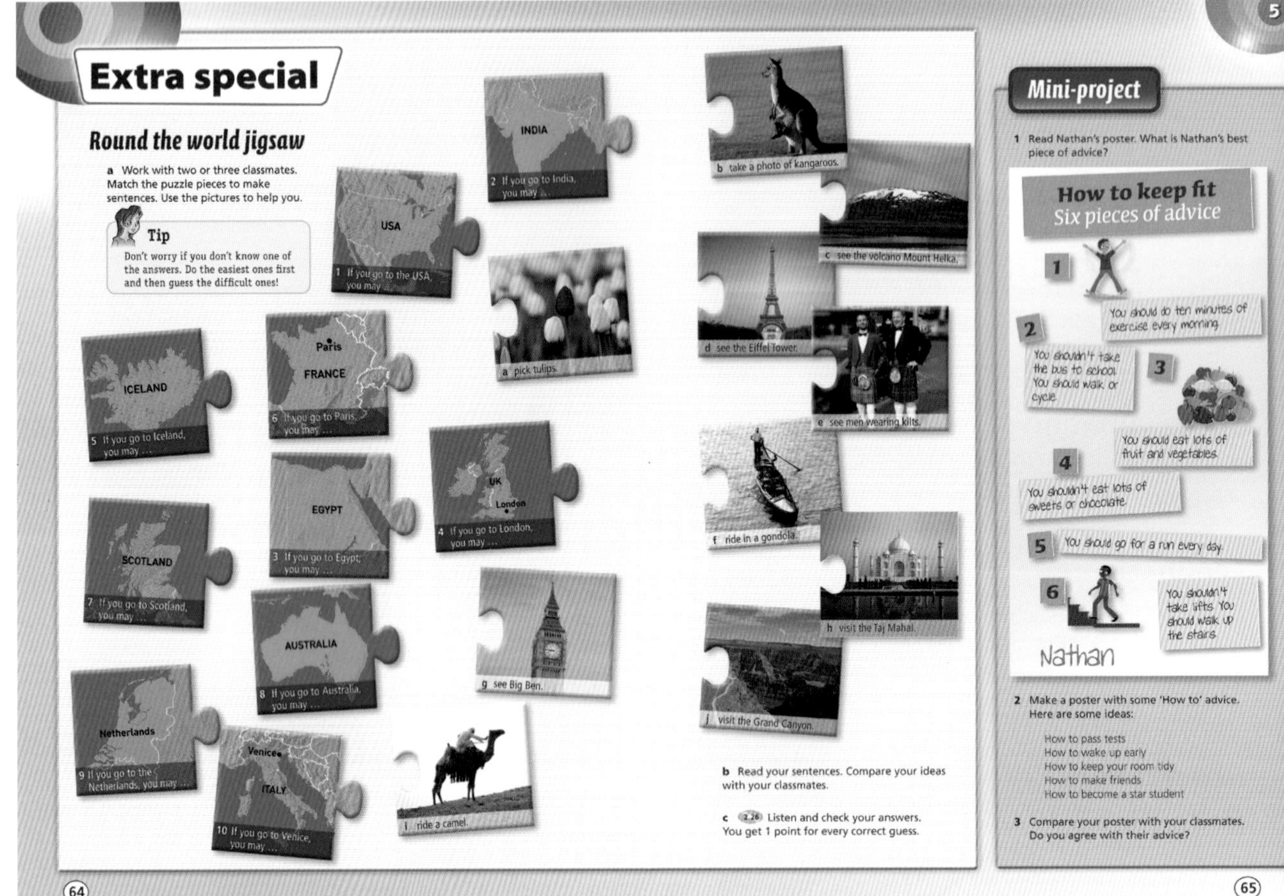

Extra special

Round the world jigsaw

a Work with two or three classmates. Match the puzzle pieces to make sentences. Use the pictures to help you.

Tip
Don't worry if you don't know one of the answers. Do the easiest ones first and then guess the difficult ones!

b Read your sentences. Compare your ideas with your classmates.

c 2.26 Listen and check your answers. You get 1 point for every correct guess.

64

5

Mini-project

1 Read Nathan's poster. What is Nathan's best piece of advice?

2 Make a poster with some 'How to' advice. Here are some ideas:

How to pass tests
How to wake up early
How to keep your room tidy
How to make friends
How to become a star student

3 Compare your poster with your classmates. Do you agree with their advice?

65

Round the world jigsaw

a) Divide students into groups of three or four. Explain that they are going to find out about tourist attractions and customs round the world by matching puzzle pieces. Ask them to read the tip in the box and encourage them to make guesses about the answers.

b) Ask the groups to read out their sentences and compare their ideas with other groups. Do not reveal the answers yet. Ask groups not to change their original answers.

c) [2.26] Play the CD for students to check their answers. Groups get one point for each correct guess. Elicit what else students know about the places in the activity and what else a tourist may see or experience there.

Tapescript and Answer key

1 If you go to the USA, you may **j:** visit the Grand Canyon.
2 If you go to India, you may **h:** visit the Taj Mahal.
3 If you go to Egypt, you may **i:** ride a camel.
4 If you go to London, you may **g:** see Big Ben.
5 If you go to Iceland, you may **c:** see the volcano Mt. Helka.
6 If you go to Paris, you may **d:** see the Eiffel Tower.
7 If you go to Scotland, you may **e:** see men wearing kilts.
8 If you go to Australia, you may **b:** take a photo of kangaroos.
9 If you go to the Netherlands, you may **a:** pick tulips.
10 If you go to Venice, you may **f:** ride in a gondola.

Extra activity

In the same groups, students write a similar quiz about the places within their own country. They should write the phrases separately as in the jigsaw above. Groups exchange their quizzes with other groups and try to solve them.

Mini-project

1 Check students know the phrase: *keep fit*. Explain to students that a boy called Nathan has made a poster with pieces of advice on how to keep fit. Ask students to read his project and choose the best piece of advice. Clarify any vocabulary in the project if necessary. Ask students to vote for the best piece of advice.

2 Students make a poster with *How to* advice. They can use one of the suggested topics or their own ideas. They should write at least six pieces of advice. Encourage them to make a draft copy first. Students can illustrate projects. Monitor their work and provide help if necessary.

3 In groups of six, students present their projects and decide if they agree with the advice in their classmates' projects. Individual students share their answers.

Extra activity

Divide students into groups of four. Ask them to imagine that a group of foreign tourists is going to visit their country. They should talk about where these people should go, how they should travel, what sights they should see and what food and drink they should try. They can add any other advice they think is important. Set a time limit of ten minutes. Groups report the results of their discussion to the whole class.

Lesson objective

Talking about what is going to happen

21 DIY disasters

1 Vocabulary

2.27 Find these things in the picture.

hammer ladder window toolbox paint drill wallpaper

hammer c

2 Presentation

a Match the names in A with the phrases in B to make sentences about what you think is going to happen.

1 Helga is going to spill the paint.

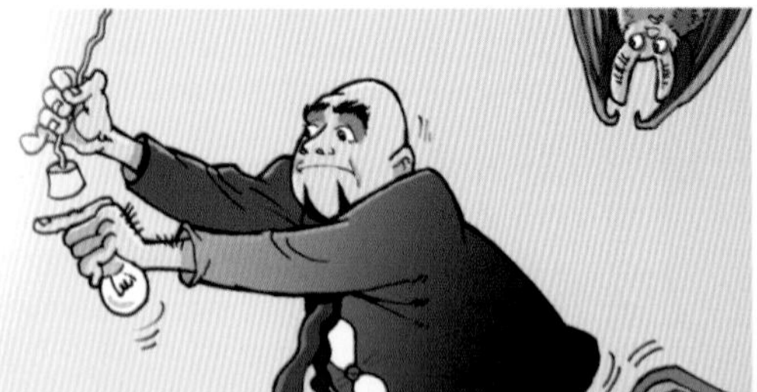

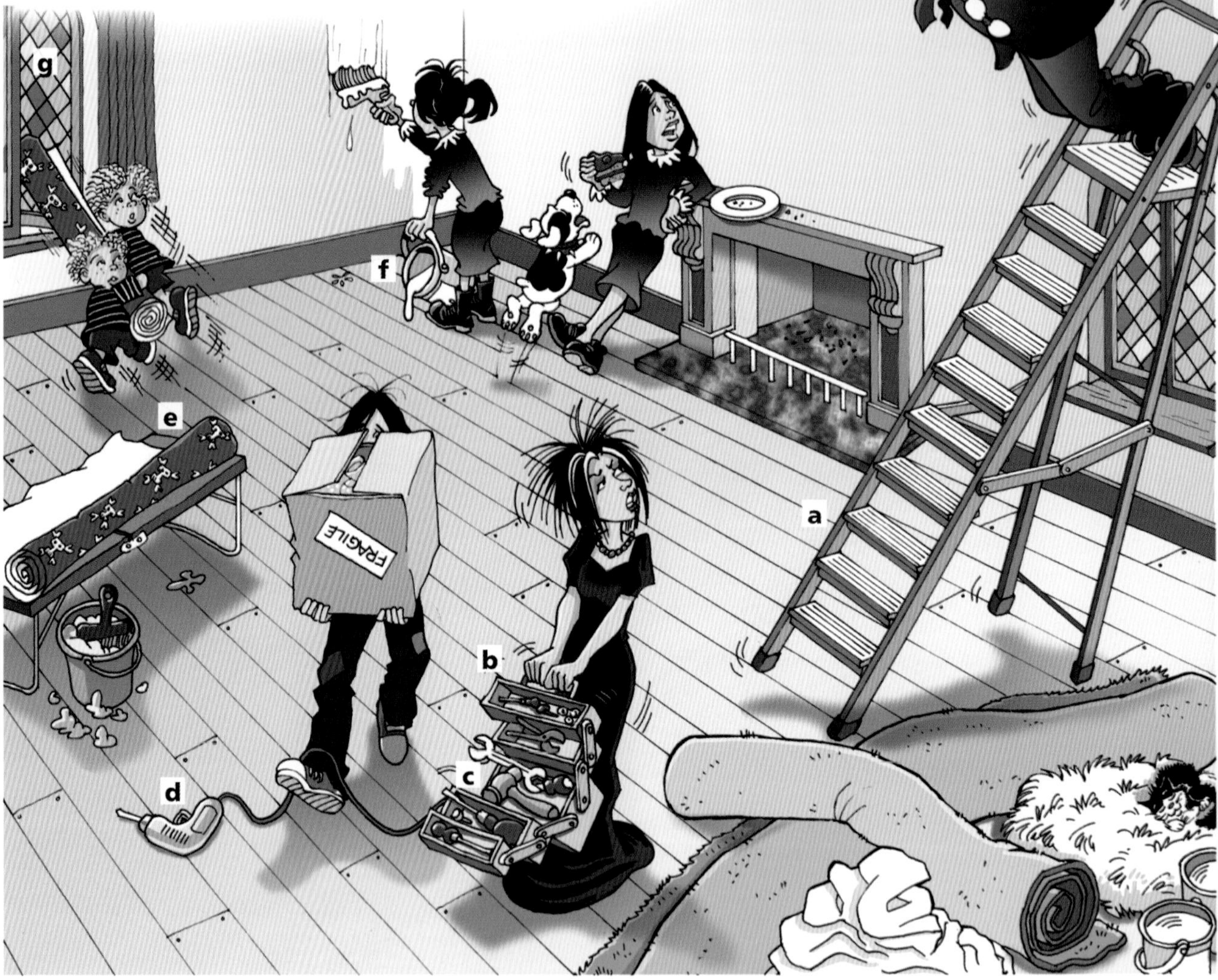

	A		B
1	Helga	**a**	is going to eat Mandy's cake.
2	Martha	**b**	are going to break the window.
3	Rudolph	**c**	is going to spill the paint.
4	Vincent	**d**	is going to fall off the ladder.
5	Pam and Sam	**e**	is going to drop the toolbox.
6	Bonehead	**f**	is going to trip over the drill.

b 2.28 Listen to the Glooms and check your answers.

21 DIY disasters

Grammar • future predictions with *going to*; verbs and prepositions **Vocabulary** • DIY tools and actions	**Optional materials** • an age-appropriate film on DVD; a tall glass, a fresh egg, a tray, a bottle of water **Optional Activity Book activities** • Fast finishers p70, Extra practice p71 **Photocopiable activity** • *What am I going to do?* p122

PART 1

Introduction

Divide students into groups of four and ask them to tell their classmates what changes their family have made in their flat/ house since they started living there, e.g. *We've painted the rooms, we've bought new kitchen furniture,* etc.

❶ Vocabulary

[2.27] Ask students to look at the picture in Activity 2 and elicit what the title of the lesson means. The students look at the words related to DIY and listen as you play the CD. Then they match the words to the objects in the picture in Activity 2. They should make guesses about new vocabulary.

Students work individually on the task and then compare their answers in pairs. Play the CD again and elicit the letters labelling the corresponding objects. Make sure everybody understands all the words now and drill the pronunciation.

Mixed-ability classes

Fast finishers check what other things related to DIY they can name in the picture. Elicit their ideas when everyone has finished working on Activity 1.

Teaching tip: *Vocabulary learning strategies*

Teach students a variety of vocabulary learning strategies so that they can test them and identify the ones which work best. Here are some suggestions appealing to different learning styles:

- copying new words into your notebook and writing translations or definitions next to them
- illustrating the words with drawings or magazine pictures
- writing down collocations, i.e. words which go together
- making sentences with new words
- writing the new words on Post-it™ notes and sticking them to the corresponding objects
- making word cards and playing with them
- repeating the words
- saying the words in your head
- rapping or singing the words
- recording the words and listening to them
- walking around the room while saying the words
- tapping fingers while saying the words
- saying words and touching objects they refer to.

Elicit from students any other strategies they use to remember new vocabulary.

Tapescript

see Student's Book Activity 1

Answer key

hammer – **c**	ladder – **a**	window – **g**	toolbox – **b**
paint – **f**	drill – **d**	wallpaper – **e**	

❷ Presentation

a) Ask students to look at the picture carefully and elicit or explain that the Glooms are renovating their house. Point to different characters and elicit their names. Ask students to match the names in A with the phrases in B to make sentences about what is going to happen to members of the Gloom family. Before students begin the task, use mime to pre-teach the following verbs: *spill, fall off, drop, trip over.* Students compare their answers in pairs.

b) [2.28] Ask students to listen to Mandy and check their answers. Play the CD. Refer them to the **Study tip** to explain that some verbs often go with certain prepositions and it is useful to note them down together. Point out that illustrations help you remember vocabulary. Encourage students to add simple drawings to the words in their notebooks when possible.

Refer students to the **Grammar spot** on the next page to explain *going to* for future predictions. Elicit that we also use *going to* to talk about future plans. Point out that we use *going to* when we want to talk about a future situation which is connected to the present, e.g. by visual evidence.

Tapescript

1 **Mandy:** Watch out, Helga! You're going to spill the paint!
Helga: Ooh.
2 **Vincent:** Careful, Martha! You're going to drop the toolbox.
Martha: Oh my!
3 **Mandy:** Rudolph, be careful! You're going to trip over the drill!
Rudolph: Ooops!
4 **Martha:** Watch out, Vincent! You're going to fall off the ladder!
Vincent: Don't worry, I'm OK. I'm fine.
5 **Mandy:** Take care, Pam and Sam. You're going to break the window.
Pam and Sam: Uh oh!
6 **Vincent:** Look at Bonehead! He's going to eat Mandy's cake!

Answer key

1 c **2** e **3** f **4** d **5** b **6** a

❸ Grammar practice

a Look at these pictures and make predictions with *going to*.

1 He's going to fall off the chair.

1 he/fall off/the chair.

2 she/spill/her cereal.

3 they/trip over/the ladder.

4 he/drop/the books.

5 the ball/break/the window.

b 2.29 Listen and check.

Grammar spot
Future predictions with *going to*

She**'s going to** spill the paint.
They**'re going to** break the window.

Grammar page 104

❹ Writing

Look at the picture and make predictions about what is *going to* happen.

break spill drop eat fall off trip over

the tins the chair the broom
the glass the biscuits the water

1 Vincent is going to spill the water.

1 Vincent ____.
2 Martha ____.
3 Sam and Pam ____.
4 Rudolph ____.
5 Mandy ____.
6 Bonehead ____.

❺ Game

Pretend you are *going to* do something. Choose one of the ideas below. Mime it to your friends. Can they guess what you are *going to* do?

fall off a chair
fall asleep
sneeze
drink a glass of water
drop a plate
eat some soup
go swimming
run in a race

You're going to drop a plate!

No, I'm not.

You're going to fall off a chair!

Yes, I am.

❻ Check your English

Match the phrases in A with the phrases in B to make sentences.

A

1 Look! The apples
2 Look at the clouds. It
3 Jack has got tennis racket and a tennis ball. He
4 Helen is shouting very loudly. She

B

a 's going to play tennis.
b 's going to wake the baby.
c 's going to rain.
d are going to fall off the tree.

❸ Grammar practice

a) Focus students' attention on the pictures and ask them to predict what is going to happen. They should use the prompts to make sentences with *going to.* Go through the example before they begin the task. Ask students to compare their answers in pairs.

b) [2.29] Play the CD for students to check their answers.

Extra activity

In pairs, students tell each other if they have ever had any of the accidents from Activities 2 and 3 and explain the details.

Tapescript and Answer key

1 He's going to fall off the chair.
2 She's going to spill her cereal.
3 They're going to trip over the ladder.
4 He's going to drop the books.
5 The ball's going to break the window.

Homework suggestions

1 Activity Book page 44, Activities 1–3
2 Students write their own sentences with the words in Activity 1. Encourage them to make these sentences true about their home, e.g. *There are ten windows in my flat. Our ladder is made of metal.*

PART 2

Introduction

Divide students into pairs. Student A in each pair should sit with their back to the board. Write the following verbs from the previous lesson on the board for Student B to define for Student A to guess: *trip over, drop, eat.* Ask them to try to make definitions rather than mime the words. You can write the following sentence beginning for students to use: *It's something you do when ….* When Student As have guessed the words, they change roles. Write these words for Student A to define and Student B to guess: *fall off, break, spill.*

❹ Writing

Focus students' attention on the picture and ask them to identify all the members of the Gloom family. Go over the words in the box. Use the picture to explain *tins* and *broom.* Ask students to make predictions about the picture, using *going to* and the verbs and the nouns in the box. Point out that the verbs and the nouns are in mixed order.

Students compare their answers in pairs. Individual students read out the sentences.

Answer key

1 Vincent is going to spill the water.
2 Martha is going to fall off the chair.
3 Sam and Pam are going to eat the biscuits.
4 Rudolph is going to drop the tins.
5 Mandy is going to trip over the broom.
6 Bonehead is going to break the glass.

Extra activity

Play a suspenseful scene from an age-appropriate film on a DVD. Pause before the climax and ask students to predict what is going to happen, what the characters are going to do or say next. Encourage students to justify their predictions, e.g. *She is going to cry because she is very sad.* Play the rest of the scene for students to check their predictions.

❺ Game

Divide students into groups of four. Ask them to take turns to choose one activity in the box and pretend that they are going to do it, using mime. Their classmates try to guess what they are miming. Make sure students understand they have to mime getting ready to do the action and not doing it, e.g. they could stand on a chair and wobble to elicit: *You're going to fall off the chair,* but they should not actually fall off it. Go over the example dialogue before students begin the game. Each student should mime two activities. They can repeat activities used previously by another classmate, provided they use different gestures.

Photocopiable activity

What am I going to do? p122; instructions p98

Extra activity

You can conduct simple physics experiments and ask students to predict the results, using *going to.* For example, you can put a fresh egg at the bottom of a tall thin glass standing on a tray. Ask students to predict what is going to happen when you pour water into the glass. Listen to their ideas and pour the water quickly. The egg should go up and then back down. If students are curious, you can explain in L1 that moving water has a lower pressure than water that is still. When you pour water into the glass, the water above the egg starts moving and has lower pressure than the pressure below, so the egg rises. Then the pressure goes back to normal and the egg sinks.

❻ Check your English

Students match the phrases in A with the phrases in B to make predictions. Students compare their answers in pairs. Check the answers with the whole class.

Answer key

1 d **2** c **3** a **4** b

Homework suggestions

1 Activity Book page 45, Activities 4–6
2 Students find a magazine picture of a busy scene and make predictions about what is going to happen next. They should write at least four sentences.

22 My home

Lesson objective

Talking about where you live

❶ Presentation

a 2.30 Listen and read. Match the pictures to the texts.

a

b

c

What is your home like?

1 I don't get many visitors to my house and it's very peaceful here. That's because I live in an old **lighthouse**! Sometimes it's very quiet and not exciting enough, but I've got a beautiful view of the sea. There's another problem – there are too many stairs in my house!!

2 I live in a **caravan** with my mum and dad. It hasn't got many rooms and I sleep on a sofa in the living room. Some people think our caravan is very small, but it's big enough for us. We've got enough **furniture**: a TV, a sofa, a table and three chairs. And I've got some books and DVDs, so I'm happy. We can travel around and meet different people in different places.

3 I live in the outback of Australia on a big **ranch**. I don't go to school; it's 200 kilometres away. But I have some online lessons every day and I talk to my teacher on the radio. I like living on a ranch but there aren't enough people here, so sometimes I get a bit lonely.

4 I live in a pretty **cottage** in a village. In the summer a lot of tourists visit this village and there's too much **traffic** and noise. I don't like it then because it's very busy and it's not quiet enough. But in the winter there aren't many people here and it's quiet and beautiful.

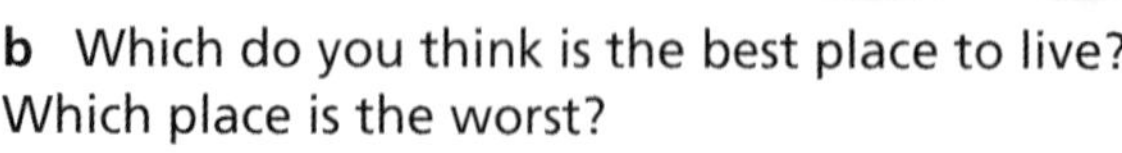

b Which do you think is the best place to live? Which place is the worst?

d

❷ Vocabulary

Find the words in bold in the text and match to these definitions.

1 furniture

1 Things in a house like beds, chairs and tables.
2 Cars and other vehicles in one place.
3 A very large farm in Australia or America.
4 A small house in the country.
5 A vehicle that people can live in.
6 A tower next to the sea. It usually has a big light.

22 My home

Grammar	**Optional Activity Book activities**
• *too much/many; enough*	• Fast finishers p70, Extra practice p71
Vocabulary	**Photocopiable activity**
• types of houses; furniture; adjectives	• *Complaints* p123

PART 1

Introduction

Write the following questions on the board:

How many doors are there in your house?
What is the colour of your front door?
Where is the radio in your house/flat?
What is the first thing you hear in the morning?
What is your favourite place in your house/flat?

Put students into pairs, preferably with a classmate they rarely work with. Ask them to interview each other with the questions on the board. They should give a false answer to one of the questions. When they have finished asking questions, they try to guess which of their classmate's answers was false.

1 Presentation

a) [2.30] Point to the pictures and the heading and elicit that the photos show different places where people live. Ask students to listen and read and match the texts to the pictures. They should ignore the words they do not know, but encourage them to underline words and phrases which helped them choose the corresponding photo. Play the CD. Elicit the answers and the words individual students underlined.

Tapescript

see Student's Book Activity 1a

Answer key

1 b **2** a **3** d **4** c

b) Ask students to decide which place is the best and which is the worst to live. Point to the pictures in turn and get students to vote: they should raise both their hands for the best place and stand up for the worst place. Volunteers can justify their choices.

Extra activity

In pairs, students tell each other about their dream place to live. They can talk about the area as well as the building. Encourage them to take notes of their classmate's answers. Set a time limit of six minutes and then put students into different pairs. They should tell each other about the dream place of the previous classmate they talked to.

2 Vocabulary

Ask students to read the definitions. Clarify any vocabulary if necessary. Then ask students to look at the words in bold in the texts in Activity 1a and match them to the definitions. Students compare their answers in pairs before you check them with the whole class.

Find out if students know/can guess the meaning of the following words and phrases: *peaceful, quiet, stairs, outback, online, get a bit lonely, busy.* Provide explanation if necessary.

Extra activity

Ask students to brainstorm other types of houses where people live. Write their ideas on the board. You can teach students the English names of types of houses where they live, e.g. *a block of flats, a semi-detached house, a terraced house,* etc.

Dyslexia tip: *Making notes*

Some dyslexic students have poor visual and spatial awareness. Encourage them to leave enough space between the lines as they are noting down new vocabulary or writing their own sentences. They will find it easier to read their notes and to spot and edit their mistakes. You can ask them to put the index finger of the non-writing hand between the lines to make sure there is adequate space.

Answer key

1 furniture
2 traffic
3 ranch
4 cottage
5 caravan
6 lighthouse

Grammar spot
Determiners

***too many/much* + noun**
too many stairs (countable)
too much traffic (uncountable)

adjective + *enough*	***enough* + noun**
not exciting *enough*	*enough* furniture
big *enough*	not *enough* people

Grammar page 105

3 Grammar practice

a Look at these words. Put them under the correct heading.

tourist money visitor homework
noise book water chair tree time

Countable	**Uncountable**
tourist	*money*

b Now use *enough* or *too much/many* to complete these sentences.

1 enough

1. We haven't got ____ money. We can't buy that TV.
2. There isn't ____ space for my computer because there are ____ books on my desk.
3. I've got ____ homework. I can't finish it all tonight.
4. There isn't ____ hot water in this bath. I'm cold!
5. It's very busy in the shopping centre and there are ____ people. Let's go home.

4 Listening

a 2.31 Listen to David. Are these sentences true (T) or false (F)?

1 F

1. David's house has got a huge garden.
2. David's mum thinks that David has got too many books and games in his room.
3. David likes his house because he can ride his bike outside.
4. David sometimes can't sleep at night because it's not quiet enough.
5. David's friends don't live close enough.

b 2.31 Listen again and check your answers.

My English file

Write about where you live. What is it like? Use *too much, too many,* and *(not) enough*.

My Home

I live in a large flat. It's very noisy here. There are too many cars on the street and there is too much noise but it's close enough to the park.

5 Speaking

What's your school like? Think of three good things and three bad things about your school. Tell your classmate.

Bad things	**Good things**
There's too much traffic outside.	*It's warm enough in the winter.*
There aren't enough windows.	*The playground is big enough.*

6 Pronunciation

a Put these words under the correct heading /uː/ or /ʌ/.

view enough mum school another too

/uː/	/ʌ/
view	*enough*

b 2.32 Listen and check your answers.

7 Check your English

Choose the correct words to complete the sentences.

1. There are too *much/many* people in our house and it hasn't got *enough space/space enough*! It's *too small/small enough*.
2. Our bedroom has got too *much/many* furniture.
3. This house *isn't/is* quiet enough. There's *too much/enough* traffic outside.
4. There *are/aren't* enough flowers in my garden. I want to get some more.

Grammar spot

Go over the example sentences to elicit or explain the use of *too much/many* and *enough*. Review countable and uncountable nouns. Elicit that they go with *many* and *much* respectively. Point out the different position of *enough* with a noun and an adjective. Explain it goes both with countable and uncountable nouns. Students can find more examples of *too much/many* and *enough* in Activity 1. Refer them to the **Grammar summary** on page 105 for more information on *too much/many* and *enough.*

Teaching tip: *Noticing a target grammar point*

Once you have explained a given grammar point introduced in a text, you can play the text again. Students listen and raise their hands every time their hear the target grammar point. Pause the recording when you see a show of hands for students to note down the relevant words related to the grammar point. As a follow-up they can use their notes to make sentences relating to the text or the corresponding pictures, e.g. *The lighthouse is not exciting enough.*

Extra activity

Review *too* + adjective. Ask individual students questions to receive two responses for each one: with *too* +adjective and adjective + *enough*, e.g. *Can you vote for president? I'm too young/I'm not old enough.* You can use these questions: *Can you buy a Ferrari? Can you play basketball in the NBA? Can you lift 200 kilograms?*

3 Grammar practice

a) Students read the words in the box and put them in the correct category: *uncountable* and *countable.* Remind them that the same words can belong to a different category in students' L1 so it is important to note down any differences. In pairs, students compare their answers. Check the answers with the whole class.

Answer key

Countable: tourist, visitor, book, chair, tree; **Uncountable:** money, time, homework, noise, water

b) Students use *too much/many* and *enough* to complete the sentences. All the sentences are complaints. Students should choose the right determiners to make them logical.

Mixed-ability classes

Less confident students underline the nouns following the gaps to help them decide whether to use *too much* or *too many* when *enough* is not the right option.

Answer key

1 enough **2** enough … too many **3** too much **4** enough **5** too many

Photocopiable activity

Complaints p123; instructions p99

Homework suggestions

1. Activity Book page 46, Activities 1–3
2. Students write their own sentences with *too much/many* and the words in the box in Activity 3a.

PART 2

Introduction

Write the following pairs of words on the board: *romantic comedies/sitcoms, sea/mountains, cars/motorbikes, local shops/shopping centres.* In pairs, students tell each other which option they prefer and say why the other one is worse, using *too much/many or enough,* e.g. *I prefer sitcoms, because romantic comedies are not funny enough.*

4 Listening

a) [2.31] Students listen to David talking about the place where he lives. Play the CD and ask students to decide if the sentences are true or false.

Tapescript

I live in a house in the centre of town. It's not huge, but it's big enough for us and we've got a small garden. My bedroom is really great and it's right at the top. My mum says I've got too many books and games in my room. But I like it! But outside, the road isn't safe enough for me to ride my bike or play football. There's too much traffic and it's really noisy. At night time I sometimes can't sleep because it's not quiet enough. But my friends live close enough, so I can visit them quite often.

b) [2.31] Play the CD again for students to check their answers. Elicit the answers and encourage students to correct the false statements.

Tapescript

see Activity 4a

Answer key

1 false (It's small) **2** true **3** false (His road isn't safe enough) **4** true **5** false (They live close enough)

My English file

Students write about the place where they live, using *too much/many and (not) enough.* They should write at least three sentences. They can just write about the area around their house if they prefer to. Go through the example first.

When students have finished, they exchange their notebooks in pairs. They read each other's texts and point out orally any mistakes they notice.

5 Speaking

In pairs, students tell each other three good things and three bad things about their school. They should talk about the building and the area. Elicit the answers from different pairs.

6 Pronunciation

a) Model the sounds /uː/ and /ʌ/. Students say the words in the box quietly and put them under the correct heading, depending on the sound they contain.

b) [2.32] Play the CD for students to check their answers. Drill the pronunciation of the words.

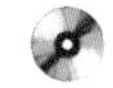

Tapescript

/uː/ view, school, too; /ʌ/ enough, mum, another

7 Check your English

Students choose the correct words to complete the sentences. Check the answers with the whole class.

Answer key

1 many … enough space … too small **2** much **3** isn't … too much **4** aren't

Homework suggestions

1. Activity Book page 47, Activities 4–6
2. Students choose a magazine picture of a room or house they do not like. They write what they do not like about it, using *too much/many* and *enough.*

23 The eco-village

Lesson objectives
- Using large numbers
- Talking about processes

1 Guessing

a How much rubbish do people in the UK throw away?

1. 76,000 tonnes per day.
2. 76,000 tonnes per month.
3. 76,000 tonnes per year.

b 2.33 Listen and check. Are you surprised?

Facts and figures

A tonne = 1,000 kilos
% = per cent
17.5 = seventeen point five (or seventeen and a half)
A million = 1,000,000
A billion = 1,000,000,000

2 Presentation

a 2.34 Listen and read. Complete the text with the words and numbers in the box.

kitchens	17	paper	17.5	food
15	farm	28	electricity	Scotland

1 28

Darcy, 11

Kyle, 13

Did you know ...?

- [1]_____ million tonnes of rubbish are thrown away every year in the UK. That's the same as 6 million elephants!
- Only [2]_____ % of rubbish in Britain is recycled.
- [3]_____ million plastic bottles are used every day.
- [4]_____ billion plastic bags are produced every year.

But in some places, people live in eco-villages, where lots of things are reused and recycled. Darcy and Kyle live in an eco-village called Melford, in [5]_____.

Fruit and vegetables are grown at the village [8]_____ for everyone in the village. 70% of Melford's [9]_____ is produced here.

The houses are specially designed. They don't use much gas and electricity. They are kept warm with special [6]_____ in the walls. [7]_____ and laundry rooms are shared so that very little energy is used.

100% of their [10]_____ is made in Melford. They make their own power with wind turbines.

b 2.34 Listen again and check.

23 The eco-village

Grammar:
- present passive

Vocabulary:
- large numbers; ecology; environment; verbs to describe processes

Optional materials:
- a plastic bottle per group of four

Optional Activity Book activities:
- Fast finishers p70, Extra practice p71

Photocopiable activity:
- *Plastic bags* p124

PART 1

Introduction

Write *eco-village* on the board. Ask students what they think it means. If necessary, explain that it is a village where people try to live ecologically. Divide students into groups of four and ask them to imagine what an eco-village looks like and what people do there to protect the environment. Set a time limit of four minutes. Elicit the ideas from different groups. Explain that in this lesson they are going to find out about an eco-village in Britain and they will be able to check their ideas.

1 Guessing

a) Go over the **Facts and figures** box. Ask students to compare how we write and/or say the numbers in English with their L1 and if there are any significant differences.

Ask students to read the question and the answers. Clarify any vocabulary students do not understand. Ask students to guess which answer is correct.

b) [2.33] Play the CD for students to check their guesses. Find out if they are surprised by any facts.

Extra activity

Students write three different large numbers and percentages. They cannot show their notes to their classmates. In pairs, they dictate the numbers to each other and then check if their classmate has written them correctly.

Dyslexia tip: *Working with numbers*

Dyslexic students whose visual tracking is poor struggle with reading, copying and writing numbers. Encourage them to use the following techniques when dealing with longer numbers:

- break a long number into chunks of two or three digits by making larger spaces between them
- with numbers with a string of zeroes, cover the number with a piece of paper to see a maximum of three zeroes at a time
- highlight various sections of the number with different colours
- if there are similar numbers in consecutive lines, cover them and look only at the number you are trying to read or copy at a given moment.

Tapescript

In the UK, we throw away 76,000 tonnes of rubbish every day!

2 Presentation

a) [2.34] Point to Darcy and Kyle in the photo. Explain that they live in the eco-village in the pictures below. Ask students to listen and read to find out more about life in their village. If you did the introduction activity, students are now able to compare their ideas with the text.

Ask students if the eco-village in the text is the same as they imagined or if anything surprises them about it. Then ask them to complete the texts with the words and numbers in the box. They should compare their answers in pairs.

Tapescript

see Activity 2a

b) [2.34] Play the CD for students to check their answers.

Check if students know/can guess the meaning of the following words and phrases: *reused, laundry rooms, power, wind turbines.* Provide explanation if necessary.

Refer students to the **Grammar spot** on the next page to elicit or explain the present passive. Point out the structure of the present passive: verb *be* in the correct present form and the past participle, which is also used in the present perfect. Explain that we use the passive when we do not know or it is not important who does something.

Elicit more examples of the passive voice in the text in Activity 2a, and write them on the board. Explain that in English if we have a number and a noun, we use the form of verb *be* which goes with the noun, e.g. *15 billion plastic bottles are produced.* Ask students to compare that with their L1. Refer students to the **Grammar summary** on page 105 for more information on the present passive.

Tapescript and Answer key

see Student's Book Activity 2a.

The missing answers are:

1 28	**5** Scotland	**9** food
2 17	**6** paper	**10** electricity
3 15	**7** kitchens	
4 17.5	**8** farm	

Cultural information

The text in Activity 2 is based on a real eco-village near the village of Findhorn in the north-east of Scotland. The village was established in 1985 to show that sustainable living is possible in the industrialised world. Various ecological techniques are used in housing and farming in the village, including wind turbines and solar water-heating system. The average resident uses half of the resources and produces half of the waste of the average British citizen. The village won the Best Practice designation from the United Nations in 1998. You can find out more information about the eco-village at www.ecovillagefindhorn.com.

❸ Comprehension

Read about Melford again. Are these sentences true or false? Correct the false sentences.

1 T

1 The UK doesn't recycle a lot of its rubbish.
2 Melford is the name of a house in Scotland.
3 The houses at Melford use a lot of gas and electricity.
4 There is special paper in the walls of the houses.
5 70% of the village's food is not produced at Melford.
6 Melford's power comes from wind turbines.

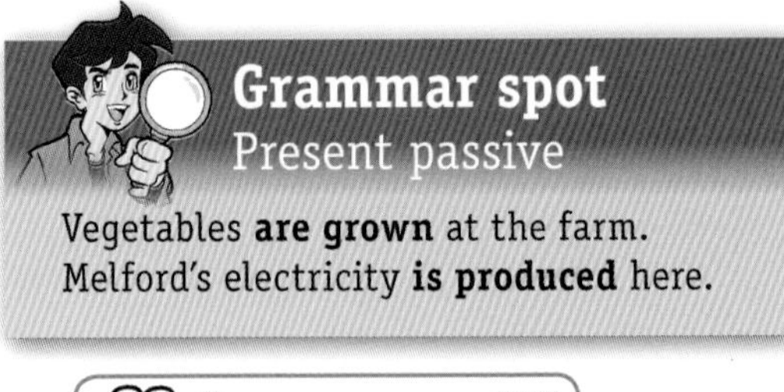

Grammar page 105

❹ Class poll

What do you think about Melford? Would you like to live there? Have a class vote. Write the results on the board.

Yes	No

❺ Grammar practice

a Complete these passive sentences with the correct form of the verb in brackets.

1 A lot of things are recycled at Melford.

1 A lot of things (recycle) ____ at Melford.
2 Electricity (produce) ____ for the village.
3 The houses (build) ____ from wood.
4 Vegetables (grow) ____ at the farm.
5 The kitchens (share) ____.

b 2.35 Listen and check.

❻ Listening

a 2.36 Darcy is talking about how her fleece top is made. Listen and put the pictures in the correct order.

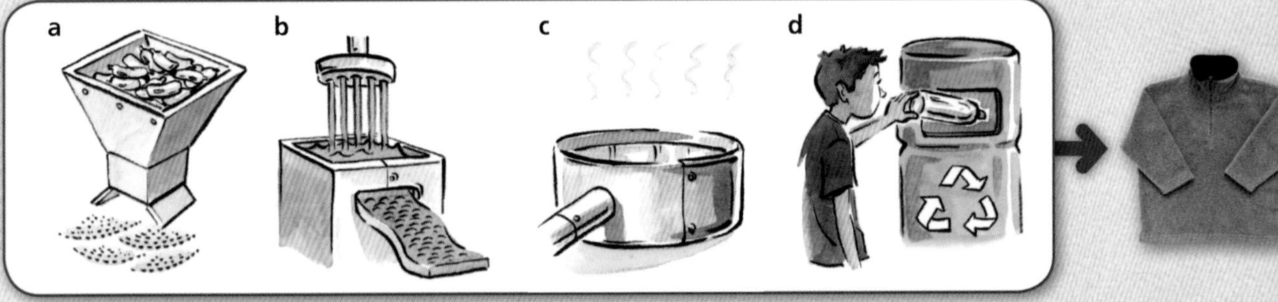

b 2.36 Listen again and complete the sentences. Use the passive form of the verbs in the box.

make melt collect dry pull cut clean

1 are collected

1 First, old plastic bottles ____ from recycling bins.
2 Then they ____ up into very small pieces.
3 The pieces ____ and then they ____.
4 After that, they ____.
5 The melted plastic ____ into long, thin strings.
6 The fleece material ____ from these strings.

❼ Check your English

Match the phrases in A with the phrases in B to make sentences.

A

1 Fruit and vegetables
2 12.5 million tonnes of paper and cardboard
3 This fleece top
4 Old plastic bottles
5 The houses in Melford

B

a is made from recycled plastic bottles.
b are built from wood.
c are collected from recycling bins.
d are grown on a farm near the village.
e are used in the UK every year.

❸ Comprehension

Students read the text in Activity 2a again and decide if the sentences are true or false. Then they discuss their answers in pairs. Check the answers with the whole class and ask volunteers to correct the false statements.

Answer key

1 true
2 false (It's the name of the eco-village)
3 false (They do not use much gas and electricity)
4 true
5 false (70% of the village's food is produced at Melford)
6 true

❹ Class poll

In pairs, students tell each other what they think about Melford and if they would like to live there. They should give their reasons. Ask the whole class if they would like to live in Melford. If the answer is *yes,* they should raise their hands. Ask volunteers to count the votes and write them on the board.

Homework suggestions

1 Activity Book page 48, Activities 1–4
2 Students write reasons why they would or would not like to live in Melford.

PART 2

Introduction

Write the following questions on the board: *Which cars are produced in your country? What is done with the rubbish? Which vegetables are grown? How is electricity produced? What are houses built from?* Divide students into groups of four and ask them to answer these questions about their country, using the present passive. Help with any new vocabulary. Elicit the answers from different groups.

❺ Grammar practice

a) Ask students to complete the passive sentences with the correct form of verb *be* and the past participle of the verb in brackets. If necessary, refer students to the **Grammar spot** to review the present passive. Ask students to compare their answers in pairs.

Mixed-ability classes

Less confident students underline the nouns preceding the gaps to help them decide which form of the verb *be* to use.

b) [2.35] Play the CD for students to check their answers.

Tapescript and Answer key

1 A lot of things are recycled at Melford.
2 Electricity is produced for the village.
3 The houses are built from wood.
4 Vegetables are grown at the farm.
5 The kitchens are shared.

❻ Listening

a) [2.36] Point to the pictures and ask students if they know how fleece tops are made. Ask them to listen to Darcy to check their predictions and then to put the pictures in the correct order.

Tapescript

This is my favourite top! It's fleece and it's amazing because it's made out of recycled plastic bottles. First, old plastic bottles are collected from recycling bins. Then they are cut up into very small pieces. The pieces are cleaned and they are dried. After that, they are melted. The melted plastic is pulled into long, thin strings. The fleece material is made from these strings. 25 big plastic bottles are used to make one fleece top. Cool!

Answer key

1 d **2** a **3** c **4** b

b) [2.36] Students listen to the recording again and complete the sentences with the passive form of the verb in the box. Make sure students understand all the verbs in the box. Play the CD. Set a time limit of four minutes.

Students compare their answers in pairs. Check the answers with the whole class.

Extra activity

Divide students into groups of four and give each group an empty plastic bottle. Ask them to imagine and write down as many ways as possible to reuse this bottle, e.g. as a pot for plants, as a bowling pin, etc. Set a time limit of four minutes. The group with the longest list wins the game. Ask the winners to read out their list. Other groups cross out the ways which repeat on their lists and add any other that have not been mentioned.

Tapescript

see Activity 6a

Answer key

1 are collected
2 are cut up
3 are cleaned … are dried
4 are melted
5 is pulled
6 is made

❼ Check your English

Students match the phrases in A with the phrases in B to make sentences. In pairs, they compare their answers. Check the answers with the whole class.

Answer key

1 d **2** e **3** a **4** c **5** b

Photocopiable activity

Plastic bags p124; instructions p99

Homework suggestions

1 Activity Book page 49, Activities 5–7
2 Students choose an object or a type of food and find information on the Internet or in the library on how it is made. They describe the process in a simple way in English with the present passive. They should use Activity 6 as a model. Encourage them to look up new words in a dictionary.

24 The eco-family

1 Reading

a 2.37 Listen and read the article. Match the questions to the correct answers.

1 What's your family like?

What's your home like?	What's your school like?	What's your family like?	What do you usually eat?

In this week's issue of 'My Life', we talk to Chloe Evans

1 ___

We're a big family. I've got four brothers and three sisters! My mum is an artist and my dad works at home. He's a researcher. My gran also lives with us. Sometimes I think there are too many people in our family – there are eleven people in our house!

2 ___

We live in the Rhondda Valley in Wales. Our house is big enough for our family and we've got a fantastic garden. In our garden we've got a goat and a few chickens! The goat's called Milly. She eats everything in our garden: the flowers, the grass, sometimes even our clothes!

3 ___

We grow our own food. We have fruit trees and a special vegetable garden. We have eggs from our chickens and milk from our goat. We make our own cheese. It's made from Milly's milk!

4 ___

We don't go to school. Our mum and dad teach us at home. Art is taught by Mum, of course, and all the other subjects are taught by Dad. We do lots of interesting things every day but we always do Maths and English.

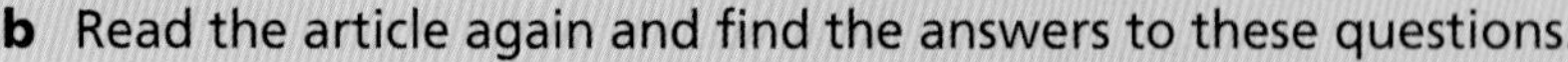

b Read the article again and find the answers to these questions.

1 How many people are there in Chloe's family?
2 Where does Chloe live?
3 Who is Milly?
4 Where does Chloe go to school?
5 Who teaches Art?

24 The eco-family

Optional materials	**Photocopiable activity**
• a map of the UK	• *Families* p125

PART 1

Introduction

Write *eco-family* on the board. Put students into groups of four and ask them to discuss what a family has to do to be an eco-family, e.g. *reuse plastic, grow fruit and vegetables*. Elicit the ideas from different groups onto the board. Ask students if their families do any of the activities on the board.

1 Reading

a) [2.37] Introduce the girl in the photo, Chloe Evans. Explain that her family is an eco-family. Then go over the questions in the box. Ask students to listen and read the article and match the questions to the correct paragraphs. Play the CD.

Elicit the answers. If you have a map of the UK, you can show students where Chloe lives – the Rhondda Valley is in the south-east of Wales.

Check if students know/can guess the meaning of the following words and phrases from the article: *researcher, gran, goat*. Provide explanation if necessary.

Mixed-ability classes

Fast finishers write two more questions they would like to ask Chloe. Elicit the questions when everyone has finished Activity 1a and ask the class what they think Chloe's responses could be.

Tapescript

see Student's Book Activity 1a

Answer key

1 What is your family like?
2 What is your house like?
3 What do you usually eat?
4 What is your school like?

b) Ask students to read the article again and answer the questions. In pairs, students compare their answers. Check the answers with the whole class.

Mixed ability classes

Fast finishers write more questions about the article. They can ask their questions to the whole class when everyone has completed the task in Activity 1b.

Extra activity

Divide the class into two teams. Ask Team A to discuss and write down all the good points of home education and Team B to find all the bad points. Set a time limit of four minutes. Team representatives read out their lists. Get students to vote by raising their hands if they would like to be home educated. Ask individual students to share their reasons.

Cultural information

Home education is the education of children at home by parents or tutors as an alternative to formal education. In the UK this form of education has been growing in popularity in recent decades. There can be different reasons for choosing home education, e.g. dissatisfaction with the schools in one's local area, religious beliefs or living in isolated areas without schools. People who teach children at home in the UK are not required to be trained teachers and they are free to choose what they want to teach. Some use a structured curriculum and school textbooks while others use their own resources and ideas. For more information on home education you can go to *home-ed.info*.

Answer key

1 Eleven people
2 In Wales
3 The goat
4 She doesn't go to school
5 Chloe's mum

❷ Listening

a 2.38 Listen to this interview with Fred Braithwaite. Find and correct the seven mistakes below.

my two sisters

Hello, Fred. Tell us about yourself.

Hi. Well, there are four people in my family. There's me, my two brothers and my mum.

And what's your home like?

We live in a big flat in Glasgow, Scotland. There's too much space for four people really, but it's a nice place. We don't have a garden but we have a great view of the city. Oh, and we've got two crazy dogs called Ginger and Tilly.

What do you usually eat, Fred?

We eat very healthy food. We don't eat too many chips or chocolate. We have lots of fruit and vegetables, pasta and cheese.

What's your school like?

It's OK, but there are too many desks in my class! There are thirty-two students and there's only one teacher!

b 2.38 Listen again and check your answers.

❸ Speaking

Work in pairs.

Student A: You are a reporter for 'My Life' magazine. Interview Student B about his/her life. Ask questions about family/home/school.

Student B: You are an unusual person. Answer Student A's questions about your life. Make up some interesting facts! You can use the ideas below:

I'm … an alien/a Hollywood star/a famous footballer/an explorer
I live in … a space rocket/a castle/ a house with a gym/a tent
I've got … not much space/a lot of money/ a few pets/not much furniture

Study tip
Remembering vocabulary

Write down words in lexical groups.

Animals	**Garden**
chicken	*flowers*
goat	*grass*

❹ Writing

Write about your unusual life. Use the facts you made up for Activity 3. Start like this:

I'm a/an … I live in …

Word race

Play in teams. How many more words can you write for each heading?
You have three minutes.
The team with the most words is the winner!

Things you can recycle
plastic bottles

Types of houses
cottage

Furniture
chair

Brown food
chocolate

❷ Listening

a) [2.38] Point to the photo and introduce Fred Braithwaite, who lives in Scotland. If you have a map of the UK, you can show students where Glasgow is. Ask students to listen to the interview with Fred and remember as much as possible. Play the CD. Then ask students to read the printed interview and find seven mistakes in it. In pairs, students compare their answers.

Tapescript

see Activity 2b

b) [2.38] Play the CD again for students to check their answers.

Tapescript and Answer key

Hello, Fred. Tell us about yourself.

Hi. Well, there are four people in my family, there's me, my two <u>sisters</u> and my mum.

OK. And what's your home like?

We live in a <u>small</u> flat in Glasgow, Scotland. There's <u>not enough</u> space for four people really, but it's a nice place. We don't have a garden but we have a great view of the city. Oh, and we've got two crazy <u>cats</u> called Ginger and Tilly.

What do you usually eat, Fred?

We eat very healthy food. We don't eat too many <u>sweets</u> or chocolate. We have lots of fruit and vegetables, pasta and <u>rice</u>.

What's your school like?

It's OK but there are too many <u>students</u> in my class! There are thirty-two students and there's only one teacher!

Photocopiable activity

Families p125; instructions p99

Homework suggestions

1 Activity Book page 50, Activity 1
2 Students write who they would like to visit in their home: Chloe from Activity 1 or Fred from Activity 2. They should give their reasons.

PART 2

Introduction

Elicit from the whole class examples of unusual families they know from magazines, TV series and books. Write them on the board. In pairs, students should choose one family and discuss what they know about them. They should say what is good and what is difficult about being a member of this family. Pairs report the results of their discussion to the whole class.

❸ Speaking

Divide students into pairs. Explain that they are going to role-play an interview. Students A and B in each pair should read their respective role instructions. Student A prepares a series of at least five questions about family/home/school for Student B, Student B prepares his/her fictional answers to the questions, using the suggestions in the book or their own ideas. Allow five minutes for preparation.

When the time is up, students act out the interview within their pairs. Monitor the activity. When everybody has finished, ask Student As in different pairs to report Student Bs' answers. You can then ask one or two pairs to act out their interview for the whole class.

❹ Writing

Students imagine they have unusual lives. They should write a paragraph about their fictional life, e.g. their family, home, school. Encourage them to use the ideas from Activity 3. Go over the example before they begin the task.

Encourage students to make a draft copy first and rewrite it after editing. Monitor their work, providing help. Then they should exchange their texts in pairs. If they notice any mistakes in their classmate's text, they should point these out orally.

Dyslexia tip: *Writing paragraphs or compositions*

It is best to provide a structured plan before asking dyslexic students to complete a writing task. On the board write key topics, e.g. *who you are, where you live, what your family is like*, suggested grammar to use, set phrases to use and the minimum number of sentences. Inform students what you are going to evaluate. You can provide the whole plan and answer students' questions about it in class and then assign the actual writing for homework to let dyslexic students work at their own pace.

Word race

Divide students into groups of four and ask them to add as many words to each heading as possible. Set a time limit of three minutes. The group with the most words altogether wins the game.

Teaching tip: *Rewards*

Students often find competitive games engaging and you can motivate them further by providing rewards for the winners. These should be free so that other students do not feel too envious. You may use the following ideas:

- printed home-made awards or certificates
- printed home-made homework passes which students can use when they forget their homework and they will not be penalized
- an extra point to add to students' next test results. It is unlikely to influence their grade, but still feels valuable
- a letter or phone call to students' parents to praise their achievement in class
- when playing a game against the whole class, you can promise them a homework-free weekend or their favourite song/game in class if they win.

Homework suggestions

1 Activity Book page 50, Activity 2
2 Students write a paragraph about an unusual family they know. It can be a real family or a fictional one from films/TV/books.

Module 6 Review

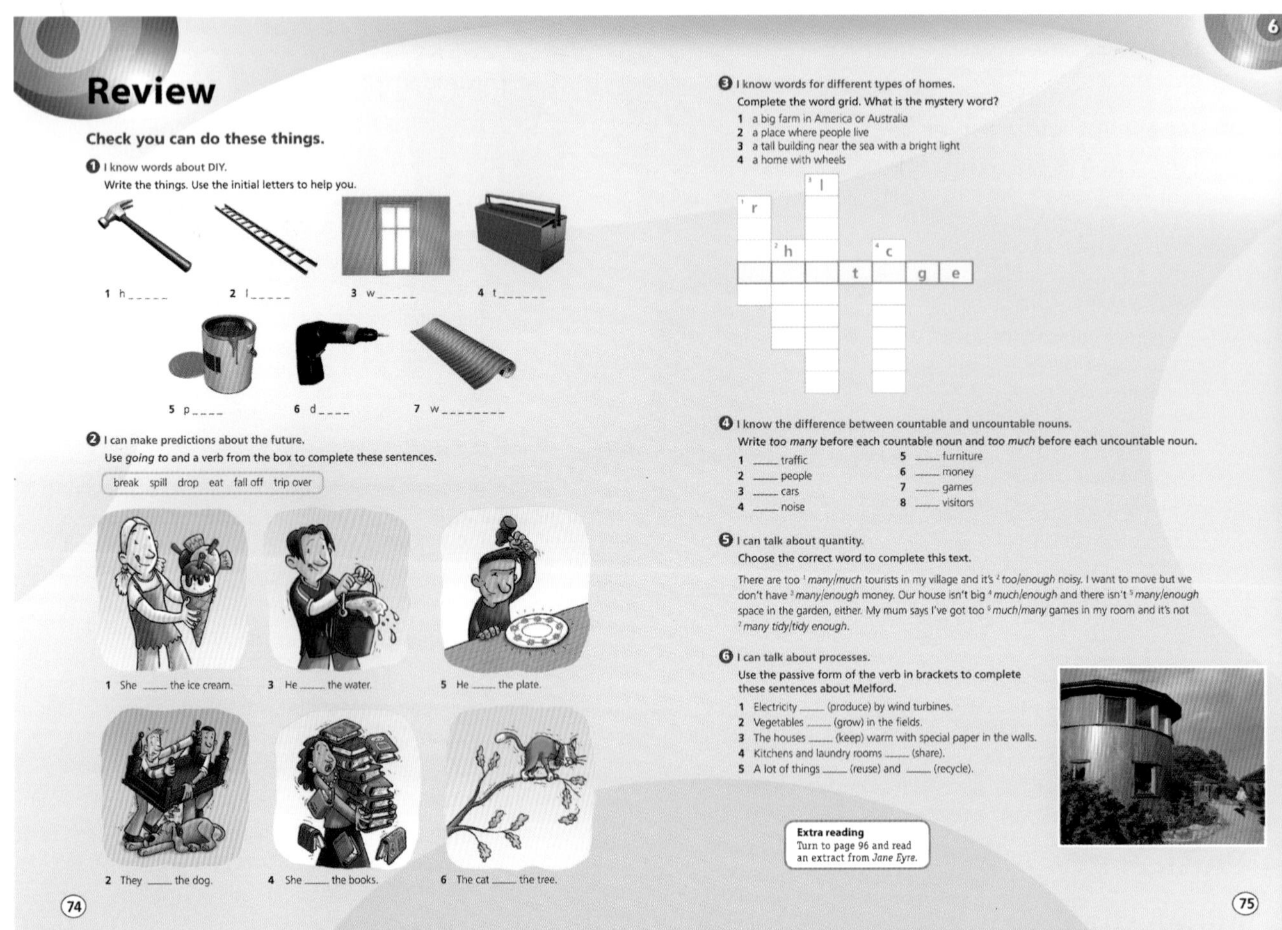

Review

Check you can do these things.

1 I know words about DIY.

Write the things. Use the initial letters to help you.

1 h_ _ _ _ _
2 l_ _ _ _ _
3 w_ _ _ _ _
4 t_ _ _ _ _ _
5 p_ _ _ _
6 d_ _ _ _
7 w_ _ _ _ _ _ _ _

2 I can make predictions about the future.

Use *going to* and a verb from the box to complete these sentences.

break spill drop eat fall off trip over

1 She ___ the ice cream.
2 They ___ the dog.
3 He ___ the water.
4 She ___ the books.
5 He ___ the plate.
6 The cat ___ the tree.

74

3 I know words for different types of homes.

Complete the word grid. What is the mystery word?

1 a big farm in America or Australia
2 a place where people live
3 a tall building near the sea with a bright light
4 a home with wheels

1 r
2 h
3 l
4 c
_ _ _ t _ g e

4 I know the difference between countable and uncountable nouns.

Write *too many* before each countable noun and *too much* before each uncountable noun.

1 ___ traffic
2 ___ people
3 ___ cars
4 ___ noise
5 ___ furniture
6 ___ money
7 ___ games
8 ___ visitors

5 I can talk about quantity.

Choose the correct word to complete this text.

There are too [1] *many/much* tourists in my village and it's [2] *too/enough* noisy. I want to move but we don't have [3] *many/enough* money. Our house isn't big [4] *much/enough* and there isn't [5] *many/enough* space in the garden, either. My mum says I've got too [6] *much/many* games in my room and it's not [7] *many tidy/tidy enough*.

6 I can talk about processes.

Use the passive form of the verb in brackets to complete these sentences about Melford.

1 Electricity ___ (produce) by wind turbines.
2 Vegetables ___ (grow) in the fields.
3 The houses ___ (keep) warm with special paper in the walls.
4 Kitchens and laundry rooms ___ (share).
5 A lot of things ___ (reuse) and ___ (recycle).

Extra reading
Turn to page 96 and read an extract from *Jane Eyre*.

75

Optional materials

- two scraps of paper per each student; a non-transparent bag

Optional revision

Before your students start this Review, you may want to direct them to the **Grammar summary** at the back of their coursebooks and to the **Word lists** at the back of their Activity Books. This will remind them of the main grammar and vocabulary in the module. Give them ten minutes to read through those in small groups and ask you any questions they may have.

- Activity Book: Refer your students to pages 85–86: *DIY*; *Recycling an ecology*; *Places*
- **Grammar summary**: Refer your students to pages 104–105 sections 15–17

Module 6 Review

The purpose of this section is revision and consolidation of the material studied in Module 6.

Completing the activities

Go over all the activities with the class, explaining rubrics and giving examples to make sure students know what to do. There are written and oral tasks, but you may decide yourself how they should be completed by students. Generally students should do the writing tasks individually and the oral tasks in pairs, testing each other's knowledge. Make sure they do not treat the *Review* as a formal test, but complete the activities in a friendly, stress-free atmosphere. Fast finishers can write down the answers to the oral tasks.

Checking answers

When students have finished, check the answers with the whole class by asking volunteers to copy their answers onto the board or to say them aloud. If necessary, explain the more difficult issues, ask additional questions about the activities and solve any problems that arise.

Self-evaluation

Tell students to evaluate themselves. They should tick the activities where at least half of their answers were correct.

Feedback

Ask students which activities were difficult, which were easy and if there is anything they would like to review. Make a note of common language problems to go over in future lessons.

Teaching tip: *Making checking answers engaging*

Make sure you do not just present students with a list of correct answers, but have them work out which answers are correct and why. You can use the following options:

- put students in pairs or groups so that they can compare and discuss the answers together
- give a prepared list of answers to one student in each group to act as 'teacher', choosing a less confident student for that role
- put the answers on the board in mixed order for students to match to the correct questions
- assign each exercise to a different pair or group to give answers to other groups. Check that their answers are correct first.

Be ready to listen to various versions of the answers students come up with as there may be more possible answers than one.

Answer key

1
1 hammer
2 ladder
3 window
4 toolbox
5 paint
6 drill
7 wallpaper

2 Students study the pictures and predict what is going to happen. They complete the sentences with ***going to*** and the verbs in the box.

1 is going to eat
2 are going to trip over
3 is going to spil
4 is going to drop
5 is going to break
6 is going to fall off

3
1 ranch
2 house
3 lighthouse
4 caravan
mystery word: cottage

4
1 too much
2 too many
3 too many
4 too much
5 too much
6 too much
7 too many
8 too many

5
1 many
2 too
3 enough
4 enough
5 enough
6 many
7 tidy enough

6
1 is produced
2 are grown
3 are kept
4 are shared
5 are reused … recycled

Extra activity

Ask students to write on scraps of paper two words they have learnt in Module 6. They can look through their books to review the words. Put all the words in a non-transparent bag. Divide students into pairs. One pair begins by one player picking a word from the bag and defining it for their classmate to guess as quickly as possible. They can also answer *yes/no* questions. When the word is guessed, the player picks another word and so on until the time limit of one minute is up. If they do not guess within a minute, the word goes back into the bag. Then it is another pair's turn. The pair who guessed the most words wins.

Extra reading

Refer students to pages 96 and 97 of their books to find an extract from *Jane Eyre*.

1 Students read the background information about the book and its author and say if they know any famous authors from their own country who lived at the same time as Charlotte Brontë.

2 Students read the extract from the book and put the events in the correct order.

Answer key

1 c **2** e **3** a **4** d **5** b

3 Students discuss the questions in groups of three.

Homework suggestions

If students enjoyed the extract, they may want to read the whole story. There is a Macmillan Reader available of *Jane Eyre*. Visit macmillanenglish.com/readers for details.

Module 6 Tests (A and B) are on the Tests CD

Learning diary

You can refer students to page 51 of the Activity Book for further review, more study tips and self-assessment activities.

Extra special

6

Extra special

Mini-play

Look at the picture. What is Jane doing?

a 2.39 **Listen and read. Who has an accident?**

Jane Mark, I need a few things. Can you go to the shops for me?
Mark What do you need?
Jane I need a little more paint. And I need another paintbrush.
Mark Why? What are you doing?
Jane I'm painting the window.
Mark Why are you painting the window?
Jane Because it's old and dirty.
Mark Well, I don't think it's a good idea.
Jane Why not?
Mark Well … it's dangerous.
Jane No, it's not!
Mark Watch out! You're going to fall off the ladder!
Jane No, I'm not! I'm fine.
Mark Well, be careful. You're going to spill the paint!
Jane Don't be silly. I'm not going to fall off the ladder and I'm not going to spill the paint.
Mark OK, OK. I'm sorry. But you usually have a lot of accidents.
Jane Accidents? No, I don't. I never have accidents.
Mark Yes, you do. You … STOP!
Jane What?
Mark You're going to break the window with your paintbrush!
Jane No, I'm not! Really, Mark, calm down. Look, I haven't got enough paint here. Can you get some more?
Mark Oh well, OK.
Jane Thank you!
Mark Watch out! You're going to drop your paintbrush onto the floor.
Jane Mark! Stop it! I'm not going to fall off the ladder. I'm not going to spill the paint. I'm not going to break the window and I'm not going to drop my paintbrush on the floor.
Mark Hmm. OK. Look, here's the paint and the new paintbrush. I'll bring it over to you.
Jane No, Mark, wait! I think that's a bad idea.
Mark Why?
Jane Because you're going to …
Mark Ow!
Jane … trip over the paint pot!

b 2.39 **Listen again. Then choose your part: Jane or Mark and read the play with a classmate.**

Memory challenge
Learn your lines by heart.

Mini-project

1 Read Shivani's general knowledge quiz. Write answers to the questions.

General knowledge quiz

Honda cars are made in …
A Sweden B Japan C France

Paper is made from …
A grass B hair C wood

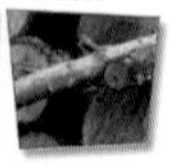

Cocoa beans are grown in ...
A Austria B Kenya C Canada

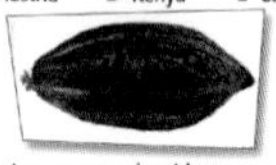

Omelettes are made with …
A rice B eggs C sugar

Glass is made from …
A sand B plastic C water

Shivani

2 Write a general knowledge quiz. Use the present passive.

3 Ask your classmates to write answers to your quiz.

76 77

Mini-play

Focus students' attention on the picture and introduce Jane and Mark. Elicit that Jane is painting the window.

a) [2.39] Students listen and read the play to find out who has an accident. Play the CD and elicit that Mark has an accident – he trips over the paint pot.

Ask comprehension questions, e.g. *What does Jane need? Why is she painting the window? Why isn't Mark happy that Jane is painting the window? Has he been to the shop? What did he buy?*

Tapescript

see Student's Book Activity a

b) [2.39] Divide students into pairs and ask them to choose the parts from the play. Play the CD for students to listen carefully to their lines. Get students to read out the play in pairs. Then go over the **Memory challenge** and encourage students to learn their lines by heart. Give them five minutes to practise and memorise their lines. Then ask volunteers to act out the play to the rest of the class, saying as many lines from memory as possible. Get the class to vote for the best performance.

Extra activity

In groups of four, students tell each other if they or their family members had any accidents when redecorating or renovating their flats or houses.

Mini-project

1. Explain to students that a girl called Shivani has written a general knowledge quiz. Ask students to read her quiz and choose the correct answers. Encourage them to use the pictures to help them understand the questions. Check the answers with the whole class. You can award students one point for each correct answer.

Answer key

1 B **2** C **3** B **4** B **5** A

2. Ask students to write a general knowledge quiz, using the present passive. To each question they should add three answers, one of which should be correct. You can assign research for homework on a previous lesson, use the Internet in class if available or set the project as a homework activity.
3. In groups of four, students present their quizzes and ask their classmates to write the correct answers using full sentences.

Extra activity

You can ask students to engage in a long-term project on becoming an eco-class. Encourage the class to brainstorm all the ways in which they can personally protect the environment, e.g. replace long baths with quick showers, turn off water when brushing teeth, use both sides of writing paper, recycle plastic, glass and paper, etc. They should make a copy of these guidelines for each student. Students can then try to apply these guidelines and write weekly reports on how they are progressing.

Lesson objectives
- Talking about rules
- Giving directions

25 Rules of the road

1 Presentation

a 2.40 Listen and read. Match the traffic rules with the Glooms. Write the letters.

1 f

Traffic rules

1 You mustn't drive more than 30 mph.
2 You must stop when the traffic light is red.
3 You mustn't enter this street.
4 You must keep straight on. You mustn't turn left.
5 You mustn't park here.
6 You must cycle in the cycle lane. You mustn't cycle on the pavemen
7 You must wear a crash helmet when you ride a motorbike.
8 You mustn't cross the road. You must wait for the green man.

b 2.40 Listen again and check your answers. Then point to the Glooms in the picture and read out the traffic rules.

You mustn't cross the road. You must wait for the green man.

Grammar spot
Obligation *must, mustn't*

You **must stop** when the traffic light is red.
You **mustn't turn** left.

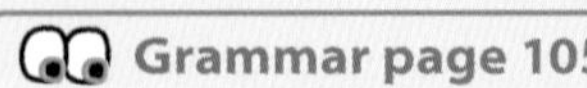

25 Rules of the road

Grammar
- *must/mustn't* for obligation; imperative

Vocabulary
- traffic rules; words connected with traffic; directions

Optional materials
- bilingual dictionaries, one per group of four students

Optional Activity Book activities
- Fast finishers p72, Extra practice p73

Photocopiable activity
- *Rules* p126

PART 1

Introduction

Divide students into groups of four and ask them to brainstorm all vehicles they know in English. Set a time limit of four minutes. Elicit the words from different groups onto the board. Then ask students to compare the list on the board with the vehicles in the picture in Activity 1. Elicit or teach the names of the vehicles in the picture: *car, tandem, penny-farthing bicycle, moped, van, beach buggy, tricycle, motorbike, double-decker bus, limousine.* Ask the following questions: *Which of these vehicles do you usually see on the streets in your country? Have you ever seen a penny-farthing bicycle/tandem/beach buggy/tricycle/limousine? Where did you see them?*

1 Presentation

a) [2.40] Focus students' attention on the picture. Elicit that the scene is taking place in the UK and all the vehicles are driving on the left. Ask students to identify the members of the Gloom family, who are labelled with letters in the picture. Elicit that they are all breaking different traffic rules, because they do not live in a city and do not know the rules.

Students listen and read the rules in the box. Then they match each rule with the member of the Gloom family who is breaking the rule.

Play the CD. Encourage students to make guesses about new vocabulary. Students work individually on the task and then compare their answers in pairs.

Mixed-ability classes

Put fast finishers into pairs to make sentences about what different people are doing in the picture, using the present continuous.

Cultural information

Left-hand traffic used to be predominant worldwide as it was more convenient for a right-handed person to mount a horse from the left side, their sword worn on the left did not hit other people and fighting was easier with swords held in the right hand. When wagons pulled by several pairs of horses started transporting farm products in France and the USA, the driver sat on the left rear horse to control all the horses with the whip in his right hand. It was easier for the driver to see the oncoming traffic from the left, so he kept on the right side of the road. After the French Revolution of 1798 more countries switched to the right. Nowadays, only about one quarter of the world drives on the left. In Europe there are only four countries with left-hand traffic: Cyprus, Malta, Great Britain and Ireland. For more information, see *www.users.telenet.be/worldstandards/driving*.

Check if students know/can guess what the following words and phrases mean: *30 mph, traffic light, enter, keep straight on, park, pavement, crash helmet, cross.* Provide explanation if necessary.

Refer students to the **Grammar spot** to elicit or explain *must* and *mustn't* for obligation. If students ask about the difference between *have to,* which they know from *Hot Spot Student's Book 2,* and *must,* explain that both can be used to talk about rules referring to the present. Point out that there is a difference in meaning in the negative: *don't have to* means that something is not necessary, whereas *mustn't* means that something is prohibited. Refer students to the **Grammar summary** on page 105 for more information on *must* and *mustn't*.

Tapescript

see Student's Book Activity 1a

b) [2.40] Play the CD again and pause after each rule to check the answers with the whole class. Then put students into pairs. Ask them to take turns to point to the Glooms in the picture and read out the corresponding traffic rules.

Extra activity

Divide students into groups of four. Ask them to discuss which traffic rules people in their town or city usually break. Elicit the answers from different groups. Encourage students to explain why it is important to follow traffic rules.

Tapescript

see Activity 1a

Answer key

1 f **2** h **3** g **4** c **5** d **6** b **7** e **8** a

❷ Grammar practice

Look at the traffic signs. Make sentences with *You must/mustn't* and these words.

turn left stop wear a crash helmet
cross the road park keep straight on

You must keep straight on.

❸ Vocabulary

a 2.41 Look at the picture in Activity 1. Listen and find these things.

parking meter – 4

parking meter traffic sign
cycle lane pedestrian crossing
traffic lights traffic warden
pavement crossroads

b 2.42 Listen and check.

❹ Speaking

a Look at the map. Find *You are here* and follow the instructions. What are the missing words?

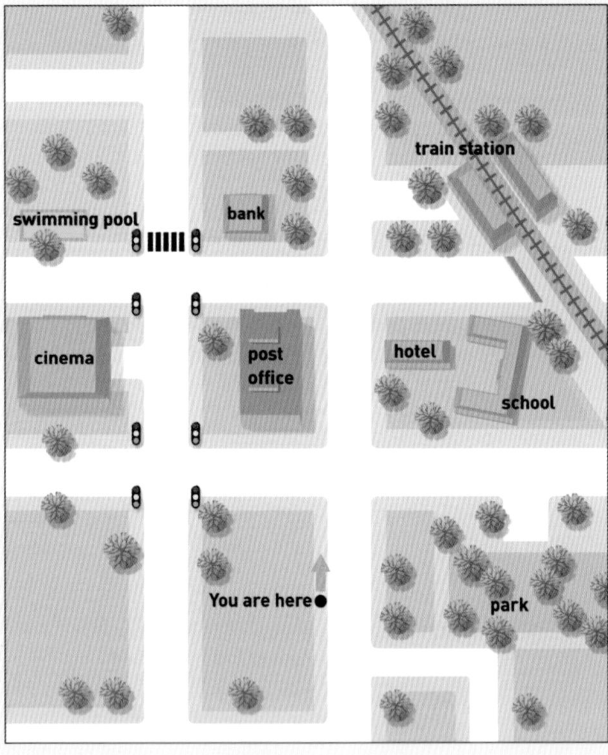

Excuse me, where is the ____, please?

Turn left at the crossroads. Keep straight on until the traffic lights and turn right. Then keep straight on until the pedestrian crossing. Cross the road. Keep straight on. The ____ is on the right.

b 2.43 Listen and check.

c Work with a classmate. Take it in turns to give directions to the different places on the map. Use the phrases in the box to help you.

turn left/right keep straight on (until)
cross the road it's on the left/right
walk along (the road)

Excuse me, where is the bank, please?

Walk along the road and turn right at the …

❺ Class poll

a In groups think about where you live and write some traffic rules on the board. Use *You must …* or *You mustn't …*

You must stop when the traffic light is red.

You mustn't drive on the left.

b Look at your ideas and vote for the rule you think is the most important.

❻ Check your English

a Complete the sentences with *must* or *mustn't* and an appropriate verb.

In my country …

1 You ____ a crash helmet when you ride a motorbike.
2 You ____ in the cycle lane.
3 You ____ at more than 50 kph in a city.
4 You ____ when the traffic light is red.

b Look at the map in Activity 4 and write the instructions from *You are here* to the train station.

Walk along the road …

❷ Grammar practice

Students look at the traffic signs and make sentences about the rules they illustrate with *You must/mustn't* and the words in the box. In pairs, students compare their sentences. Check the answers with the whole class.

Extra activity

In groups of four, students think of other signs illustrating different rules they see in public places, e.g. at a swimming pool, in a library, etc. Students draw the signs and write the rules below them, using *must/mustn't*. Give them dictionaries to look up new words. Groups present their projects to the whole class.

Answer key

1 You must keep straight on.
2 You mustn't park.
3 You mustn't turn left.
4 You must stop.
5 You must wear a crash helmet.
6 You mustn't cross the road.

Photocopiable activity

Rules p126; instructions p100

Homework suggestions

1. Activity Book page 52, Activities 1–3
2. Students imagine that a foreign exchange student is going to live in their home for a month. They write a list of at least four rules for the student, e.g. about meals, watching TV, going out, homework, chores, etc. They should use *must* and *mustn't*.

PART 2

Introduction

Give students two minutes to write down as many things as they can see on the street outside their school as possible, e.g. *trees, pavement, shops*. When the time is up, divide students into pairs. They should compare their lists and find out how many words are the same.

❸ Vocabulary

a) [2.41] Students look at the words in the box and listen as you play the CD. Then they match them with the numbered elements of the picture in Activity 1. They should make guesses about new vocabulary.

Students work individually on the task and then compare their answers in pairs.

Tapescript

see Student's Book Activity 4a

b) [2.42] Play the CD for students to check their answers. Make sure everybody understands all the words now and drill the pronunciation.

Tapescript and Answer key

parking meter **4**
traffic sign **5**
cycle lane **7**
pedestrian crossing **6**
traffic lights **3**
traffic warden **1**
pavement **2**
crossroads **8**

❹ Speaking

a) Students look at the map and find *You are here*. They should follow the instructions from that point with their finger on the map as they are reading them. Students' task is to find the missing words.

b) [2.43] In pairs, students compare their answers. Play the CD to check. Point out that we use the imperative to give instructions. Clarify any vocabulary students do not understand.

Extra activity

In pairs, with the text in Activity 4a covered, students follow the route and try to reconstruct the instructions. When they have finished, they uncover the text and check their answers.

Tapescript

see Student's Book Activity 4

Answer key

missing word: *swimming pool*

c) In pairs, students take turns to ask for directions to different places and respond, using the phrases in the box. Read out the example with a confident student first. Ask a pair to repeat their dialogue to the whole class.

Extra activity

Individually, students write instructions on how to get from their school to a destination within walking distance, e.g. a bakery. They should keep the destination a mystery. In groups of four, students take turns to read out their instructions and guess their classmates' mystery places.

❺ Class poll

a) In groups of four, students make a list of different traffic rules in their country, using *must* and *mustn't* and the vocabulary from Activity 3 when appropriate. Set a time limit of four minutes. Group representatives write the rules from their lists on the board. They should not repeat any rules that are already written there.

b) Students look at all the ideas on the board and individually choose the most important one. Read out the ideas in turn and get students to vote for the most important one by raising their hands. They can vote only once. Write the votes next to the rules and find out which one most students chose as the most important. Ask students to give their reasons for choosing it.

❻ Check your English

a) Students complete the traffic rules with *must* or *mustn't* and an appropriate verb. In pairs, students compare their answers. Check the answers with the whole class.

Mixed-ability classes

For less confident students write the missing verbs in mixed order on the board.

Answer key

1 must wear
2 must cycle
3 mustn't drive
4 must wait

b) Students look at the map in Activity 4 and write their own instructions from the *You are here* point to the bus station. Elicit the instructions from different students.

Homework suggestions

1. Activity Book page 53, Activities 4–6
2. Students draw a simple map of the area where they live and write instructions on how to get from their home to a place they often walk to, e.g. the nearest shop.

26 My secret identity

Lesson objective

Giving information about yourself and others

1 Presentation.

a 2.44 Listen and read. Is the man's name really Mr King?

Guard Hello, Mr King. Why do you want to visit our country?
Mr King I'm here to paint pictures of your beautiful mountains.
Guard But there aren't any mountains in Sylvania, Mr King.
Mr King Er … I mean your beautiful countryside.
Guard Umm … I think I must ask you some questions. What is your full name?
Mr King It's Graham Anthony King.
Guard I see. And where are you staying in Sylvania?
Mr King At the Ritz Palace Hotel.
Guard Ah, the Ritz. It's a very good hotel. So, you're an artist, Mr King. How long have you been an artist?
Mr King I've been an artist for two years.
Guard Two years? Umm … and I see you can fly a plane, Mr King.
Mr King Yes, I can.
Guard How long have you had a pilot's licence?
Mr King I've had a pilot's licence since 2008.
Guard Umm … since 2008. And how long have yo lived in New York?
Mr King I've lived there for six months.
Guard For six months? I see. What is your telepho number there?
Mr King It's … let's see, er … 01 834 875 1006.
Guard Umm. And how long have you had a passport?
Mr King I've had a passport since August.
Guard I'm afraid you cannot enter Sylvania. You have made four mistakes and I don't believ you are Mr King … I think you are the worl famous secret agent Mr X.

b 2.44 Look at the information on the computer and listen again. What four mistakes does Mr X make?

26 My secret identity

Grammar
- present perfect with *for* and *since*; questions with *How long ...?*

Vocabulary
- personal information; time expressions

Optional Activity Book activities
- Fast finishers p72, Extra practice p73

Photocopiable activity
- *How long have you ...?* p127

PART 1

Introduction

Write the following topic on the board: *Passport control.* Explain to students that in some countries for safety reasons there is a detailed passport control when we arrive at the border. Elicit what questions border guards usually ask during passport control. If students have had any interesting personal experiences with going through passport control, encourage them to share these with the whole class.

❶ Presentation

a) [2.44] Focus attention on the picture and introduce the characters: Mr King and the border guard. Elicit that Mr King has just arrived in the fictional country of Sylvania and he is answering the guard's questions. Point to the close-up of the guard's computer screen for an overview of the information the guard is asking about. Ask students to listen and read the conversation and decide if the man's name is really Mr King. Play the CD. Elicit that the man is not really Mr King.

Tapescript
see Student's Book Activity 1a

b) [2.44] Students study the information about Mr King that the guard has on the computer. Ask them to listen and read the conversation again and compare Mr King's answers with the information on the computer to find four mistakes he makes. Play the CD. Check the answers with the whole class.

Check if students know/can guess the meaning of the following words and phrases: *full name, fly a plane, pilot's licence, secret agent.* Provide explanation if necessary.

Refer students to the **Grammar spot** on the next page to elicit or explain the present perfect with *for* and *since* to talk about situations that started in the past and continue up to the present. Point out that we use *since* to say when something started and *for* to say how long something has been going on. You can draw timelines to illustrate this point. Ask *How long ...?* questions to students about their individual interests to elicit responses with *since* or *for*, e.g. *How long have you played baseball/ watched your favourite TV series?* Refer students to the **Grammar summary** on page 101 for more information on the present perfect with *for* and *since*.

Extra activity
Ask students which other secret agents they know from TV series, films or books. Elicit what a typical secret agent looks like and what skills he or she has. Ask: Why is Mr King a bad secret agent?

Tapescript
see Activity 1a

Answer key
the full name, how long he has had his pilot's licence, how long he has lived in New York, his telephone number.

Teaching tip: *Know your students' interests*

Make sure that you know your students' interests so that you can illustrate new language material or invent fun practice activities with examples students can relate to. The easiest way is to do a survey where students write down their favourite TV series, computer and video games, films, actors, sports, music, books, magazines, Internet websites. Try to incorporate them into your lessons to increase students' motivation. This can also help you establish good rapport with your students as they will appreciate your efforts and will have common topics to discuss with you.

Grammar spot
Present perfect with *for* and *since*

How long **have** you **been** an artist?
I've **been** an artist **for** two years.
I've **lived** there **for** six months.

How long **have** you **had** a pilot's licence?
I've **had** a pilot's licence **since** 2008.
I've **had** a passport **since** August.

Grammar page 101

2 Grammar practice

a Work with a classmate. Copy and complete the lists with the words below.

six days Tuesday a week ten years
my birthday last year a few minutes
an hour 1999 February

For	**Since**
six days	*Tuesday*

b 2.45 Listen and check.

3 Speaking

a Make notes about yourself.

1 I've lived in my home for 13 years.

1 I've lived in my home for …
2 I've been at this school since …
3 I've known my friend ____ for …
4 I've had my Hot Spot book since …

b Work with a classmate. Take it in turns to ask and answer these questions.

How long have you lived in your home?

For thirteen years.

1 How long have you lived in your home?
2 How long have you been at this school?
3 How long have you known your friend ____?
4 How long have you had your Hot Spot book?

c Report back to the class.

Tomas has lived in his home for thirteen years.

4 Game

a Work in a small team. Write a secret agent's identity. Fill in the form below.

1 Name:	
2 Name of hotel in Sylvania:	
3 Profession:	How long: **for …**
4 Driving licence:	How long: **for …**
5 Address:	How long: **since …**
6 Telephone number:	
7 Passport:	How long: **since …**
8 Favourite food:	

b Exchange identities with another team. Memorise your new identity. Then give back your identity to the other team.

c Now take it in turns to ask and answer questions. You get 1 point for every correct answer.

5 Writing

Write a dialogue between a border guard and a secret agent. Use your secret identity from Activity 4 to help you.

A: What is your full name?
B: My full name is Maria Luisa Gonzales.
A: Where are you staying in Sylvania?
B: I'm staying at the …

6 Check your English

a Work with a classmate. Use your information from Activity 4. Ask and answer.

What is her name?

Maria Luisa Gonzales.

Where is she staying?

At the Queen Hotel.

b Complete these sentences with *for* or *since*.

1 I've had my bag ____ two years.
2 My sister has worked in a shop ____ April.
3 My brother has played football ____ he was six.
4 We have studied English ____ three years.

❷ Grammar practice

a) In pairs, students copy and complete the lists by writing the words in the box under the correct heading: *for* or *since.* Remind students that *for* refers to the general period of time and *since* to the point in time when something started.

b) [2.45] Play the CD for students to check their answers.

Extra activity

Students stand in a line. Name different time expressions, e.g. *last Monday, three hours, January, five minutes.* Students step to the left if the expressions go with *since* and to the right if they go with *for.* If they make a mistake, they are out of the game. Set a time limit of three minutes. Students who remain in the line until the end win the game.

Tapescript and Answer key

For: six days, a week, ten years, a few minutes, an hour
Since: Tuesday, my birthday, last year, 1999, February

Homework suggestions

1 Activity Book pages 54–55, Activities 1–3
2 Students write true sentences with three time expressions from Activity 2, using the present perfect and *for* or *since,* e.g. *I have had my bike since last year.*

PART 2

Introduction

Before class interview one student with *How long have you …?* questions about their hobbies, possessions, home, e.g. *How long have you played the piano/had your own room/ used your own mobile phone?* Ask the student not to tell their classmates about your conversation. In class, write the student's responses on the board, e.g. *He/She has lived in his/ her house … five years.* Do not reveal the student's gender. Students complete the sentences with *for* and *since,* and then guess which of their classmates these sentences are true about.

❸ Speaking

a) Students write true sentences about themselves with the provided sentence beginnings and adding an appropriate time expression.

b) In pairs, students take turns to ask and answer the questions. Before their classmate asks them question 3, they should tell each other the name of the friend they wrote in Activity 3a. Students should memorise or take notes of their classmate's answers.

Extra activity

Ask the first question *How long have you lived in your home?* to one student in the class and say *for* or *since.* The student has to answer truthfully with the word you chose and the appropriate time expression. Then the student asks the same question to another classmate and adds *for* or *since* to use in the answer. Continue with several students and then repeat the procedure with questions 2–4.

c) Individual students report their classmate's answers to the whole class. Go over the example first. If you have a large class, do this activity in groups.

Photocopiable activity

How long have you…? p127; instructions p100

❹ Game

a) Put students into groups of three or four so that there is an even number of teams in the class. Ask them to write a secret agent's identity by filling in the form below. Set a time limit of four minutes.

b) Pair each team with another one. They exchange the identities they wrote about. Each team should imagine that they are secret agents and they need to memorise the details of the new identity they received. Set a time limit of four minutes. Teams should return the notes on the identity to the other team.

c) Teams take turns to ask the other team about their identity and compare the answers with the notes. Team members have 30 seconds to agree on the answer and one of them gives it to the other team. They get one point for each correct answer. Before students begin the task go through the example and review the questions students need to ask about the topics in the form.

❺ Writing

Students write a dialogue modelled on Activity 1 between a border guard and a secret agent. The border guard should ask at least five questions related to some of the topics in the form in Activity 4. Encourage students to use the secret identity from Activity 4 for the secret agent. Go through the example first.

When students have finished, they exchange their notebooks in pairs. They read each other's texts and point out orally any mistakes they notice.

❻ Check your English

a) Pair each student with a classmate they worked with in one group in Activity 4. Students take turns to ask and answer about Maria Luisa Gonzales, using the details from the completed form in Activity 4.

b) Students complete the sentences with *for* or *since* and complete the answers in pairs. Check the answers with the whole class.

Answer key

1 for
2 since
3 since
4 for

Homework suggestions

1 Activity Book page 55, Activities 4–6
2 Students write *How long have you …?* questions with the following prompts: *study/English, know/your teacher, have/ school bag.* Then they answer the questions about themselves with *for* or *since.*

27 My amazing year

Lesson objectives
- Describing recent experiences
- Talking about plans for the future

1 Vocabulary

2.46 Find these things in the pictures.

Malaysian food belt tomato balcony seeds pot

2 Presentation

a 2.47 Listen and read Charlie's web page. Which experience or plan do you think is the most interesting?

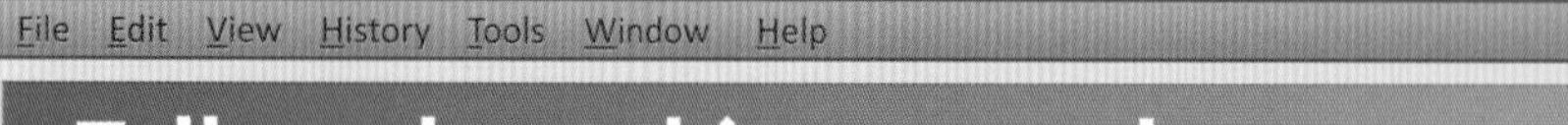

Tell us about this year and next year!

Tell us about some amazing, interesting or unusual things you have done this year. Then tell us about what you're going to do in the future.

My name's Charlie Fisher and I'm thirteen years old.

What have I done this year?

- I've joined a karate club and I've got my orange belt! I started lessons in February – it's hard work but it's also great fun.

- I've eaten Malaysian food. I went to my friend Mel's house last weekend. Mel's mum is from Malaysia and she cooked a typical Malaysian meal with rice, chicken and peanuts. It was delicious!

- I've started guitar lessons. My dad gave me his old guitar. I can play six chords now and I've written a song. Hey – I'm going to be a pop star!

What am I going to do next year?

- I'm going to form a band with some of my friends. Mel's a really good singer and Mike can play drums. We're going to be famous!

- I'm going to learn how to swim. All my friends can swim but I can't. My Uncle Pete's going to teach me how to swim during the summer holidays. I'm a bit scared!
- I'm going to grow some vegetables! We don't have a garden, but I can grow tomatoes in small pots on our balcony. I'm going to plant the seeds next week. Yum! I love tomatoes!

b Listen again. Then match the words in A to the words in B to make phrases from the text.

	A		B
1	join	a	Malaysian food
2	eat	b	how to swim
3	learn	c	some vegetables
4	grow	d	a karate club
5	plant	e	the seeds

27 My amazing year

Grammar
- present perfect; past simple; *going to*

Vocabulary
- experiences; future plans; everyday activities

Optional materials
- objects representing the teacher's experiences this year, e.g. train/plane tickets, cinema/theatre/concert tickets, receipts of interesting purchases, wedding invitations

Optional Activity Book activities
- Fast finishers p72, Extra practice p73

Photocopiable activity
- *How well do you know them?* p128

PART 1

Introduction

Write the current year on the board. Show students objects representing your experiences this year, e.g. train/plane tickets, cinema/theatre/concert tickets, receipts of interesting purchases, wedding invitations, etc. Students study the objects and make guesses about your experiences, e.g. *You have seen STOMP at the theatre.* Tell students if they have guessed correctly and encourage them to ask you questions to find out more about the experiences.

1 Vocabulary

[2.46] Students look at the words in the box and listen as you play the CD. Then they match the words to the pictures. They should make guesses about new vocabulary.

Students work individually on the task and then compare their answers in pairs. Play the CD again and elicit the corresponding pictures. Make sure everybody understands all the words now and drill the pronunciation.

Mixed-ability classes

Fast finishers make their own sentences with two or three words in the box. Elicit their sentences when everyone has finished working on Activity 1.

Teaching tip: *Making associations*

Encourage students to associate something that is familiar to them with new words they are learning. It is useful to make L1 associations and build mental images or draw pictures based on the connections, e.g. in Polish 'pot' means 'sweat' so Polish students can be told to imagine a pot sweating in the sun to remember the word. The more absurd or funnier the associations are the better we remember them.

Tapescript

see Student's Book Activity 1

2 Presentation

a) [2.47] Divide students into groups of four. Encourage them to make guesses about how the words in Activity 1 are connected with Charlie's experiences and plans. Then ask students to listen and read the text on Charlie's website to check their guesses and choose the most interesting experience or plan. Play the CD.

In pairs, students tell each other which experience or plan they find the most interesting.

Tapescript

see Student's Book Activity 2a

b) [2.47] Ask students to listen and read Charlie's website again. Play the CD. Then students match the words in A with the words in B to make phrases from the text describing Charlie's plans and experiences.

Check if students know or can guess the meaning of *peanuts and chords*. Explain any words students still find difficult.

Extra activity

Ask students if they write their answers to online questionnaires like Charlie does in Activity 2. Find out on which websites they post their answers or where they copy the questionnaires from if they post them on their own blogs. Elicit example questions they answer.

Tapescript

see Activity 2a

Answer key

1 d **2** a **3** b **4** c **5** e

❸ Comprehension

Are these sentences true (T) or false (F)? Correct the false sentences.

1 F Charlie started guitar lessons this year.

1 Charlie's going to learn how to play the guitar next year.
2 He's eaten Malaysian food.
3 He's formed a band with his friends.
4 He's going to plant some tomato seeds next week.
5 He's got his orange belt in karate.

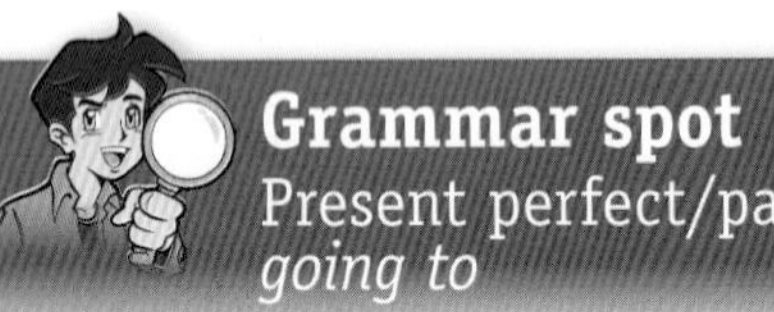

Grammar spot
Present perfect/past simple/*going to*

Present perfect
I've **joined** a karate club.

Past simple
I **started** lessons in February.

***going to* for future plans**
I'**m going to form** a band.

Grammar pages 99, 101, 104

❹ Grammar practice

Read and complete Mel's web page. Put the verbs in brackets into the correct tense: present perfect, past simple or *going to*.

1 I've visited
2 I went

What have I done this year?

- I [1]_____ (visit) my friend, Michelle, in France. I [2]_____ (go) to her house in Montpellier for Easter.
- I [3]_____ (join) the eco-club at school. Last week we [4]_____ (make) a poster about recycling.
- I [5]_____ (start) horse riding lessons. I [6]_____ (have) five lessons in January. They were great!

What am I going to do next year?

- I [7]_____ (stay) with my aunt in Scotland for the summer holidays. She's got a beautiful little cottage in the Highlands.
- I [8]_____ (invite) Michelle to stay with me next month. She's never been to the UK.
- I [9]_____ (learn) how to cook Malaysian food. My mum [10]_____ (teach) me.

❺ Pronunciation

a 2.48 Listen to this tongue twister.

/g/

Gregory's going to grow gorgeous green grapes in his grandfather's garden.

b 2.49 Listen again and repeat. How fast can you say it?

❻ Speaking

a Use the words below to make questions.

1 Have you visited an interesting place this year?

What have you done this year?

1 visit/an interesting place
2 start/violin/riding/piano/karate lessons
3 join/a club
4 eat/some unusual food
5 get/a new pet

b Now ask and answer with a classmate.

Have you visited an interesting place this year?

Yes, I have. I've been to Prague. I went …

My English file

a Write about your year. Describe three unusual, interesting or amazing experiences.
I've learnt how to ski. I went to Kamchatka in Russia with my cousins. I've started …

b Write about three plans for next year.
I'm going to join a football team in my village. I'm going to …

❼ Song

2.50 Find the song *We are the Champions* on page 91.

❽ Check your English

Complete these sentences with the present perfect, the past simple or the *going to* form of the verbs in brackets.

1 Next summer I _____ (start) violin lessons.
2 I _____ (form) a band with my brother. We _____ (play) at our first concert last week.
3 I _____ (get) a new cat tomorrow.
4 We _____ (play) basketball next weekend.

❸ Comprehension

Students read the sentences and decide if they are true or false. They should correct the false sentences. Students compare their answers in pairs before you check them with the whole class.

Answer key

1 false (Charlie started guitar lessons this year) **2** true **3** false (He's going to form a band with his friends next year) **4** true **5** true

Grammar spot

Go over the example sentences to review the present perfect and the past simple to talk about experiences and *going to* for future plans. Elicit when we use the present perfect and when the past simple to talk about experiences. Ask students to find more examples of the two tenses in Activity 2. Refer students to the **Grammar summary** on page 101 and 104 for more information on the tenses in the **Grammar spot**.

❹ Grammar practice

Ask students to read Mel's web page where she answers similar questions to Charlie's in Activity 2. They should complete the gaps with the verbs in brackets in the correct tense: the present perfect, the past simple or *going to*. Students compare their answers in pairs. Check the answers with the whole class and elicit why students used a particular tense in each gap.

Homework suggestions

1. Activity Book page 56, Activities 1–4
2. Students write sentences with the verbs in part A in Activity 2b. They should use different words than in part B of the same activity to make new collocations.

Answer key

1 've visited **2** went **3** 've joined **4** made **5** 've started **6** had **7** 'm going to stay **8** 'm going to invite **9** 's going to learn **10** 's going to teach

PART 2

Introduction

On the board write sentences about your experiences this year and plans for next year in mixed order. Put the verbs in the brackets. Make sure you add relevant time expressions in each sentence, e.g. *I _____ (learn) how to drive next year.* One sentence should be false. Students complete the sentences with the present perfect, the past simple or *going to* and guess which sentence is false about you.

❺ Pronunciation

a) [2.48] Explain that in English the letter *g* can be pronounced within a word as /g/, as in *great*, or /dʒ/, as in *gym*. Encourage students to compare that with their L1. The tongue twister in their books practises words with the /g/ sound. Play the CD and ask students to read the tongue twister in their books.

Tapescript

see Student's Book Activity 5a

b) [2.49] Play the CD again and ask students to repeat it. Then encourage students to practise saying the tongue twister as fast as they can.

Teaching tip: *Mouthing*

Mouthing is a useful technique for correcting pronunciation errors. If you see that students mispronounce a sound in a word, you can mouth the correct pronunciation without making a sound. Do it in an exaggerated way, emphasising the sound that was mispronounced so that students can easily spot the mistake and correct themselves.

❻ Speaking

a) Students use the words in the box to make present perfect questions to ask their classmate about their experiences this year. Go through the example before they begin the task. Set a time limit of five minutes and elicit the correct questions.

b) In pairs, students take turns to ask each other the questions from Activity 6a. If they have done a given activity, encourage them to add more information about the experience, using the past simple. Read out the example with a confident student. Individual students report their classmate's answers to the whole class.

Extra activity

In pairs, students use the same prompts as in Activity 6a to ask each other about their plans for next year, e.g. Are you going to visit an interesting place next year?

My English file

Go through the example and ask students to write about their three unusual, interesting or amazing experiences from this year, using the present perfect and the past simple. Then they write about their three plans for next year.

When students have finished, they exchange their notebooks in pairs. They read each other's texts and point out orally any mistakes they notice. They can ask additional questions about the information in their classmate's text.

❼ Song

[2.50] Refer students to page 91. Ask them to look briefly at the lyrics and play a few seconds of the recording. Find out if students recognise the song and play the CD through.

Explain any words students do not understand. Play the song again, encouraging students to join in singing. Elicit what the song is about and ask students to read the background information.

Tapescript

see lyrics on page 91 of the Student's Book

❽ Check your English

Students complete the sentences with the present perfect, the past simple or the *going to* form of the verbs in brackets. In pairs, students compare their answers. Check the answers with the whole class.

Mixed-ability classes

Encourage less confident students to underline time expressions in the sentences to help them choose the correct tense.

Answer key

1 'm going to start
2 've formed … played
3 'm going to get
4 're going to play

Photocopiable activity

How well do you know them? p128; instructions p100

Homework suggestions

1. Activity Book page 57, Activities 5–6
2. Students write six sentences about interesting experiences and plans of different people they know. They can illustrate the sentences.

28 Amazing places

1 Reading

a 2.51 Listen and read the emails. What are they about?

wonderful homes
interesting buildings in Britain
unusual holiday places
amazing fruits

a

Diana,

Hello from the Pineapple House in Scotland! I've been here for a week and this place is amazing! It's 250 years old and it's got a 23-metre stone pineapple on the roof! You can rent the house for the weekend or for a week. We're having a great time. We've walked around the beautiful gardens, we've visited a castle and tomorrow we're going to take a boat trip.

Carly

b

Hi John,

Brrr! It's cold! I'm in Oymyakon, Russia – the coldest town in the world! It's -50°C today. I've been here since yesterday and it's fantastic! I'm staying with a family in a log cabin. There's a big festival on at the moment. It's called 'The Pole of Cold Festival'. There are fishing competitions, fireworks and music. Tomorrow, I'm going to watch a reindeer race!

Ben

c

Susie,

This is an amazing place! It's a hotel in a cave in Cappadocia, Turkey. We've been here for a week and we've seen some fantastic houses in the caves. My bedroom is more than 1400 years old. It's very beautiful, with stone walls and a big window. We're going to go home tomorrow but I want to come back here next year.

Ursula

b Read again. Find words to match these definitions.

1 Pineapple

1 (email a) a kind of fruit
2 (email a) pay money to stay in a place
3 (email b) a house made of wood
4 (email c) a large hole in the side of a hill

28 Amazing places

Optional materials

- a selection of magazine photos of different types of holiday places; a soft ball/a crumpled newspaper; a dice per group of four

Photocopiable activity

- *Game show* p129

PART 1

Introduction

Ask students to imagine that an international teenage magazine wants to find out which are the best holiday places in their country. In groups of four, students make a list of five places they can recommend. They should take notes to explain why these places are the best. Set a time limit of five minutes. Elicit all the places onto the board and ask students to justify why they are the best. Ask students to vote for the best five from all the places on the board.

1 Reading

a) [2.51] Focus students' attention on the topics in the box. Then ask students to read the emails and decide which topic they are all about. Play the CD.

Elicit that the emails are about unusual holiday places. Ask volunteers for a brief description of the places in the emails. Explain that these are real places and find out if students have ever heard of them or know someone who has visited them.

Extra activity

In groups of four, students talk about the most unusual places they have visited. They should describe the places and the activities they did there.

Tapescript

see Student's Book Activity 1a

b) Ask students to read the definitions and then read the emails again to find the words to match the definitions. In pairs, students compare their answers. Check the answers with the whole class. Clarify any other vocabulary students do not understand.

Answer key

1 pineapple
2 rent
3 log cabin
4 cave

Extra activity

Bring to class a selection of magazine photos of different types of holiday places. Divide students into pairs. Give each pair one photo and ask them not to show it to their classmates. Pairs write a short description of the place in the photo. Set a time limit of five minutes and collect the photos. Stick the photos on the board. Ask pairs to read out their descriptions and encourage the rest of the class to guess which photos these describe.

Cultural information

The Pineapple or the *Dunmore Pineapple* is one of the most remarkable buildings in Scotland. It is located within a walled garden of Dunmore Park near the village of Airth in central Scotland. It was built as a summer house. The pineapple was a common decorative motif in the 18th century. Airth Castle, which dates from the 14th century, is near Dunmore.

Oymyakon is located in Siberia in Russia. In 1926 the temperature of –71.2 °C degrees was recorded, which is the lowest temperature for any permanently inhabited place. In winter, the temperature is often between –50 and –60 °C. Tourists visit Oymyakon and stay with the families in their log cabins to see how people live in such extreme weather conditions.

The Cappadocia region in central Turkey is a natural wonder. Its dramatic landscape with chimney rock formations was shaped by eruptions of volcanoes. For centuries people carved out the volcanic rocks to form houses, churches, monasteries and underground cities which served as hiding places for early Christians. Nowadays a lot of houses in the rocks have been converted to hotels.

❷ Speaking

a Work in small groups. Choose one place from Activity 1 to go on holiday. Why?

I want to go to … because … is more exciting/unusual/interesting than …

I don't like cold weather/hot weather/caves so I'd like to …

b Tell the class about your choice.

We want to go to …

❸ Listening

(2.52) Teri is talking about her holiday plans. Listen then choose the correct words.

1 Teri is going to stay *in a caravan/in a teepee.*
2 A teepee is a kind of *tent/boat.*
3 Teri and her family are going to *go cycling/go horse riding.*
4 In the evenings they're going to cook their food *on a fire/in a stove.*

❹ Writing

a Invent an unusual holiday place. Make notes about these things.

Is it a house/a hotel/a tent?
What can you do during the day?
How old is it?
Is it expensive or cheap?

b Now imagine you are staying in your holiday place. Write an email to a friend.

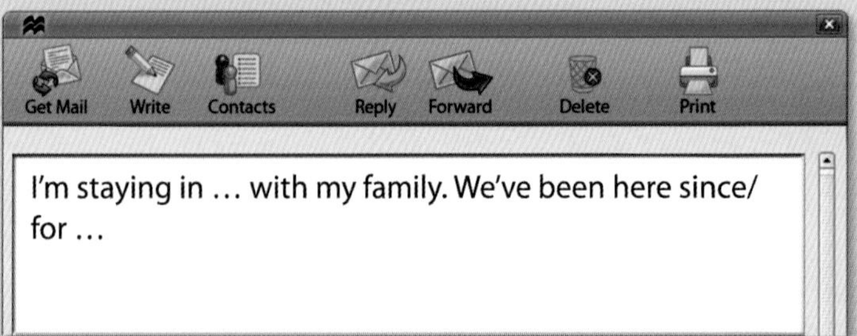

Writing tip

Use adjectives to describe things.

*We've walked around the **beautiful** gardens.*

*I've had some **delicious** hot chocolat*

Talk about it!

Work in small groups. Throw the dice and land on a segment. Talk about that subject for 30 seconds.

❷ Speaking

a) Divide students into groups of three or four. They should discuss the places in Activity 1 and choose one to go on holiday. They should give the reasons behind their choice. Encourage them to use the language in the example.

b) Ask groups to tell the class about their choice and give their reasons.

Homework suggestions

1 Activity Book page 58, Activity 1

2 Students write about a place where they would like to go on holiday. They should write a short description of the place and explain why they would like to go there. They can illustrate their text with drawings or magazine pictures.

PART 2

Introduction

Students stand in a circle. Give them a minute to think about their dream holiday place and one reason they want to go there. Throw a soft ball/a crumpled newspaper to a student and tell them about your dream place, e.g. *I want to go to the Canary islands because I love sunbathing.*

The student memorises your words, throws the ball to another classmate and makes a sentence about their own dream holiday place and so on, until everyone has had a chance to speak. The last student throws the ball back to you. Throw it back, trying to recall his or her words, e.g. *Marek wants to go to Nepal because he loves trekking.* The student then throws the ball back to the person who previously threw it to him and recalls their sentence. Continue until the ball reaches you again.

❸ Listening

[2.52] Students look at the picture and make guesses where Teri is going on holiday. Play the CD for students to check their guesses and ask them to choose the correct words to complete sentences about her plans. Explain any words students do not understand.

In pairs, students compare their answers. Check the answers with the whole class. Find out if students think Teri's holiday plans are fun or not. They should explain their reasons.

Tapescript

For our holiday in August, we're not going to stay in a hotel or in a caravan. We're going to stay in a teepee near the Rocky Mountains in Montana, USA. A teepee is a Native American tent. We're going to stay there for two nights. We're going to go horse riding with real cowboys and we're going to learn about Native American art. In the evenings we're going to cook our food on a fire inside the teepee.

Answer key

1 in a teepee
2 tent
3 go horse riding
4 on a fire

❹ Writing

a) Ask students to invent an unusual place and make notes about it by answering the questions. They can add any other information about the place if they want to.

Mixed-ability classes

You can show less confident students pictures of unusual places in art or architecture publications, e.g. presenting Antonio Gaudi's or Hundertwasser's designs to prompt their ideas.

b) Ask students to imagine that they are staying in their unusual holiday place. They should write an email to their friend based on their notes and using Activity 1 as a model. Before they begin writing, refer them to the **Writing tip** to point out adjectives describing holiday places and experiences. Explain that adjectives make texts more interesting. Encourage students to use the provided adjectives in their texts.

Students make a draft copy first and rewrite it after editing. Monitor their work, providing help. Then they should exchange their texts in pairs. If they notice any mistakes in their classmate's text, they should point these out orally.

Extra activity

Display students' emails around the classroom. Students read all the emails and stand next to the place they would most like to visit based on the description.

Dyslexia tip: *To-do lists*

Organisational tips are particularly helpful to dyslexic students who often get lost while following long instructions. Help them plan and prioritise tasks by encouraging them to make to-do lists to manage more complicated tasks. They can draw pictures of particular steps or write short notes. You can suggest time limits to add to each item, e.g. *1 Think of unusual place* (1 minute).

Talk about it!

Divide students into groups of four and give each group a dice. Each student places their counter, e.g. a badge, on the *Start* square. The student who throws the highest number starts the game. Students take turns to throw the dice and move their counters along the number of squares indicated by the dice. When they land on a *Talk about it!* square, they talk about a given topic for at least thirty seconds. If they finish early, they miss the next turn. When they land on other squares, they move forward or miss their turn as told. The first person to reach the end is the winner. Demonstrate the task with a confident student first.

Photocopiable activity

Game show p129; instructions p101

Homework suggestions

1 Activity Book page 58, Activity 2

2 Students make sentences about places they have visited or their experiences with all the adjectives in the **Writing tip**.

Module 7 Review

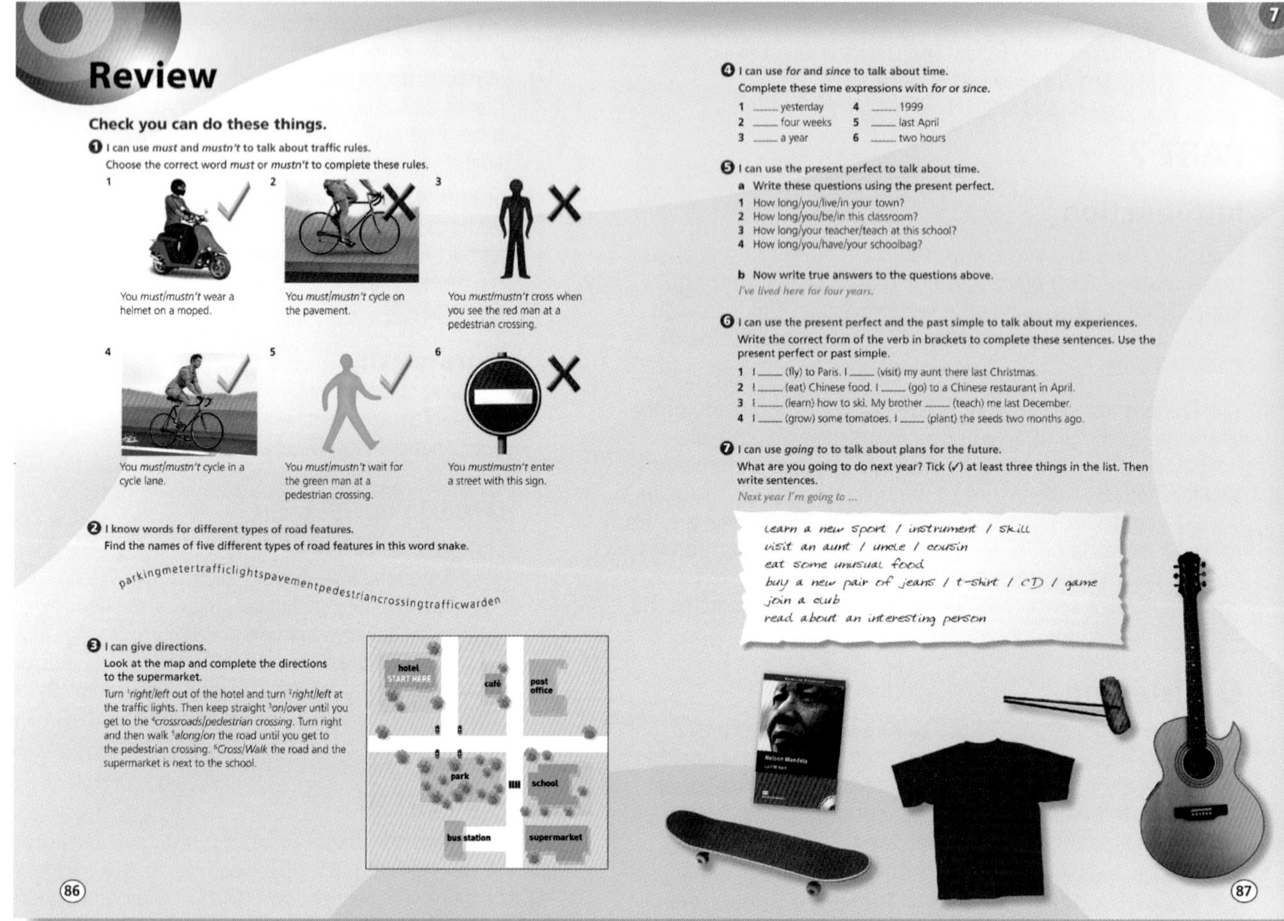

Review

Check you can do these things.

1 I can use *must* and *mustn't* to talk about traffic rules.
Choose the correct word *must* or *mustn't* to complete these rules.

1 You *must/mustn't* wear a helmet on a moped.
2 You *must/mustn't* cycle on the pavement.
3 You *must/mustn't* cross when you see the red man at a pedestrian crossing.
4 You *must/mustn't* cycle in a cycle lane.
5 You *must/mustn't* wait for the green man at a pedestrian crossing.
6 You *must/mustn't* enter a street with this sign.

2 I know words for different types of road features.
Find the names of five different types of road features in this word snake.

parkingmetertrafficlightspavementpedestriancrossingtrafficwarden

3 I can give directions.
Look at the map and complete the directions to the supermarket.

Turn [1]*right/left* out of the hotel and turn [2]*right/left* at the traffic lights. Then keep straight [3]*on/over* until you get to the [4]*crossroads/pedestrian crossing*. Turn right and then walk [5]*along/on* the road until you get to the pedestrian crossing. [6]*Cross/Walk* the road and the supermarket is next to the school.

4 I can use *for* and *since* to talk about time.
Complete these time expressions with *for* or *since*.

1 ___ yesterday
2 ___ four weeks
3 ___ a year
4 ___ 1999
5 ___ last April
6 ___ two hours

5 I can use the present perfect to talk about time.

a Write these questions using the present perfect.

1 How long/you/live/in your town?
2 How long/you/be/in this classroom?
3 How long/your teacher/teach at this school?
4 How long/you/have/your schoolbag?

b Now write true answers to the questions above.

I've lived here for four years.

6 I can use the present perfect and the past simple to talk about my experiences.
Write the correct form of the verb in brackets to complete these sentences. Use the present perfect or past simple.

1 I ___ (fly) to Paris. I ___ (visit) my aunt there last Christmas.
2 I ___ (eat) Chinese food. I ___ (go) to a Chinese restaurant in April.
3 I ___ (learn) how to ski. My brother ___ (teach) me last December.
4 I ___ (grow) some tomatoes. I ___ (plant) the seeds two months ago.

7 I can use *going to* to talk about plans for the future.
What are you going to do next year? Tick (✓) at least three things in the list. Then write sentences.

Next year I'm going to …

learn a new sport / instrument / skill
visit an aunt / uncle / cousin
eat some unusual food
buy a new pair of jeans / t-shirt / CD / game
join a club
read about an interesting person

86 87

Optional revision

Before your students start this Review, you may want to direct them to the **Grammar summary** at the back of their coursebooks and to the **Word lists** at the back of their Activity Books. This will remind them of the main grammar and vocabulary in the module. Give them ten minutes to read through those in small groups and ask you any questions they may have.

- Activity Book: Refer your students to pages 85–86: *On the road*; *Other nouns*; *Prepositions*; *Nationalities*; *Places*
- **Grammar summary**: Refer your students to pages 101, 104 and 105

Module 7 Review

The purpose of this section is revision and consolidation of the material studied in Module 7.

Completing the activities

Go over all the activities with the class, explaining rubrics and giving examples to make sure students know what to do. There are written and oral tasks, but you may decide yourself how they should be completed by students. Generally students should do the writing tasks individually and the oral tasks in pairs, testing each other's knowledge. Make sure they do not treat the *Review* as a formal test, but complete the activities in a friendly, stress-free atmosphere. Fast finishers can write down the answers to the oral tasks.

Checking answers

When students have finished, check the answers with the whole class by asking volunteers to copy their answers onto the board or to say them aloud. If necessary, explain the more difficult issues, ask additional questions about the activities and solve any problems that arise.

Self-evaluation

Tell students to evaluate themselves. They should tick the activities where at least half of their answers were correct.

Feedback

Ask students which activities were difficult, which were easy and if there is anything they would like to review. Make a note of common language problems to go over in future lessons.

Answer key

❶ **1** must
2 mustn't
3 mustn't
4 must
5 must
6 mustn't

❷ Students find names of five types of road features in the word snake. Point out that some of the features are made of two words.

parking meter, traffic lights, pavement, pedestrian crossing, traffic warden

❸ **1** right
2 left
3 on
4 crossroads
5 along
6 Cross

❹ **1** since
2 for
3 for
4 since
5 since
6 for

❺ **a)** **1** How long have you lived in your town?
2 How long have you been in this classroom?
3 How long has your teacher taught at this school?
4 How long have you had your schoolbag?

b) Students write their own true answers to the questions in Activity 5a. They should ask you an appropriate question in English to find the answer to question 3 if they do not know it.

❻ **1** have flown … visited
2 have eaten … went
3 have learnt … taught
4 have grown … planted

❼ Students choose three plans from the list and write sentences about them with *going to.*

Dyslexia tip: *Providing answers to exercises*

It is beneficial for dyslexic students to receive printed answers to exercises. They may have troubles reading the answers from the board and a printed key can be placed next to the relevant activities, limiting visual discomfort. The key makes self-checking easier, because checking answers with the whole class may go too fast for dyslexic students to be able to spot and analyse their own mistakes.

Extra activity

Ask two volunteers to leave the room. The rest of the class should stand in the circle. Explain the rules of the game: when asked a question, each student should answer as the classmate on their left would. If they do not know how this person would answer to a given question, they should say: *I don't know.* Invite the volunteers back to the classroom. They should ask their classmates any questions they want and try to work out the rules of the game.

Module 7 Tests (A and B) are on the Tests CD

Teaching tips: *Correcting tests*

When students receive their marked tests, they focus on the marks rather than on their mistakes. To make students analyse their answers, on the lesson following the test give them more difficult tasks from the test to review in small groups. Once they have discussed the task, tell them the correct answers and give them their corrected tests. They should now understand their mistakes more easily, having had an opportunity to work through them with their classmates.

Learning diary

You can refer students to page 59 of the Activity Book for further review, more study tips and self-assessment activities.

Extra special

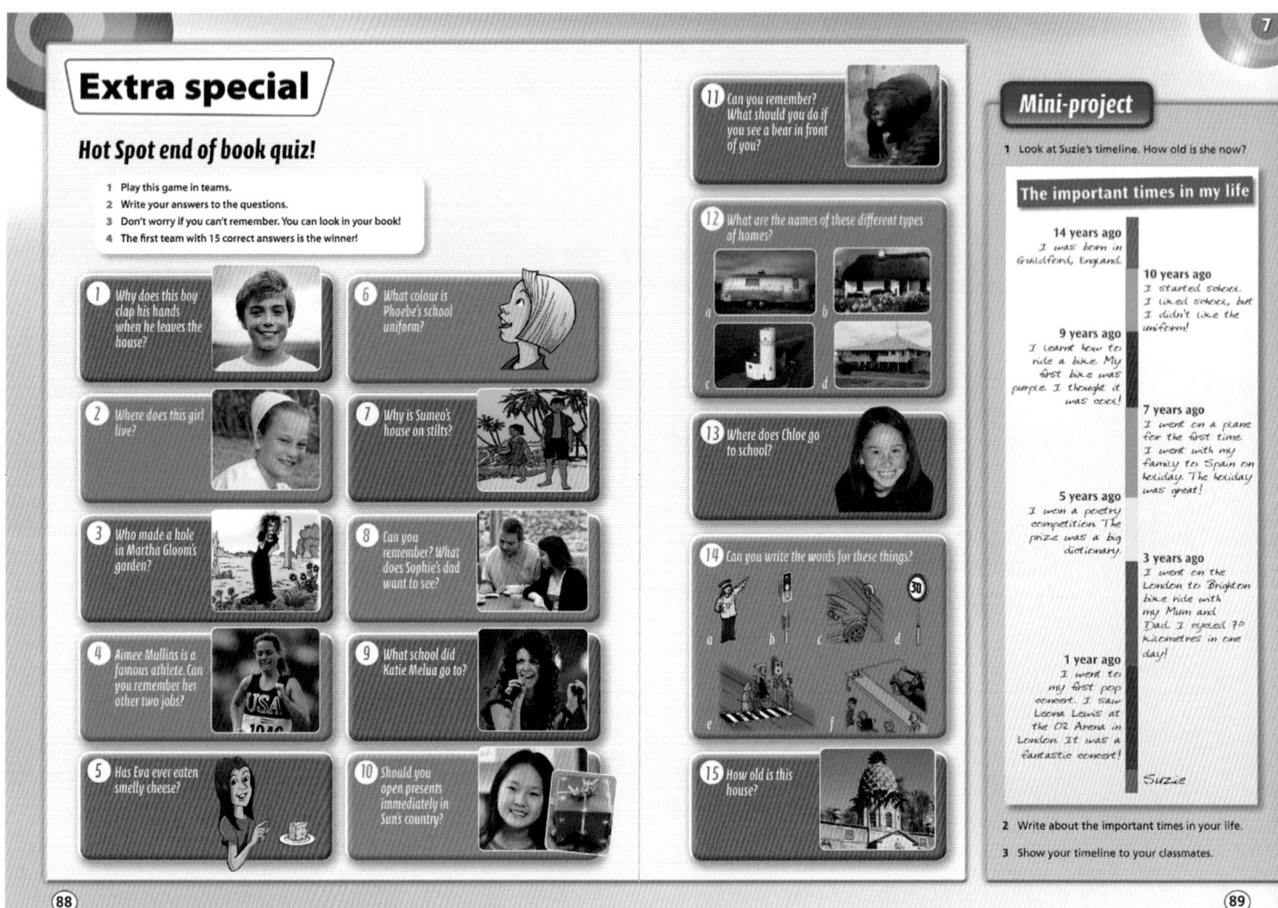
Extra special

Hot Spot end of book quiz!

1 Play this game in teams.
2 Write your answers to the questions.
3 Don't worry if you can't remember. You can look in your book!
4 The first team with 15 correct answers is the winner!

1 Why does this boy clap his hands when he leaves the house?

2 Where does this girl live?

3 Who made a hole in Martha Gloom's garden?

4 Aimee Mullins is a famous athlete. Can you remember her other two jobs?

5 Has Eva ever eaten smelly cheese?

6 What colour is Phoebe's school uniform?

7 Why is Sumeo's house on stilts?

8 Can you remember? What does Sophie's dad want to see?

9 What school did Katie Melua go to?

10 Should you open presents immediately in Sun's country?

11 Can you remember? What should you do if you see a bear in front of you?

12 What are the names of these different types of homes? a b c d

13 Where does Chloe go to school?

14 Can you write the words for these things? a b c d e f

15 How old is this house?

88

7

Mini-project

1 Look at Suzie's timeline. How old is she now?

The important times in my life

14 years ago I was born in Guildford, England.

10 years ago I started school. I liked school, but I didn't like the uniform!

9 years ago I learnt how to ride a bike. My first bike was purple. I thought it was cool!

7 years ago I went on a plane for the first time. I went with my family to Spain on holiday. The holiday was great!

5 years ago I won a poetry competition. The prize was a big dictionary.

3 years ago I went on the London to Brighton bike ride with my Mum and Dad. I cycled 70 kilometres in one day!

1 year ago I went to my first pop concert. I saw Leona Lewis at the O2 Arena in London. It was a fantastic concert!

Suzie

2 Write about the important times in your life.

3 Show your timeline to your classmates.

89

Optional materials
- one slip of paper and one sheet of A4 paper per each student

Hot Spot end of book quiz

Go over the rules with the whole class. Divide students into groups of three or four and ask them to choose a team secretary to note down their answers.

Ask team secretaries to write numbers 1–15 in a vertical column on a sheet of paper. When you say *Start,* teams begin reading questions and looking for the answers. Secretaries write the answers next to the numbers of the corresponding questions.

When students from one team have finished, they give you their answers. Go over these as quickly as you can. If you notice wrong answers, hand the answer sheet back for the team to correct. The winner is the first team with 15 correct answers.

Answer key

1 He does this because bears usually walk away when they hear humans
2 In the USA
3 Bonehead
4 An actress and a model
5 No, she hasn't
6 Purple
7 Because sometimes the sea floods his island
8 Shakespeare's play (Romeo and Juliet)
9 The Brit School
10 No, you shouldn't. People think it's very rude
11 You should speak to the bear in a quiet voice and walk away
12 caravan, cottage, lighthouse, ranch
13 She doesn't go to school. Her parents teach her at home
14 a) traffic warden
b) traffic lights
c) parking meter
d) traffic sign
e) pedestrian crossing
f) cycle lane
15 250 years old

Extra activity

Ask students to look through their books. Give each student a slip of paper to write one task or question connected with what they studied this year, e.g. *Name five musical instruments; What should you do when you are lost in the jungle?* They must know the answer and they should not repeat any questions from the quiz above. Students mingle and take turns to ask a classmate their question, helping them with the answer if necessary. Then they swap their slips of paper and ask the new question to another student. Continue the game for five minutes.

Mini-project

1. Explain to students that a girl called Suzie has made a timeline with important times in her life. Ask students to read her project and find out how old she is. Clarify any vocabulary in the project if necessary. Elicit that Suzie is 14 years old. Point out that Suzie used the past simple to talk about past events.
2. Students make their own timeline with the important times in their life, using the past simple to describe details. You can write the following topics on the board to prompt their ideas: *school, competitions, holidays, concerts, theatres, theme parks, brothers and sisters, moving house.* They should write about at least six important times. Encourage them to make a draft copy first. Monitor their work and provide help if necessary.
3. In groups of six, students present their projects and answer any questions that their classmates may have about their timelines.

Dyslexia tip: *Proofreading*

Encourage dyslexic students to write at the back of their notebook a list of issues they should pay attention to when proofreading, e.g. capital letters, punctuation, spelling, omissions (especially the *-es* ending in 3rd person singular in the present simple, *am/is/are* in the present continuous/ *going to* and *have/has* in the present perfect). They should look at the list when they are proofreading their written tasks to remind themselves what typical mistakes they should be looking for.

Extra activity

Ask students to sit in a circle. Give each student a sheet of A4 paper and ask them to sign their name at the top and pass the paper to the person on their left. Students should write in English a present they would like to give the person whose page they are holding, e.g. *a plane ticket to Australia, a racing car, a house at the seaside.* They can illustrate their presents. Then they pass the page to the person on their left. Students continue the activity until they receive their own page back. Ask students to report to the class which presents they received are the best.

Grammar summary key

1 Present simple

1 *Do you read a lot of books?*
2 *Do your friends live near you?*
3 *Does it snow a lot in your country?*
4 *Does your teacher give you a lot of homework?*
5 *Do you like chocolate?*

2 Present continuous

Students' own answers

3 Possessive pronouns

1 *This is yours.*
2 *This is his.*
3 *This is mine.*
4 *These are ours.*
5 *These are theirs.*
6 *This is hers.*

4 Comparatives and superlatives

Students' own answers

5 Past simple

1 *Did you meet your friends last weekend?*
2 *Did you watch TV last night?*
3 *Did you swim in the sea last year?*
4 *Did you go to bed early yesterday?*
5 *Did you make your bed this morning?*

Students' own answers

6 Past continuous

1 *Ben wasn't watching TV.*
2 *They were eating.*
3 *Kate was not standing up.*
4 *They were not doing their homework.*
5 *They were not drinking cola.*
6 *Kate was watching TV.*
7 *Ben was reading a magazine.*

Students' own answers

7 Past continuous and past simple

1 *He was skateboarding when he fell over.*
2 *We were having a picnic when it started to rain.*
3 *They were swimming when they saw a shark.*
4 *I was looking out the window when it began to snow.*
5 *She was telling a joke when the teacher came into the classroom.*

8 Present perfect

1 *Have you ever gone skiing?*
2 *Have you ever ridden a horse?*
3 *Have you ever flown in a plane?*
4 *Have you ever met a famous person?*
5 *Have you ever broken your leg?*

1 *I've just heard a funny story.*
2 *I've just eaten lots of sweets.*
3 *I've just lost my purse.*
4 *I've just been on a long walk.*

1 *for*
2 *since*
3 *for*
4 *since*
5 *for*

9 Future predictions with *will*

1 *I think it'll snow tomorrow.*
2 *I think I'll buy a CD.*
3 *I think we'll/they'll win the match.*
4 *I think I'll make a cake.*
5 *I think I'll be a scientist.*

10 *can, could, I'll* (requests, offers)

1 *I'll get you a drink.*
2 *Can you close the door, please?*
3 *Could you pass me the pen?*
4 *I'll open the window.*

11 Making suggestions

1 *How about*
2 *Let's*
3 *Would you like to*
4 *Let's*
5 *How about*

12 First conditional

1 *If it rains, I won't go out.*
2 *If you go to bed early, you won't be tired tomorrow.*
3 *If we don't run, we won't catch the bus.*
4 *If I go out, I'll do some shopping.*
5 *If you don't study, you won't pass the exam.*
6 *If it's sunny, I'll go to the beach.*

13 *may* (possibility)

1 *It may rain tomorrow.*
2 *My friend may phone me.*
3 *I may not go to school today.*
4 *We may go on holiday this summer.*
5 *I may buy some new jeans.*

14 *should, shouldn't* (obligation and advice)

1 *You should do your homework.*
2 *You shouldn't eat in the classroom.*
3 *You shouldn't shout.*
4 *You should listen to your teacher.*
5 *You should/shouldn't write in your course book.*

15 *going to*

1 *She's going to throw the ball.*
2 *They're going to sit down.*
3 *He's going to kick the ball.*
4 *They're going to play tennis.*

16 Determiners

1 *Please be quiet. You are making too much noise.*
2 *My sister doesn't go to school. She's not old enough.*
3 *I'm hungry. I didn't eat enough breakfast.*
4 *My bag is heavy. There are too many books in it.*
5 *I'm not going swimming. It's not warm enough.*

17 Present passive

1 *Football is played all around the world.*
2 *Cheese is made from milk.*
3 *Grapes are grown in Spain and Italy.*
4 *Bridges are built from steel.*
5 *This key is used a lot.*

18 *must, mustn't* (obligation)

1 *You're very ill. You must see a doctor.*
2 *I'm tired. I must go to bed.*
3 *We are bored. We must do something exciting.*
4 *Your room is untidy. You must tidy it.*
5 *I'm having a party. You must come to it.*
6 *We're late for school. We must run.*

Resource section
Photocopiable worksheets

Teacher's instructions 92

Photocopiable worksheets 102

Module 1
Lesson 1 *Getting to know you* 102
Lesson 2 *Plans* 103
Lesson 3 *Clothes* 104
Lesson 4 *What's my word?* 105

Module 2
Lesson 5 *Last week* 106
Lesson 6 *Find out the truth* 107
Lesson 7 *The missing bag* 108
Lesson 8 *Famous people* 109

Module 3
Lesson 9 *Experiences* 110
Lesson 10 *Do you know anybody who ...?* 111
Lesson 11 *What's just happened?* 112
Lesson 12 *Interesting stories* 113

Module 4
Lesson 13 *The future* 114
Lesson 14 *Problems and solutions* 115
Lesson 15 *Youth club* 116
Lesson 16 *Two schools* 117

Module 5
Lesson 17 *Telepathy* 118
Lesson 18 *What may happen?* 119
Lesson 19 *Dear Teen Dreams* 120
Lesson 20 *Survival kit* 121

Module 6
Lesson 21 *What am I going to do?* 122
Lesson 22 *Complaints* 123
Lesson 23 *Plastic bags* 124
Lesson 24 *Families* 125

Module 7
Lesson 25 *Rules* 126
Lesson 26 *How long have you ...?* 127
Lesson 27 *How well do you know them?* 128
Lesson 28 *Game show* 129

Module 1
Lesson 1
Getting to know you

Type of activity: Survey
Organization: Whole class work
Time: 15 minutes
Preparation: Make one copy of the worksheet for up to 15 students and cut into slips as indicated.
To use: After Activity 7

Instructions

- Tell students that they are going to do a survey to find out more about their classmates. Give each student one question on a slip of paper. If there are more than 15 students in the class, make two copies of the worksheet and give some students the same questions.
- Students first decide which word is missing: *is, are* or *do*. You can write the words on the board. Students should not write anything. Elicit the missing words from each student individually.
- Students get up and mingle, asking their question to one classmate and then answering theirs. They should listen to the question asked and try to remember the answer they were given. Then they swap the questions and repeat the procedure with a different classmate and the new question. They need to remember to say the missing word in their new question.
- Students should not worry if they get some questions twice, but continue playing the game. Set a time limit of 5 minutes and then ask students to sit down in pairs and reveal which interesting things they found out about the classmates they interviewed.
- A few volunteers can report their findings to the whole class. Alternatively, if the class is not big, point to each student in turn and ask their classmates to recall this person's answers to different questions.

Module 1
Lesson 2
Plans

Type of activity: Guessing game
Organization: Pair work
Time: 15 minutes
Preparation: Copy one worksheet per pair of students and cut into A and B.
To use: After Activity 4

Instructions

- Divide the class into pairs. Give a copy of Worksheet A to Student A and Worksheet B to Student B in each pair.
- Ask students to think of their real plans for next week, these can be activities they do regularly, e.g. football practice on Mondays and Wednesdays, family dinner on Sunday or typical everyday activities. They should think of one activity for each day of the week and write it in a single word in the appropriate column in the table, e.g. *football, dinner, homework, Internet* etc. Explain that the word should be a noun, not a verb.
- Students exchange their worksheets in pairs and try to guess on the basis of the single words what their classmate's plans are. They should write the plans in full sentences in the present continuous in the appropriate column, e.g. *You're watching football on TV.*
- When they have finished, they show each other the sentences and confirm if their classmate guessed their plans correctly, e.g. *No, I'm not. I'm playing football.*
- Ask students to count how many plans they have guessed correctly.

Follow up

Put students in different pairs and ask them to tell each other from memory what the classmate they worked with previously is doing next week, e.g. *Zosia is having dinner with her family on Sunday.*

Module 1
Lesson 3
Clothes

Type of activity: Matching game
Organization: Pair work
Time: 15 minutes
Preparation: Copy one worksheet per student.
To use: After Activity 6

Instructions

- Give each student a copy of the worksheet. Divide the class into pairs.
- Ask students to work together and match the words and the clothes in the picture. All the names of the clothes come from *Hot Spot* Book 1. Set a time limit of 5 minutes. Check the answers with the whole class, drilling the pronunciation of the words if necessary.
- In pairs, students choose one symbol each: X or 0. They use the grid on one of the worksheets. They take it in turns to choose a square and make a true sentence about the clothes in the picture in Activity 1 with the word/s from the square, e.g. if they choose *more comfortable,* they can say: *These boots are more comfortable than these shoes.* If the sentence is grammatically correct, the student can put their symbol on the square. The first student to place three of their symbols in one row horizontally, vertically or diagonally is the winner. Students can play the second round with the unused grid on the other worksheet.

Module 1
Lesson 4
What's my word?

Type of activity: Team game
Organization: Group/class work
Time: 20 minutes
Preparation: Copy one worksheet and cut into cards.
To use: After Activity 4b

Instructions

- Explain that students are going to play a game where they try to guess words from definitions. All the words are related to the topic of pets. Write example phrases on the board e.g. *It's made of ... ; It's an animal which ... ; It's something you do when ... ; It's the opposite of ... ; It's a thing which ... .*
- Divide the class into two teams: A and B. One person from each team comes to the front of the classroom. Show both the students a random word from the set so that no one else can see it. Explain that they are going to make their teams guess the word by giving one-sentence definitions. They cannot make gestures or noises to help them define the word.
- The student from Team A gives a definition, e.g. *It's made of metal,* if the card reads *cage.* Team A has 10 seconds to guess the word. If they fail, the student from Team B gives another definition to Team B and so on. When the word is guessed or no one guesses after four sentences, then two different students define the next word. Team B begins the second round.
- Teams get 4 points if they guess the word after the first sentence, 3 points after the second, 2 points after the third, 1 point after the fourth. Keep the score on the board. The winner is the team with more points at the end of the game.
- If you do not want all team members to call out their guesses at once, you can appoint a captain of each team to give their team's answers.

Module 2
Lesson 5
Last week

Type of activity: Speaking
Organization: Group work
Time: 20 minutes
Preparation: Copy one worksheet per group of three and cut the squares with words into cards.
To use: After Activity 5

Instructions

- Divide the class into groups of three. Give each group a set of cards and a scoring table. Students spread the cards face down on their desk.
- Students take it in turns to pick a card and use the word on it in a positive sentence in the past simple about what they or somebody they know did last week, e.g. if they pick *break,* they can say *Last week my brother broke his leg.* The sentence can be true or false. They have 30 seconds to make a sentence.
- If the sentence is correct, they get two points. Then the other group members try to guess if the sentence is true or false. Encourage them to discuss the sentence in English, e.g. *I think it's false, because I saw your brother this morning and he was okay.* Each person who guesses correctly gets one point. Ask the groups to keep the score on the scoring table.
- If the sentence is incorrect, the student who made it places the card face down on the desk among other unused cards.
- Students take turns moving clockwise round the group, i.e. Student A makes a sentence, then Student B makes a guess and then Student C makes their guess, which can be the same as Student B's. In the next round Student B makes a sentence and Student C and Student A make guesses.
- The winner is the person with the most points when all the cards have been used.

Module 2
Lesson 6
Find out the truth

Type of activity: Survey
Organization: Group work
Time: 20 minutes
Preparation: Copy one worksheet per group of up to ten and cut into cards.
To use: After Activity 4

Instructions

- Review telling the time with the class. Remind students that when we use the 12-hour clock we use *a.m.* before noon and *p.m.* after noon.
- Divide the class into groups of up to ten students. Give each group a set of cards.
- Ask each student to pick a card and read the statement on it. Their task is to check if this statement is true about their group. In order to do that, they first have to make a question about the statement to ask their group members, e.g. *Were you watching TV at 7.30 p.m. yesterday?* Monitor their work, providing help.
- Then students get up and mingle, asking their question to everybody in their group. The person asked needs to reply with *Yes, I was/ No, I wasn't.* If the answer is *No, I wasn't,* they have to explain what they were really doing at the time, e.g. *I was visiting my aunt.* Encourage students to note down how many people were doing the activity and what other things their classmates were doing. Set a time limit of 10 minutes for this activity.
- Ask students to report their findings to the class, e.g. *It's false. Only four people were watching TV at 7.30 p.m. yesterday.* Ask them to give examples of what other classmates were doing at that time. If you have a large class, pair students from different groups and ask them to report their findings.

Module 2
Lesson 7
The missing bag

Type of activity: Story
Organization: Group work
Time: 20 minutes
Preparation: Copy one worksheet per group of four and cut into the picture cards, the word cards and the story.
To use: After Activity 5

Instructions

- Explain that students are going to listen to a true story. Pre-teach any vocabulary from the story your students may not understand.
- Divide students into groups of four. Give each group a mixed set of picture cards to spread on their desk. Give them one minute to study the pictures. Slowly read out the story from the story card. Students try to put the pictures in the correct order as they are listening. Read the story again for students to check the order of the pictures. Check the answers with the whole class.
- Give each group a set of word cards. Read out the story again and ask students to put the words in the correct order as they appear in the story. Explain that not all words from the story are on the word cards. Read out the story again and check the answers.
- Within their groups, students try to retell the story with the help of the picture cards and the word cards. They do not need to recreate the original version word by word, but they should use all the word cards. Students take turns to make a sentence each and their group members provide help. When they have finished, give them the story card to compare.

Variation

You could ask students to write the story and then compare with the text on the story card.

Module 2
Lesson 8
Famous people

Type of activity: Role play
Organization: Group/pair work
Time: 20 minutes
Preparation: Copy one worksheet per group of six and cut into six cards.
To use: After Activity 4

Instructions

- Divide the class into six groups of equal size and hand each group a set of the same role cards, one card per member of the group, e.g. the first group gets 1A cards, the second 1B and so on. If the groups are not equal, hand the reporter cards (A cards) to the larger groups.
- Students read the information on their cards. Ask students holding A cards to work with their group and write five questions they would like to ask the famous person about the adventure they had, and also personal information. Elicit a few sample questions, e.g. *How did you feel? What did you see there?*
- Explain that students with B cards are going to be interviewed, so they need to be ready to answer questions. They should make notes using *however, but, as well, because* to link ideas. Set a time limit of 8 minutes for preparation.
- Pair students who have 1A, 2A, 3A cards with students who have 1B, 2B, 3B cards respectively. If there are more with A cards, ask students with B cards to work with two reporters. Ask the reporters to do their interview.
- Ask a reporter from each situation to tell you about their interviewee.

Follow up

Each interviewee works with a reporter that interviewed them to write a short article about the famous person, linking sentences with *however, but, as well, because.*

Module 3
Lesson 9
Experiences

Type of activity: Questionnaire
Organization: Pair work
Time: 10 minutes
Preparation: Copy one worksheet per student.
To use: After Activity 4

Instructions

- Give each student a copy of the worksheet. Pre-teach any vocabulary from the questionnaire your students may not know. Ask them to complete the questions in the first column with the present perfect form of the verb. Set a time limit of 2 minutes.
- Check the answers with the whole class. Then divide students into pairs and explain that they are going to find out about various experiences in each other's lives. Students read the questions and write their own true answers in the second column. They then guess their friend's answers and complete the third column. They should not show their questionnaire to each other. Allow 5 minutes for this activity.
- Students then ask each other the questions to check their guesses. Encourage them to respond with *Yes, I have,* or *No, I haven't.* Students give themselves one point for each correct guess and write the score in the last column.
- Find out who scored the most points in the class. Ask a few students to report to the class which of their friend's experiences they found the most surprising.

Module 3
Lesson 10
Do you know anybody who ...?

Type of activity: Speaking
Organization: Whole class work
Time: 15 minutes
Preparation: Make enough copies of the worksheet so that there are two cards per student. Cut the worksheets into cards.
To use: After Activity 3

Instructions

- Explain that students are going to interview their classmates about people they know who have had unusual experiences.
- Put the mixed cards on your desk. Students get up and pick a card each. They mingle and ask their first question on the card, e.g. *Do you know anybody who has ridden a horse?* to their classmates until someone answers *Yes*. This student should then say who the person is, e.g. *my brother,* and add at least two details, using the past simple, e.g. *He rode a horse at the zoo last summer and he liked it a lot.*
- You can write questions on the board to help students decide what they can say about the experience: *When and where did he/she do it? How did he/she feel about it?*
- On their cards students should note down the details.
- Set a time limit of 6 minutes. If anyone finishes early, they can pick another card from your desk.
- Students report what they have found out to the whole class. If you have a large class, do this part of the activity in groups.

Variation

Students do the task in pairs. Cut the worksheet in half so that each student has five questions. Students ask and answer the questions to each other.

Module 3
Lesson 11
What's just happened?

Type of activity: Finding the differences
Organization: Pair work
Time: 15 minutes
Preparation: Copy one worksheet per pair of students and cut into Worksheet A and B.
To use: After *My English File*

Instructions

- Divide the class into pairs. Give a copy of Worksheet A to Student A and Worksheet B to Student B in each pair. They should not look at each other's worksheets.
- Explain that the children in the picture are on a school trip. Ask: *Where are they?* (In Paris); *How do you know?* (Because we can see the Eiffel Tower); *Have you been to Paris? Did you like it?*
- Students A and B take it in turns to tell each other what the children in their pictures have just done. Make sure they use the present perfect. They need to find 5 differences between their pictures. If necessary, pretend to be Student A and have a sample dialogue with any Student B, e.g. *Allison has just eaten a banana./ No, she hasn't. She has just eaten an apple.*
- Allow 6 minutes for this task and let students show each other their worksheets to compare the pictures at the end. Check the answers with the whole class by getting different students to make sentences showing the differences.

Extension

- Ask students to imagine that they are on the school trip together with the children in the picture and they are sitting in front of the laptop in the corner and emailing their parents about what has just happened around them. They can write the email individually or in pairs.

Module 3
Lesson 12
Interesting stories

Type of activity: Card game
Organization: Group work
Time: 20 minutes
Preparation: Copy one worksheet per group of four students and cut into cards.
To use: After *Picture quiz*

Instructions

- Divide the class into groups of four and give each group a set of cards to place face down on their desk.
- Students take it in turns (clockwise) to pick a card and ask the question on it to one of their group members. They should choose a student whose answer they genuinely do not know. The person asked has to speak for at least 20 seconds, by replying to the question truthfully and giving additional details, e.g. if they were asked: *What's the most unusual food you've eaten?* they can say: *The most unusual food I've eaten was bread pudding. I ate it in Scotland when I was visiting my cousin. Bread pudding is a type of dessert ... .*
- When they have finished speaking, other team members can ask them additional questions if they want to find out more about the experience.
- Students continue the activity until there are no cards left. Encourage groups to report the most interesting experiences to the whole class.

Module 4

Lesson 13 The future

Type of activity: Questionnaire
Organization: Pair/class work
Time: 20 minutes
Preparation: Copy one worksheet per student.
To use: After *My English file*

Instructions

- Give each student a copy of the worksheet. Ask them to close their eyes and imagine themselves in the year 2025. Allow 30 seconds for this and then ask students to read the questions and make predictions about their life in 2025. They should write their answers in note form in the second column. Set a time limit of 3 minutes.
- Ask students to mingle and find a classmate to ask questions about their predictions. They write this student's name in the third column and note down their answers below. Encourage students to explain their answers in a simple way, e.g. *I think I will live in the USA, because I speak English and I have family in New York.*
- When students have interviewed one person and answered their questions, they repeat the activity with another student.
- Set a time limit of 15 minutes.
- Ask students to read through their notes and repeat the most interesting predictions to the whole class.

Module 4

Lesson 14 Problems and solutions

Type of activity: Speaking
Organization: Group work
Time: 15 minutes
Preparation: Copy one worksheet per group of three and cut into cards.
To use: After Activity 4

Instructions

- Divide the class into groups of three. Place a set of cards with problems face down on the desk in front of each group.
- One student picks a card and reads out 'their' problem to the other group members, e.g. *I'm very hungry.* The group members have to each make a different offer with *I will*, e.g. *I'll make a sandwich for you; I'll take you to a restaurant.* Ask them to imagine that they have a lot of money and skills, so that they can be creative. The student who read out the problem chooses their favourite offer and hands the card to the student who made it. Then it is another student's turn.
- The game ends when there are no problems left. The winner is the student with the most cards in each group.

Variation

Divide students into groups of six and give each one a set of problems. One student in each group is the leader. They should read the first problem and other group members have 30 seconds to write the most obvious solution to the problem, using *I will.* The leader watches the time and when it is up, the others read out their offers. Each grammatically correct offer gets one point and students get an extra point for each group member who has written an identical offer. Groups repeat for the other problems. The winner is the person with most points at the end.

Module 4

Lesson 15 Youth club

Type of activity: Role play and discussion
Organization: Group work
Time: 20 minutes
Preparation: Copy one worksheet per group of four and cut into the question card and role cards.
To use: After Activity 5b

Instructions

- Divide the class into groups of four. Give each group a question card and distribute the role cards at random among the group members. Each group needs a watch.
- Students read the instructions on the question card together and then study their role cards. Explain any words they may not know. Make sure they understand that they all need to make suggestions as well as play their roles.
- When students are ready, they begin their discussion. Allow 15 minutes for the task. Monitor their work, making sure students remember to act out their roles.
- When the time is up, ask the groups' secretaries to report on the results of the discussion to the whole class.

Extension

Within the same groups, students make a project based on the results of their discussion. They draw and colour the new youth club on a large piece of paper, labelling the furniture and the equipment. Below the drawing they can write suggestions for the club's weekly programme.

Module 4
Lesson 16
Two schools

Type of activity: Role play
Organization: Pair work
Time: 15 minutes
Preparation: Copy one worksheet per pair of students and cut it into Worksheet A and Worksheet B.
To use: After Activity 4

Instructions

- Divide the class into pairs. Give a copy of Worksheet A to Student A and Worksheet B to Student B in each pair.
- Students work individually on the first task. They imagine the school in the task and make notes. Explain any vocabulary they may find difficult. With a less confident class, pair two Student As and two Student Bs to do the first task together. Set a time limit of 4 minutes.
- Students work in AB pairs on the second task. Student A tells Student B about their school in detail, using their notes. Student B can ask additional questions. When they have finished, Student B tells Student A if they want to join their school. They should explain their reasons.
- In the third task students change roles.

Extension

In groups of four, students discuss the questions from the first task about their own school. After 4 minutes, elicit the answers from all the groups. Ask students what they would like to change about their own school. Encourage them to use the language of making suggestions, e.g. *how about, I'd like to, I want to, I don't want to.*

Module 5
Lesson 17
Telepathy

Type of activity: Sentence completion
Organization: Individual and group work
Time: 20 minutes
Preparation: Copy one worksheet per student and fold along the line so that students can only see Activity 1.
To use: After Activity 5

Instructions

- Divide students into groups of six. Give each student a copy of the worksheet folded so that they can only see Activity 1.
- Ask students to work individually and complete the sentences in the most logical way. They cannot talk to the members of their group. Allow 8 minutes for the task.
- When the time is up, students read out their sentences within their group. They get a point for each sentence which is grammatically correct and an extra point for each person who wrote the same sentence ending. The winner is the student with the most points at the end of the game.
- In the same groups, students do Activity 2. They match the sentence endings to the sentences in Activity 1. They should choose the most logical connections. Find out if their own sentence endings were the same as the ones in Activity 2.

Answers

1g 2e 3f 4j 5c 6d 7h 8i 9a 10b

Module 5
Lesson 18
What may happen?

Type of activity: Predicting possible events
Organization: Pair work
Time: 15 minutes
Preparation: Copy one worksheet per pair of students and fold it so that students can only see Activity 1.
To use: After Activity 3

Instructions

- Divide the class into pairs. Give the worksheet to each pair. Make sure students have a folded worksheet so that they only see the pictures in Activity 1.
- Students think of two or more possible outcomes of each of the situations in the pictures and write sentences. They should use *may*, e.g. Picture 1, *He may cut his finger, He may break the knife.* Set a time limit of 10 minutes.
- Elicit sentences referring to each picture from various pairs. Then ask students to unfold the worksheet and look at Activity 2. Explain that the pictures show what really happened in each of the situations.
- Students make sentences about the new pictures orally, e.g. *He cut his finger.* They should check if they managed to guess the same outcome in the first stage of the activity, i.e. wrote the same sentences. They get a point for each correct guess. The pair with the most points wins the game.

Module 5
Lesson 19
Dear Teen Dreams

Type of activity: Problem and advice discussion
Organization: Individual and pair work
Time: 20 minutes
Preparation: Copy one worksheet per student.
To use: After Activity 5

Instructions

- Give each student a copy of the worksheet. Ask students to quickly read the emails written by teenagers to a teen magazine and decide what they all describe. Set a time limit of 2 minutes.
- Elicit that all the emails describe teenagers' personal problems and ask for advice. Ask students if they can name any magazines for children/teenagers in their own country which have advice columns.
- Individually, students read the emails again in detail and complete the missing sentences. Allow 5 minutes. Check the answers with the whole class.
- Divide students into pairs. Ask them to discuss what the authors of the emails should do. They should think of at least two pieces of advice for each person. Remind students to use *should* or *shouldn't* when giving advice.
- Elicit the suggestions from all the pairs and get the class to vote for the best advice.

Answers

1b 2a 3d 4e 5f 6c

Extension

Students choose one email each and write a reply, giving advice.

Module 5
Lesson 20
Survival kit

Type of activity: Matching and discussion
Organization: Individual and group work
Time: 15 minutes
Preparation: Copy one worksheet per student.
To use: After Activity 3

Instructions

- Give each student a copy of the worksheet. Point to the objects in Activity 1 and explain that they are all from a survival kit. Students work individually and match the words to the objects in the picture. Set a time limit of 3 minutes. Let students compare the answers in pairs before you check these with the whole class. Drill the pronunciation of the words.
- Divide the class into groups of four. Ask students to discuss how we can use the objects from Activity 1, e.g. *We can hang up the washing on a rope, We can open tins with a penknife* etc. Set a time limit of 8 minutes. Elicit the ideas for each object from different groups.

Extension

In the same groups, students discuss how important these objects are on a desert island and rank them in order of importance from 1 (the most important) to 10 (not very important). They should agree on the same order and then compare their list with other groups.

Answers

1c 2g 3f 4a 5b 6j 7i 8d 9h 10e

Module 6
Lesson 21
What am I going to do?

Type of activity: Guessing game
Organization: Group work
Time: 15 minutes
Preparation: Copy one worksheet per group of six and cut into cards.
To use: After Activity 4

Instructions

- Divide students into groups of six. Place a set of cards face down on the desk in front of each group.
- Pre-teach any names of objects from part A of each card students may not know.
- Write *I've got a …* and *You're going to …* on the board. Explain the rules of the game: one student picks a card and says what objects he/she has got on part A of the card, e.g. *I've got a kettle, a tea bag and a tea cup.* Other group members try to guess what this person is going to do based on the things he/she has got. The first person to say the sentence as on part B wins the card. Then it is another student's turn, moving clockwise round the group, to pick a card. The winner is the student with the most cards at the end.

Variation

- Make enough copies of the worksheet so that there is one card per student.
- Distribute the cards and check students know the objects on part A of their card.
- Students fold their cards so that they can see part B while part A faces outwards. Then they mingle and show part A to another student and ask them to name the objects. Then the classmate tries to guess what they are going to do. After students have finished guessing, they exchange their cards and mingle again.
- Set a time limit of 10 minutes.

Module 6

Lesson 22 Complaints

Type of activity: Word game
Organization: Individual/pairs
Time: 20 minutes
Preparation: Copy one worksheet per student.
To use: After Activity 3

Instructions

- Give each student a copy of the worksheet.
- Explain that they are going to think about places where they spend time and what they do not like about these places.
- Dictate the first place for students to write next to number 1 under the heading *PLACE: 1 my town*
- Ask students to work individually and write nouns or adjectives under the headings in the first row to express what they do not like about their town. Remind them to write uncountable nouns under *TOO MUCH* and countable nouns under *TOO MANY.* Set a time limit of 2 minutes.
- If necessary, write a completed row as an example on the board, e.g.

PLACE	1 My town
TOO MUCH	noise
TOO MANY	cars
NOT ENOUGH + NOUN	parks
NOT + ADJECTIVE + ENOUGH	interesting

- After 2 minutes, students show each other the answers in pairs and make sentences: *In my town, there are too many cars. There is too much noise,* etc.
- Continue the procedure for the places: *2 my school*; *3 my house/ flat*; *4 my bedroom*; *5 where I hang out with friends*. Students get one point for each correct word and one extra point if the word is new.
- The winner is the person with most points.

Module 6

Lesson 23 Plastic bags

Type of activity: Discussion, quiz and mini-project
Organization: Individual/pairs
Time: 20 minutes
Preparation: Copy one worksheet per student.
To use: After Activity 6b

Instructions

- Give each student a copy of the worksheet.
- Focus attention on the picture of the plastic bag. Explain that it is important to limit the number of plastic bags and re-use them, because they are dangerous for our planet.
- Ask students to work in pairs and to think about what else they can use a plastic bag for once they have brought it home from the shop. They should note down their ideas. Set a time limit of 3 minutes.
- Ask the pair with the longest list to read out their ideas. Other pairs cross out the ideas which repeat on their lists and add anything else that has not been mentioned.
- Individually, students complete the passive sentences in Activity 2. Ask which fact students find most shocking.
- In the same pairs as in Activity 1, students design their own reusable bag and draw it in the box. Allow 5 minutes and then ask students to present and describe their bags to the whole class.
- You can tell students that in 2007 a fashion designer called Anya Hindmarch designed a reusable bag with the logo *I'm not a plastic bag.* Her bags became extremely popular and now they can only be bought at Internet auctions and they cost a lot of money.

Answers

1 are given **2** are used
3 are found **4** are eaten

Module 6

Lesson 24 Families

Type of activity: Prompted speaking
Organization: Individual and pair work
Time: 15 minutes
Preparation: Copy one worksheet per pair of students and cut into Worksheets A and B.
To use: After Activity 2b

Instructions

- Divide the class into pairs. Give a copy of Worksheet A to Student A and a copy of Worksheet B to Student B.
- Ask students to look at the picture of the house on their worksheet. Ask them to imagine the family who lives in this house. Then they should read the questions and write the answers in note form. Allow 10 minutes for this task.
- When the time is up, ask students to work in pairs and tell each other about the family in their picture.

Extension

Students write a description of the family they talked about, using their notes.

Module 7
Lesson 25
Rules

Type of activity: Writing rules
Organization: Group work
Time: 15 minutes
Preparation: Copy one worksheet for the whole class and cut into cards.
To use: After Activity 2

Instructions

- Divide the class into six groups. Give each group a card with an activity. They should not show their cards to other groups. Ask them to write at least six rules for someone who is going to do the activity for the first time. They should use *must* and *mustn't*. Set a time limit of 8 minutes for this task.
- When the time is up, ask a representative of each group to read out the rules without revealing what the activity is. Other groups try to guess which activity the rules refer to.

Extension

The groups pass their list of rules on to another group and try to add more rules to the list they have received. After two minutes, they pass the list on again and repeat the task. Continue the procedure until each group has worked on all six lists.

Module 7
Lesson 26
How long have you …?

Type of activity: Survey
Organization: Group work
Time: 20 minutes
Preparation: Copy one worksheet per group of up to ten students and cut into cards.
To use: After Activity 3c

Instructions

- Divide the class into groups of up to ten students. Give each group a set of cards. Each student picks one card. If there are fewer than ten students in the group, put the remaining cards aside.
- Students read the task on their cards. Explain that to find the right person, they need to write a question based on the task and then use it to interview everyone in their group.
- They should note down everybody's answer on the back of their card, e.g. *Marek – 5 years* and then check whose answer refers to the longest period of time. Then they should write this person's name and the length of time they have done something in the space provided.
- Allow 1 minute for students to write their questions and monitor their work, providing help. Make sure their questions are correct.
- Students get up and mingle, interviewing their classmates. Set a time limit of 15 minutes.
- Elicit the answers in full sentences from each student, e.g. *Renata has known her best friend the longest. She has known her for 8 years.*

Module 7
Lesson 27
How well do you know them?

Type of activity: Questionnaire
Organization: Whole class work
Time: 20 minutes
Preparation: Copy one worksheet per student.
To use: After Activity 7

Instructions

- Give each student a copy of the worksheet.
- Students fold the questionnaire so that they can only see the *NAME* column and they write in it at random 12 names of the classmates present in class. They should not repeat the names unless there are fewer than 12.
- Students unfold the worksheet and complete each row in the *SENTENCE* column about the classmate whose name they wrote in the *NAME* column, e.g. *Patryk usually plays video games on Sunday.* They complete the gaps, using the prompts in the brackets and making the sentences true about the classmates. They cannot talk to anyone and have to make guesses if they are not sure of the answer. Allow 6 minutes for this part of the activity.
- When the time is up, students get up and mingle to check if they guessed correctly. They tell their ideas to their classmates, changing the sentences from the 3rd to the 2nd person, e.g. *Patryk, I think you usually play video games on Sunday.* He or she says if it is true or false and students mark each sentence in the last column of the questionnaire. If the sentence is false, the classmates should say the correct answer, e.g. *False. I usually go out with my parents on Sundays.* Set a time limit of 10 minutes for this task.
- Students count the true sentences to see who knows the most about their classmates.

Module 7

Lesson 28

Game show

Type of activity: Word game
Organization: Group work
Time: 25 minutes
Preparation: Make one copy of the worksheet per group of six. Have a monolingual dictionary available.
To use: After *Talk about it*

Instructions

- Divide the class into groups of six. Ask them to imagine that they are taking part in a game show. They have to try to guess words they studied in *Hot Spot 3,* based on definitions they hear. Ask one volunteer in each group to role-play a game show host.
- Ask the hosts to sit and work together. Give them each a copy of the worksheet. They read the words and try to define them in English. Point out that all the words on the worksheet are nouns. Write a few phrases on the board for students to use as a model, e.g. *It is something you use when... ; It's made of ... ; It's a place where ... ; It's something you do when ... ; It's a type of... .* You can give them a monolingual dictionary to help them with the task. Individually, they should write down the more difficult definitions. Allow 10 minutes for this task.
- In the meantime, the rest of the class look through their books to revise vocabulary from the following categories: *DIY, SPORTS, GARDEN, STREET, HEALTH, MUSIC.* Write the categories on the board.
- Ask the hosts to return to their groups. They must not show their worksheet to anyone. The group members sit in a semi-circle facing the host. The first student in the line picks a category from the board and the host gives a definition of the first word in that category. If the student guesses the word within 10 seconds, he/she gets 2 points; if not, any group member who raises their hand first has a chance to guess the same word for 1 point. Then it is the second student's turn to pick a category and so on.
- The host crosses out the words he/she has defined, whether these have been guessed or not, and keeps the score for group members. Set a time limit of 15 minutes. The winner is the student with the most points at the end.

Lesson 1 Getting to know you

This page is taken from Hot Spot 3 Teacher's Book. It is photocopiable and may be used within the class.
Published by Macmillan Education. Copyright © Macmillan Publishers Limited 2010.

Lesson 2 Plans

1 What are you doing next week? Write one word for each day of the week.

DAY OF THE WEEK	WORD	SENTENCE
Monday		
Tuesday		
Wednesday		
Thursday		
Friday		
Saturday		
Sunday		

2 Exchange the worksheet with Student B. Can you guess what Student B is doing next week? Write a sentence with Student B's word for each day of the week. Discuss the sentences with Student B.

B

1 What are you doing next week? Write one word for each day of the week.

DAY OF THE WEEK	WORD	SENTENCE
Monday		
Tuesday		
Wednesday		
Thursday		
Friday		
Saturday		
Sunday		

2 Exchange the worksheet with Student A. Can you guess what Student A is doing next week? Write a sentence with Student A's word for each day of the week. Discuss the sentences with Student A.

This page is taken from Hot Spot 3 Teacher's Book. It is photocopiable and may be used within the class.
Published by Macmillan Education. Copyright © Macmillan Publishers Limited 2010.

Lesson 3 Clothes

1 Work with a classmate. Match the words with the clothes in the picture.

1 jacket 2 hoody 3 jeans 4 T-shirt 5 skirt 6 top 7 hat 8 trainers 9 dress 10 shirt 11 boots 12 shoes

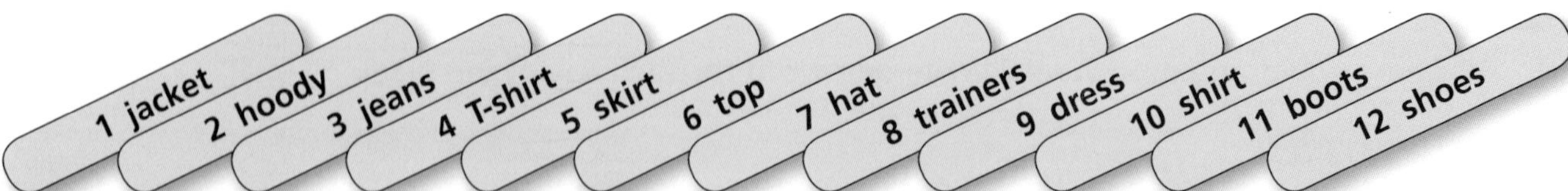

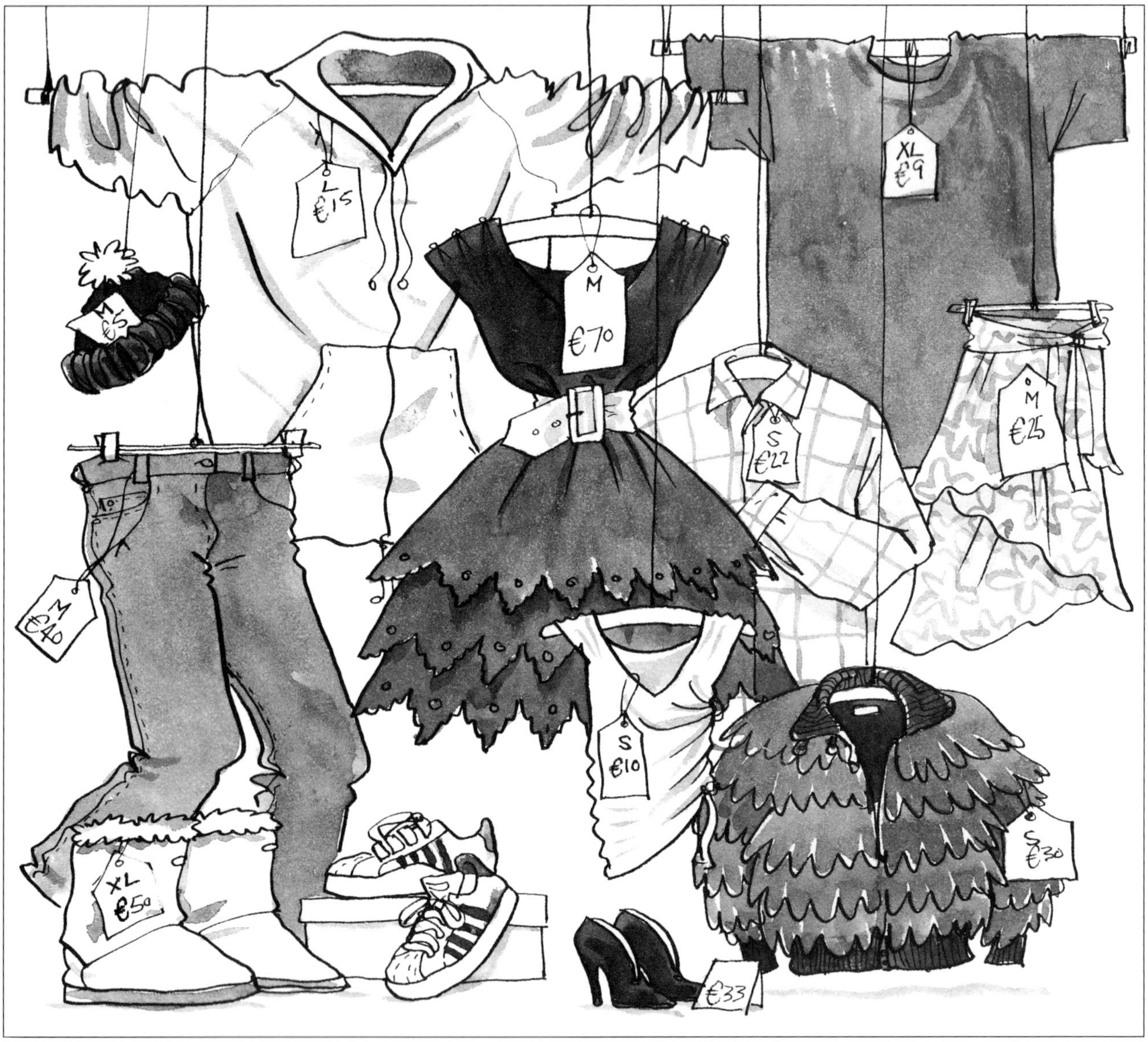

2 Play the game of Tic Tac Toe.

cheaper	nicer	the most expensive
than	more comfortable	much
smaller	the most beautiful	the biggest

This page is taken from Hot Spot 3 Teacher's Book. It is photocopiable and may be used within the class.
Published by Macmillan Education. Copyright © Macmillan Publishers Limited 2010.

Lesson 4 What's my word?

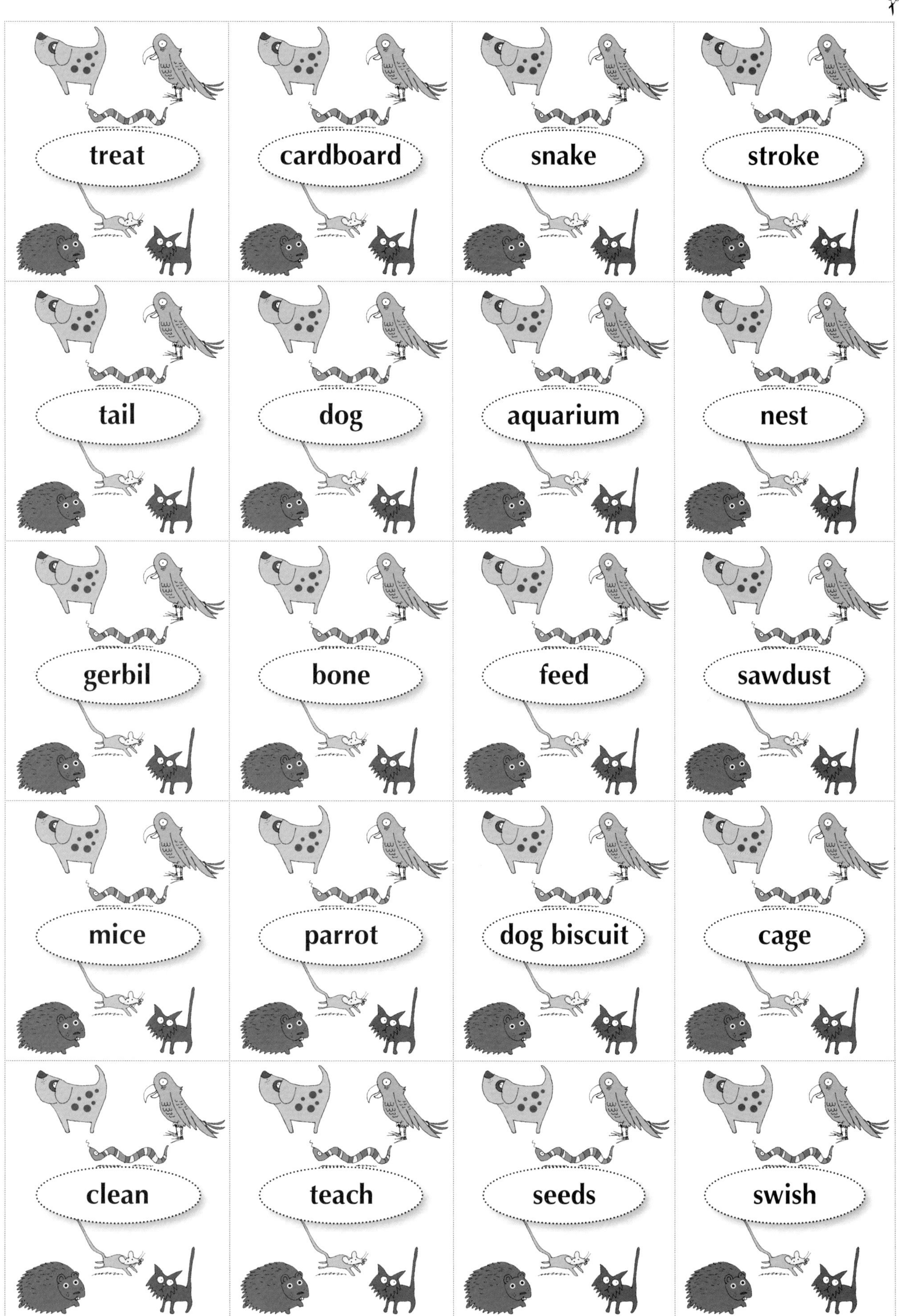

This page is taken from Hot Spot 3 Teacher's Book. It is photocopiable and may be used within the class.
Published by Macmillan Education. Copyright © Macmillan Publishers Limited 2010.

Lesson 5 Last week

break	fall	buy
run	jump	visit
look	read	get
swim	go	win
talk	throw	watch

SCORING TABLE

Name:	Name:	Name:
Score:	Score:	Score:
Total number of points:	Total number of points:	Total number of points:

This page is taken from Hot Spot 3 Teacher's Book. It is photocopiable and may be used within the class.
Published by Macmillan Education. Copyright © Macmillan Publishers Limited 2010.

Lesson 6 Find out the truth

Everybody was watching TV at 7.30 p.m. yesterday.

Question: ______________________________
______________________________?

Notes: ______________________________
____
____
____

Everybody was eating breakfast at 7 a.m. this morning.

Question: ______________________________
______________________________?

Notes: ______________________________
____
____
____

Everybody was doing their homework at 6 p.m. yesterday.

Question: ______________________________
______________________________?

Notes: ______________________________
____
____
____

Everybody was reading a book at 9 p.m. yesterday.

Question: ______________________________
______________________________?

Notes: ______________________________
____
____
____

Everybody was tidying their room last Saturday morning.

Question: ______________________________
______________________________?

Notes: ______________________________
____
____
____

Everybody was sleeping at 11.30 p.m. yesterday.

Question: ______________________________
______________________________?

Notes: ______________________________
____
____
____

Everybody was hanging out with their friends last Monday afternoon.

Question: ______________________________
______________________________?

Notes: ______________________________
____
____
____

Everybody was eating dinner at 6 p.m. yesterday.

Question: ______________________________
______________________________?

Notes: ______________________________
____
____
____

Everybody was surfing the Internet at 8 p.m. yesterday.

Question: ______________________________
______________________________?

Notes: ______________________________
____
____
____

Everybody was walking to school at 7.50 this morning.

Question: ______________________________
______________________________?

Notes: ______________________________
____
____
____

This page is taken from Hot Spot 3 Teacher's Book. It is photocopiable and may be used within the class.
Published by Macmillan Education. Copyright © Macmillan Publishers Limited 2010.

Lesson 7 The missing bag

Picture cards

Word cards

holiday	Australia	hired
a car	passports	a small black bag
driving	restaurant	lunch
getting into	dropped	one hour later
lying	car park	came back

Story

Last summer Laura and her family went on holiday to Australia. They hired a car. They put all their money and passports in a small black bag. They were driving when Laura saw a nice restaurant. They stopped for lunch: sandwiches and drinks. They were getting into the car when Laura's mobile phone rang. Laura was talking on the phone when she dropped the small black bag. One hour later Laura asked 'Where's the black bag?' Fortunately, the bag was lying on the ground in the car park when they came back to the restaurant.

This page is taken from Hot Spot 3 Teacher's Book. It is photocopiable and may be used within the class.
Published by Macmillan Education. Copyright © Macmillan Publishers Limited 2010.

Lesson 8 Famous people

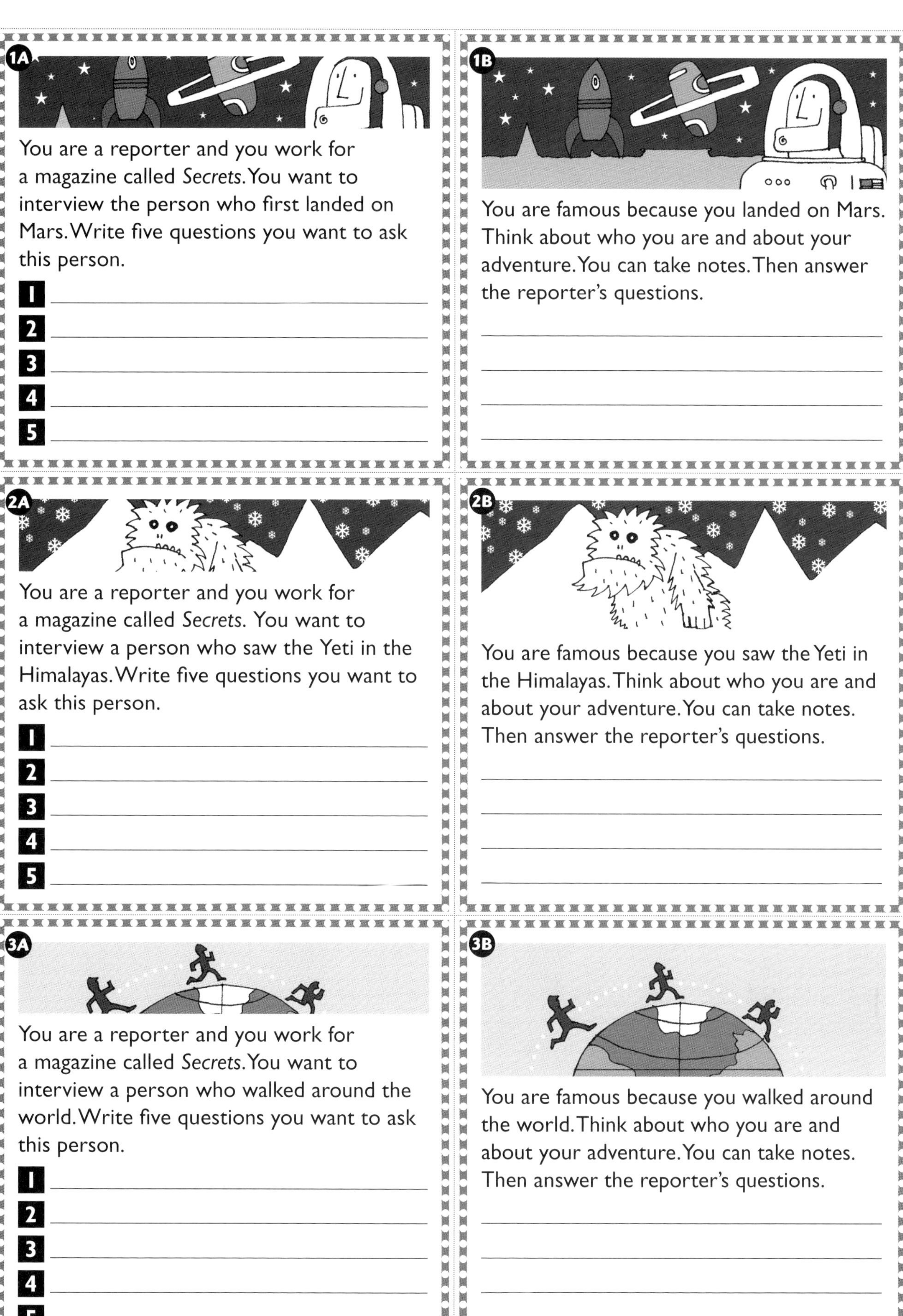

1A

You are a reporter and you work for a magazine called *Secrets*. You want to interview the person who first landed on Mars. Write five questions you want to ask this person.

1 ____________________
2 ____________________
3 ____________________
4 ____________________
5 ____________________

1B

You are famous because you landed on Mars. Think about who you are and about your adventure. You can take notes. Then answer the reporter's questions.

2A

You are a reporter and you work for a magazine called *Secrets*. You want to interview a person who saw the Yeti in the Himalayas. Write five questions you want to ask this person.

1 ____________________
2 ____________________
3 ____________________
4 ____________________
5 ____________________

2B

You are famous because you saw the Yeti in the Himalayas. Think about who you are and about your adventure. You can take notes. Then answer the reporter's questions.

3A

You are a reporter and you work for a magazine called *Secrets*. You want to interview a person who walked around the world. Write five questions you want to ask this person.

1 ____________________
2 ____________________
3 ____________________
4 ____________________
5 ____________________

3B

You are famous because you walked around the world. Think about who you are and about your adventure. You can take notes. Then answer the reporter's questions.

This page is taken from Hot Spot 3 Teacher's Book. It is photocopiable and may be used within the class.
Published by Macmillan Education. Copyright © Macmillan Publishers Limited 2010.

Lesson 9 Experiences

Use the present perfect of the verbs in brackets to complete the questions. Write your true answers. Guess your friend's answers. Ask your friend to check your guesses. You get one point for each correct guess.

EXPERIENCE	My answers Yes/No	My friend's answers Yes/No	Points
1 Have you ever ______ (play) basketball?	______	______	______
2 Have you ever ______ (be) on television?	______	______	______
3 Have you ever ______ (listen) to classical music?	______	______	______
4 Have you ever ______ (swim) in a lake?	______	______	______
5 Have you ever ______ (win) a competition?	______	______	______
6 Have you ever ______ (visit) an art gallery?	______	______	______
7 Have you ever ______ (take) an exam?	______	______	______
8 Have you ever ______ (see) a shooting star?	______	______	______
9 Have you ever ______ (eat) Japanese food?	______	______	______
10 Have you ever ______ (climb) a mountain?	______	______	______

This page is taken from Hot Spot 3 Teacher's Book. It is photocopiable and may be used within the class.
Published by Macmillan Education. Copyright © Macmillan Publishers Limited 2010.

Lesson 10 Do you know anybody who …?

Do you know anybody who has ridden a horse?

Who is it? ______________________

Details: ______________________

____

____

Do you know anybody who has climbed a very high mountain?

Who is it? ______________________

Details: ______________________

____

____

Do you know anybody who has written an email in English?

Who is it? ______________________

Details: ______________________

____

____

Do you know anybody who has broken an arm or a leg?

Who is it? ______________________

Details: ______________________

____

____

Do you know anybody who has flown in a helicopter?

Who is it? ______________________

Details: ______________________

____

____

Do you know anybody who has been to Australia?

Who is it? ______________________

Details: ______________________

____

____

Do you know anybody who has skied in the Alps?

Who is it? ______________________

Details: ______________________

____

____

Do you know anybody who has met a famous TV star or an athlete?

Who is it? ______________________

Details: ______________________

____

____

Do you know anybody who has sailed on a yacht?

Who is it? ______________________

Details: ______________________

____

____

Do you know anybody who has made a telephone call in English?

Who is it? ______________________

Details: ______________________

____

____

This page is taken from Hot Spot 3 Teacher's Book. It is photocopiable and may be used within the class.
Published by Macmillan Education. Copyright © Macmillan Publishers Limited 2010.

Lesson 11 What's just happened?

This page is taken from Hot Spot 3 Teacher's Book. It is photocopiable and may be used within the class.
Published by Macmillan Education. Copyright © Macmillan Publishers Limited 2010.

Lesson 12 Interesting stories

the most unusual food you have eaten	the best computer game you have played
the most difficult test you have taken	the scariest film you have seen
the best present you have given to someone	the most beautiful place you have visited
the most interesting TV programme you have watched	the nicest food you have eaten
the worst film you have seen	the biggest city you have been to
the best book you have read	the most dangerous sport you have done

This page is taken from Hot Spot 3 Teacher's Book. It is photocopiable and may be used within the class.
Published by Macmillan Education. Copyright © Macmillan Publishers Limited 2010.

Lesson 13 The future

In 2025…	My answers	______'s (name) answers	______'s (name) answers
1 Where will you live?			
2 What job will you have?			
3 Will you be famous?			
4 Will you have any children?			
5 What will you look like?			
6 What sports will you play?			
7 What hobbies will you have?			
8 What car will you drive?			
9 What music will you listen to?			
10 Will you have a lot of money?			

This page is taken from Hot Spot 3 Teacher's Book. It is photocopiable and may be used within the class. Published by Macmillan Education. Copyright © Macmillan Publishers Limited 2010.

Lesson 14 Problems and solutions

I'm very hungry.	It's very dark in this room.	My little sister has just broken her arm.
It's raining and I haven't got an umbrella.	My dog has to go out but I'm ill in bed.	It's very hot in this room.
I want to make a cake but I don't know how to.	I don't know how to use the camera in my mobile phone.	I don't know what to buy my brother for his birthday.
I want to learn to swim well.	I've just lost my keys somewhere in this room.	I want to see a good film.
I don't know how to do my Maths homework.	I'm very thirsty.	My computer doesn't work and I have to send an email.

This page is taken from Hot Spot 3 Teacher's Book. It is photocopiable and may be used within the class.
Published by Macmillan Education. Copyright © Macmillan Publishers Limited 2010.

Lesson 15 Youth club

Imagine that you can change your classroom into a youth club for your school. You have got a lot of money for this project. Discuss these questions. Use *Let's, How about, I'd like to, I want to, don't want to.*

1 What would you like to remove from the classroom?

____

____

2 What colour would you like to paint the walls?

____

____

3 What furniture would you like to buy?

____

____

4 What equipment would you like to buy (DVD players, computer game consoles, sound systems, etc.)?

____

____

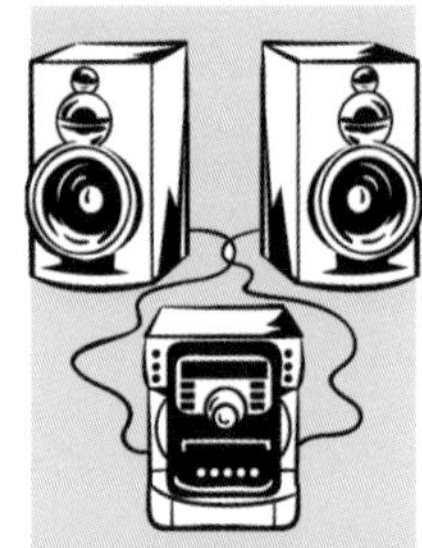

5 What other changes would you like to make?

____

____

6 What music would you like to play in the club?

____

____

7 What classes would you like to have in the club (dance lessons, karate classes, etc.)?

____

____

8 Would you like to invite any guests? Who?

____

____

ROLE CARD A

You are your group's

SECRETARY

You have to take notes of your group's final answers and then present them to all the students in your class.

ROLE CARD B

You are your group's

LEADER

You have to make sure everybody in your group makes suggestions about each topic. You have to decide what your group's final answers are.

ROLE CARD C

You are your group's

LANGUAGE OFFICER

You have to make sure everybody in your group speaks English all the time.

ROLE CARD D

You are your group's

TIME KEEPER

You have to watch the time. Your group has 15 minutes to answer all the questions. After each question tell everybody how much time you still have.

This page is taken from Hot Spot 3 Teacher's Book. It is photocopiable and may be used within the class.
Published by Macmillan Education. Copyright © Macmillan Publishers Limited 2010.

Lesson 16 Two schools

A

1 **Imagine that you are a student at a very unusual and relaxed school. What is your school like?**

- What does the school building look like? ______________________
- Do students study any unusual subjects at the school? ______________________
- What sports can students do at the school? ______________________
- What do students do during the lunch break? ______________________
- Where do students go on school trips? ______________________
- What do you like best about the school? ______________________

2 **Tell Student B about your school. Does he or she want to join your school? Why?**

3 **Listen to Student B. Do you want to join his or her school? Why? Think of at least four reasons and tell them to Student B.**

B

1 **Imagine that you are a student at a very strict and traditional school. What is your school like?**

- What does the school building look like? ______________________
- Do students study any unusual subjects at the school? ______________________
- What sports can students do at the school? ______________________
- What do students do during the lunch break? ______________________
- Where do students go on school trips? ______________________
- What do you like best about the school? ______________________

2 **Listen to Student A. Do you want to join his or her school? Why? Think of at least four reasons and tell them to Student A.**

3 **Tell Student A about your school. Does he or she want to join your school? Why?**

This page is taken from Hot Spot 3 Teacher's Book. It is photocopiable and may be used within the class.
Published by Macmillan Education. Copyright © Macmillan Publishers Limited 2010.

Lesson 17 Telepathy

1 **Complete the sentences. Use *will.* Then work in groups of six and read your sentences. You will get one point for each correct sentence and one extra point for each student who wrote the same sentence.**

Sentences	Points
1 If you miss the bus, ________________________	
2 If you eat the whole birthday cake, ________________________	
3 If you tidy your bedroom, ________________________	
4 If you don't do your homework, ________________________	
5 If you lie on the beach all day, ________________________	
6 If you don't write her address down, ________________________	
7 If you forget my birthday, ________________________	
8 If you don't eat your breakfast, ________________________	
9 If you go outside without a jacket, ________________________	
10 If you win the lottery, ________________________	
Total:	

fold

2 **Match these endings to the sentences in Activity 1. Did you write the same endings?**

a	… you'll catch a cold.	**f**	… your mum will be happy.
b	… you'll buy a big house.	**g**	… you'll be late for school.
c	… you'll get sunburn.	**h**	… I'll feel sad.
d	… you'll forget it.	**i**	… you'll be hungry.
e	… you'll get a stomach ache.	**j**	… your teacher will be angry.

This page is taken from Hot Spot 3 Teacher's Book. It is photocopiable and may be used within the class.
Published by Macmillan Education. Copyright © Macmillan Publishers Limited 2010.

Lesson 18 What may happen?

1 **Work in pairs. Look at the pictures. What may happen in each situation? Discuss your ideas together.**

fold

2 **Look what really happened. Were you right?**

This page is taken from Hot Spot 3 Teacher's Book. It is photocopiable and may be used within the class.
Published by Macmillan Education. Copyright © Macmillan Publishers Limited 2010.

Lesson 19 Dear Teen Dreams

Read the emails and complete the missing sentences.

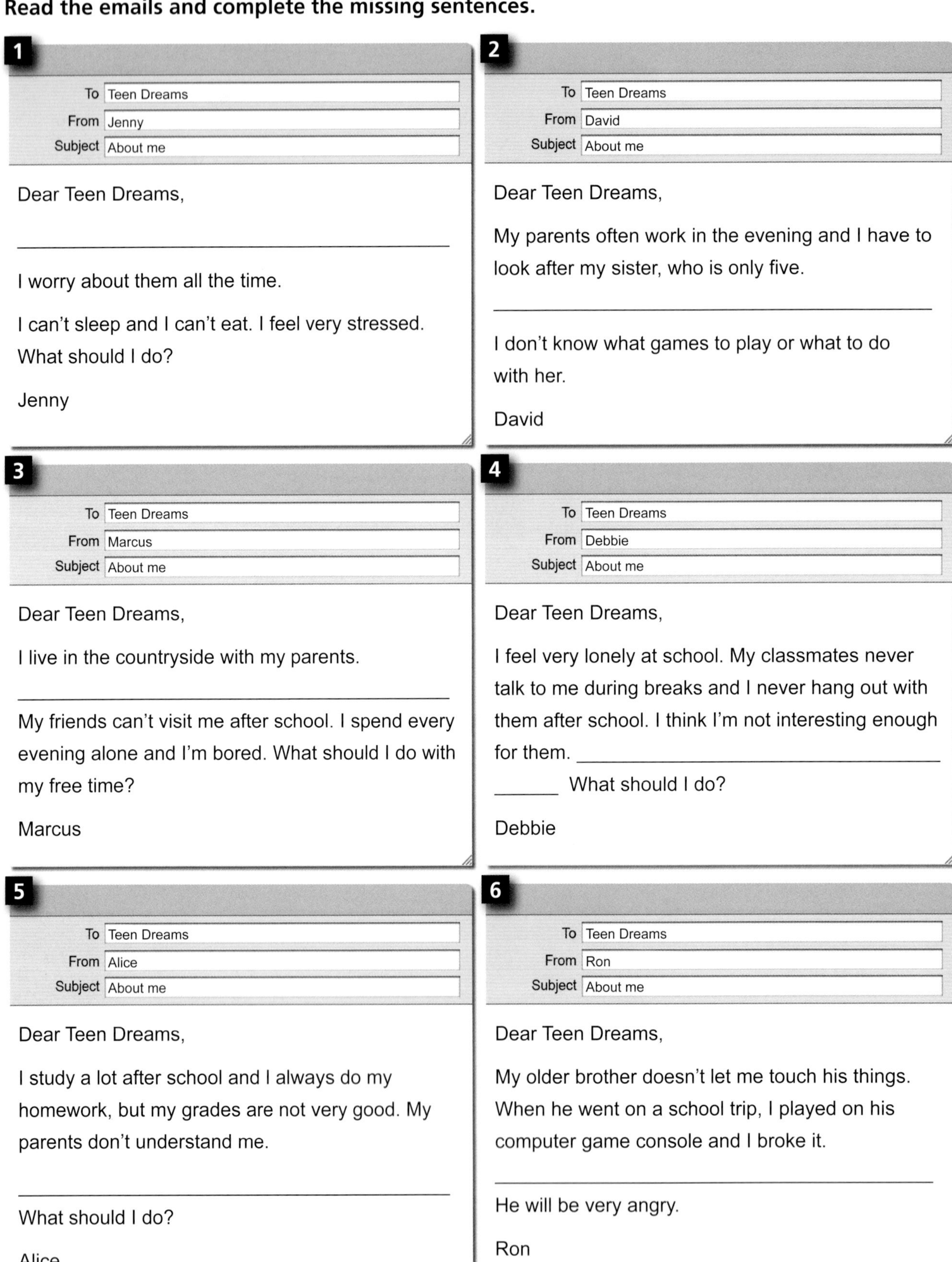

1

To: Teen Dreams
From: Jenny
Subject: About me

Dear Teen Dreams,

____

I worry about them all the time.

I can't sleep and I can't eat. I feel very stressed. What should I do?

Jenny

2

To: Teen Dreams
From: David
Subject: About me

Dear Teen Dreams,

My parents often work in the evening and I have to look after my sister, who is only five.

____

I don't know what games to play or what to do with her.

David

3

To: Teen Dreams
From: Marcus
Subject: About me

Dear Teen Dreams,

I live in the countryside with my parents.

____

My friends can't visit me after school. I spend every evening alone and I'm bored. What should I do with my free time?

Marcus

4

To: Teen Dreams
From: Debbie
Subject: About me

Dear Teen Dreams,

I feel very lonely at school. My classmates never talk to me during breaks and I never hang out with them after school. I think I'm not interesting enough for them. _______________________________ ______ What should I do?

Debbie

5

To: Teen Dreams
From: Alice
Subject: About me

Dear Teen Dreams,

I study a lot after school and I always do my homework, but my grades are not very good. My parents don't understand me.

____

What should I do?

Alice

6

To: Teen Dreams
From: Ron
Subject: About me

Dear Teen Dreams,

My older brother doesn't let me touch his things. When he went on a school trip, I played on his computer game console and I broke it.

____

He will be very angry.

Ron

a) She doesn't want to watch TV.
b) I've always got a lot of tests at school.
c) Should I tell him about it?
d) Our house is far away from the city.
e) I'd like to be more popular.
f) They say that I'm lazy.

This page is taken from Hot Spot 3 Teacher's Book. It is photocopiable and may be used within the class. Published by Macmillan Education. Copyright © Macmillan Publishers Limited 2010.

Lesson 20 Survival kit

1 Match the words and the pictures.

1 a rope

2 a penknife

3 a blanket

4 a spade

5 a water bottle

6 a compass

7 matches

8 a candle

9 a torch

10 a first aid kit

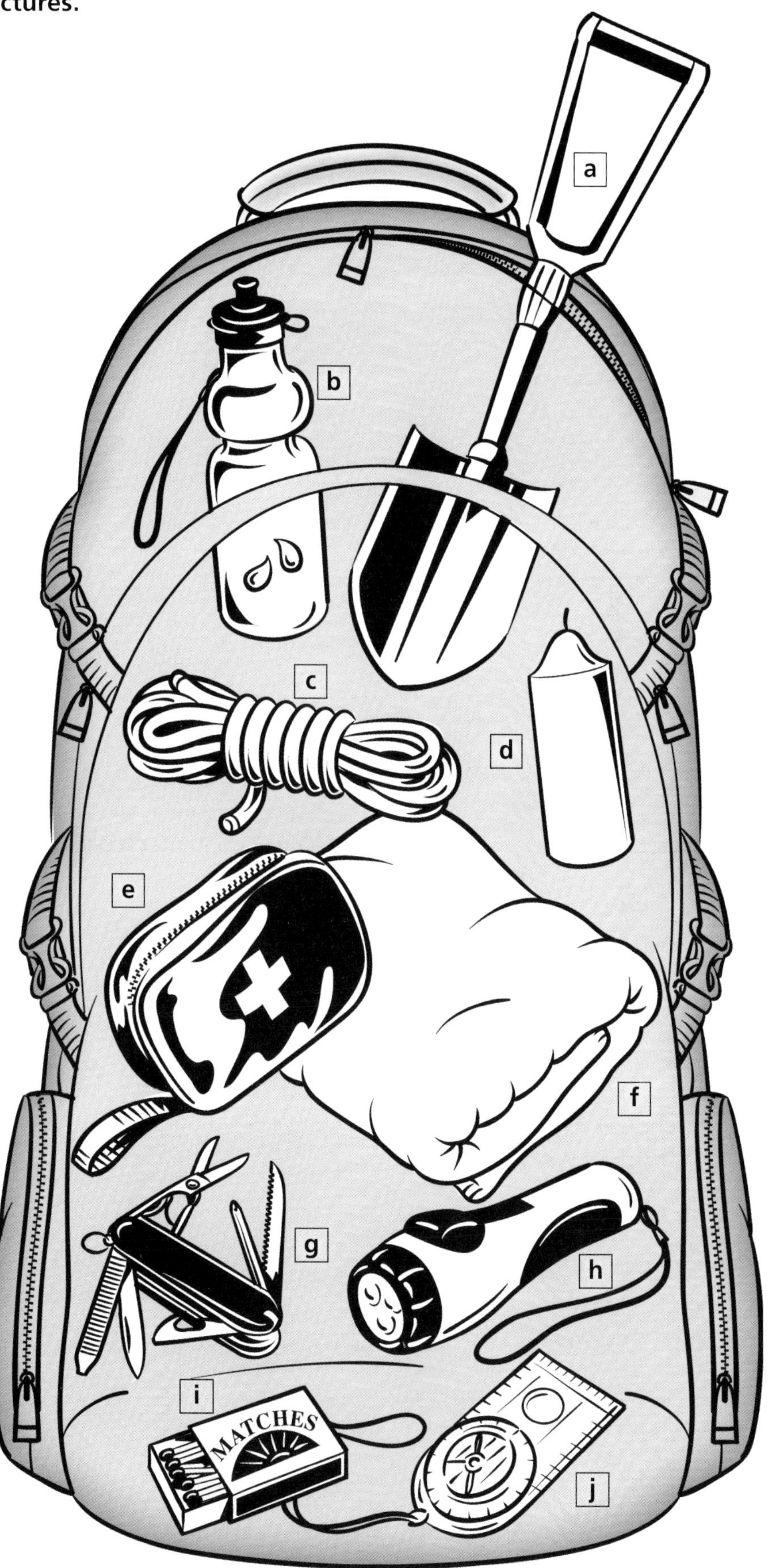

2 Work in groups of four. Discuss what we can use the objects in Activity 1 for.

This page is taken from Hot Spot 3 Teacher's Book. It is photocopiable and may be used within the class.
Published by Macmillan Education. Copyright © Macmillan Publishers Limited 2010.

Lesson 21 What am I going to do?

This page is taken from Hot Spot 3 Teacher's Book. It is photocopiable and may be used within the class.
Published by Macmillan Education. Copyright © Macmillan Publishers Limited 2010.

Lesson 22 Complaints

Listen to the teacher and write the places. What don't you like about the places? Write one word under each heading. You get one point for each correct word and one extra point if this word is new in the table.

PLACE	TOO MANY	TOO MUCH	NOT ENOUGH + NOUN	NOT + ADJECTIVE + ENOUGH	POINTS
1					
2					
3					
4					
5					
				Total:	

This page is taken from Hot Spot 3 Teacher's Book. It is photocopiable and may be used within the class.
Published by Macmillan Education. Copyright © Macmillan Publishers Limited 2010.

Lesson 23 Plastic bags

1 Work in pairs. Look at the plastic bag. What can you use this for when you bring it home? Write as many ideas as possible in 3 minutes.

____
____
____
____
____
____
____

2 Now complete the sentences to find out some shocking facts about plastic bags. Use the passive form of the verbs in brackets.

1. In Britain, over 17 billion plastic bags ________ ________________ (give) to customers by supermarkets each year.
2. Most plastic bags ________ ________________ (use) only once.
3. Plastic bags ________ ________________ (find) even in Antarctica.
4. Plastic bags ________ ________________ (eat) by animals which think they are food.

How can you help? It is very easy. Buy a reusable cloth bag and take it with you when you go shopping!

3 Work in pairs. Design your own reusable bag. Think about the following: the shape, the colour, the pictures and the slogan. Draw the bag in the box.

This page is taken from Hot Spot 3 Teacher's Book. It is photocopiable and may be used within the class.
Published by Macmillan Education. Copyright © Macmillan Publishers Limited 2010.

Lesson 24 Families

A

Look at the picture. Imagine the family who lives here and answer the questions. Tell Student B about the family.

1 How many people live in this house?

____

2 How old are they?

____

3 What are their hobbies?

____

4 Where do they work?/What school do they go to?

____

5 What do they eat for dinner?

____

6 Are they an eco-family?

____

7 Do they grow their own food?

____

8 What things do they recycle?

____

B

Look at the picture. Imagine the family who lives here and answer the questions. Tell Student A about the family.

1 How many people live in this house?

____

2 How old are they?

____

3 What are their hobbies?

____

4 Where do they work?/What school do they go to?

____

5 What do they eat for dinner?

____

6 Are they an eco-family?

____

7 Do they grow their own food?

____

8 What things do they recycle?

____

This page is taken from Hot Spot 3 Teacher's Book. It is photocopiable and may be used within the class.
Published by Macmillan Education. Copyright © Macmillan Publishers Limited 2010.

Lesson 25 Rules

Camping	Camping
Living in an eco-friendly house	Visiting your country
Cycling in a city	Studying at your school

This page is taken from Hot Spot 3 Teacher's Book. It is photocopiable and may be used within the class.
Published by Macmillan Education. Copyright © Macmillan Publishers Limited 2010.

Lesson 26 How long have you …?

Find out who has known their next-door neighbours the longest.

How long ______________________________
____
?
Name and time: _________________________

Find out who has lived in the same house the longest.

How long ______________________________
____
?
Name and time: _________________________

Find out who has had the same hobby the longest.

How long ______________________________
____
?
Name and time: _________________________

Find out who has played the same sport the longest.

How long ______________________________
____
?
Name and time: _________________________

Find out who has had their pet the longest.

How long ______________________________
____
?
Name and time: _________________________

Find out who has studied a foreign language the longest.

How long ______________________________
____
?
Name and time: _________________________

Find out who has played a musical instrument the longest.

How long ______________________________
____
?
Name and time: _________________________

Find out who has listened to the same type of music the longest.

How long ______________________________
____
?
Name and time: _________________________

Find out who has been at the school the longest today.

How long ______________________________
____
?
Name and time: _________________________

Find out who has had their own email address the longest.

How long ______________________________
____
?
Name and time: _________________________

This page is taken from Hot Spot 3 Teacher's Book. It is photocopiable and may be used within the class.
Published by Macmillan Education. Copyright © Macmillan Publishers Limited 2010.

Lesson 27 How well do you know them?

NAME	fold	SENTENCE	TRUE OR FALSE?
1		usually ______________ on Sunday. (activity)	
2		was ______________ yesterday at 6p.m. (activity+*ing*)	
3		has lived in the same house for ______________. (number of months/years)	
4		wins the lottery, he/she will buy ______________. (object)	
5		wants to be a/an ______________ in the future. (job)	
6		is ______________ after school today. (activity+*ing*)	
7		has had his/her schoolbag since ______________. (month/year)	
8		has never been to ______________. (place)	
9		must ______________ at home. (activity)	
10		is going to eat ______________ this evening. (type of food)	
11		may go to ______________ this week. (place)	
12		didn't ______________ yesterday. (activity)	

This page is taken from Hot Spot 3 Teacher's Book. It is photocopiable and may be used within the class. Published by Macmillan Education. Copyright © Macmillan Publishers Limited 2010.

Lesson 28 Game show

DIY

ladder
toolbox
drill
wallpaper
paint

SPORTS

javelin
medal
race
long jump
obstacle course

GARDEN

lawn
hammock
flowerbed
flower pot
plants

STREET

traffic sign
pavement
cycle lane
traffic lights
traffic warden

HEALTH

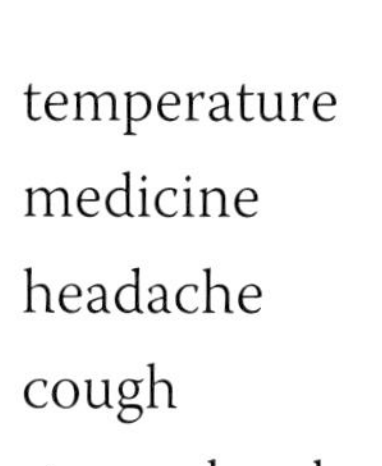

temperature
medicine
headache
cough
stomach ache

MUSIC

guitar
microphone
stage
drums
flute

This page is taken from Hot Spot 3 Teacher's Book. It is photocopiable and may be used within the class.
Published by Macmillan Education. Copyright © Macmillan Publishers Limited 2010.

Activity Book answer key

Module 1

Lesson 1

❶ Vocabulary

1 *diver*
2 *hibernate*
3 *worry*
4 *farmer*
5 *creek*
6 *clap*

❷ Grammar and vocabulary

1 *come*
2 *live*
3 *swim*
4 *hibernate*
5 *is*
6 *clap*
7 *hears*
8 *walks*
9 *worry*
10 *hibernate*

❸ Grammar and reading

1 *Where does Nicole come from? d*
2 *Where do the bears swim? e*
3 *Where do bears sleep in summer? b*
4 *When do they clap their hands? a*
5 *Where do bears hibernate? c*

❹ Grammar

1 *comes*
2 *lives*
3 *like*
4 *builds*
5 *help*
6 *doesn't go*
7 *plays*
8 *don't have*
9 *listen*

❺ Grammar and reading

1 *does / Ghana*
2 *does / in a village*
3 *do / good neighbours*
4 *does / she plays with her friends*
5 *do / the radio*

❻ Vocabulary

1 *e* 2 *c* 3 *f* 4 *a* 5 *g* 6 *b* 7 *d*

Lesson 2

❶ Vocabulary

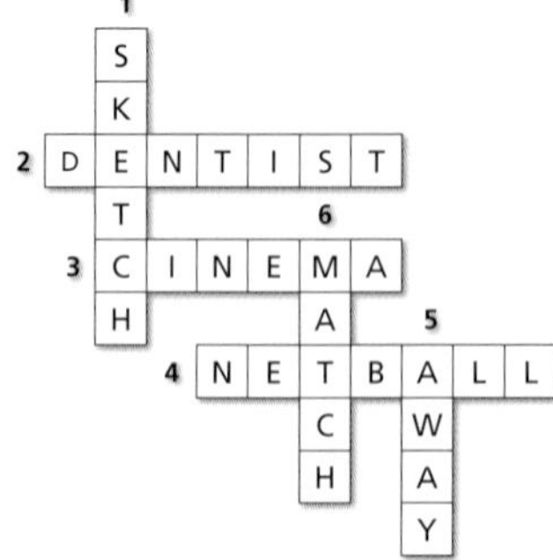

❷a Grammar and reading

1 *is watching*
2 *is seeing*
3 *is doing*
4 *is visiting*
5 *are playing*
6 *is going*
7 *practising*
8 *are going*

❷b Grammar and reading

1 *Yes, she is.*
2 *Yes, he is.*
3 *No, he isn't.*
4 *No, they aren't.*

❸ Grammar

1 *What are you doing on Friday?*
2 *I'm going to Paul's house.*
3 *What are you doing at Paul's house?*
4 *We're watching a DVD.*
5 *What are you doing on Saturday?*
6 *I'm visiting my grandma.*
7 *When are you coming back?*
8 *Because I'm having a party on Sunday night.*

❹ Grammar

1 *yours*
2 *mine*
3 *hers*
4 *his*
5 *theirs*
6 *ours*

❺ Grammar

1 *mine*
2 *yours*
3 *hers*
4 *his*
5 *ours*
6 *theirs*

Lesson 3

❶ Vocabulary

1 *are cheaper*
2 *the pattern*
3 *looks horrible*
4 *size is this*
5 *It's large*
6 *too big*

❷ Grammar

adjective + er / + r
cheap, new, tall, nice

adjective - y / + ier
tidy, friendly

more + adjective
interesting, beautiful, expensive

❸ Grammar

1 *more comfortable*
2 *messier*
3 *worse*
4 *more useful*
5 *more modern*
6 *older*

❹ Grammar

1 *the messiest*
2 *the most expensive*
3 *the best*
4 *the most horrible*
5 *the largest*
6 *the smallest*
7 *the ugliest*
8 *the most comfortable*
9 *the worst*
10 *the most beautiful*

❺ Grammar

1 *more expensive*
2 *best*
3 *prettiest*
4 *funniest*
5 *happier*
6 *hotter*

❻ Grammar and writing

1 *Teapot a is the oldest. It's older than teapots b and c.*
2 *Teapot c is the smallest. It's smaller than teapots a and b.*
3 *Teapot b is the most expensive. It's more expensive than teapots a and c.*
4 *Teapot c is the cheapest. It's cheaper than teapots a and b.*
5 *Teapot a is the biggest. It's bigger than teapots b and c.*
6 *Teapot b is the most modern. It's more modern than teapots a and c.*

7 Writing

Student's own answers.

Lesson 4

1a Reading and vocabulary

1 *b* 2 *c* 3 *a*

1a Reading and vocabulary

1 *F* 2 *F* 3 *T* 4 *F* 5 *T* 6 *T*

2 Writing

(Suggested answer)

A ferret lives for five to ten years. It likes lots of exercise. It sleeps in a cage. It eats cat food and it likes lots of clean water.

Learning diary

Study tip

1 *tall – short*
2 *boring – interesting*
3 *messy – tidy*

1
1 *come / comes*
2 *lives / live*
3 *have / has*
4 *aren't / are*
5 *goes / doesn't go*

2
1 *What are you doing on Saturday afternoon?*
2 *Are you playing football after school?*
3 *I'm going to the sports centre tomorrow.*
4 *Rory's visiting his grandmother on Sunday.*
5 *We're going to the cinema tonight.*

3
1 *friendliest*
2 *youngest*
3 *cheaper*
4 *best*
5 *more beautiful*

4
1 *his*
2 *mine*
3 *hers*
4 *ours*
5 *yours*

Module 2

Lesson 5

1 Vocabulary

1 *javelin*
2 *swimming race*
3 *metre race*
4 *obstacle course*
5 *long jump*
James

2 Grammar

1 *was*
2 *swam*
3 *threw*
4 *didn't break*
5 *broke*
6 *happened*
7 *ran*
8 *fell*
9 *didn't get*
10 *got*

3 Reading and grammar

1 *didn't do / swam in the swimming race*
2 *didn't swim / threw the javelin*
3 *didn't throw / ran in the 100-metre race*
4 *didn't run / did the obstacle course*
5 *didn't break / jumped*

4a Reading and grammar

1 *What did she buy?*
2 *What did she do in the evening?*
3 *What museum did she go to?*
4 *Who visited her?*
5 *What English homework did she do?*
6 *Did she do her maths homework?*

4b Reading and grammar

1 *She bought a CD.*
2 *She watched a football match.*
3 *She went to the History Museum.*
4 *Claire visited her.*
5 *She read a story.*
6 *No, she didn't.*

5a Grammar

1 *f* 2 *c* 3 *e* 4 *b* 5 *d* 6 *a*

5b Grammar

1 *got a new bike*
2 *went cycling*
3 *visited my friend*
4 *played tennis*
5 *watched a DVD*
6 *read music magazines*

Lesson 6

1a Vocabulary

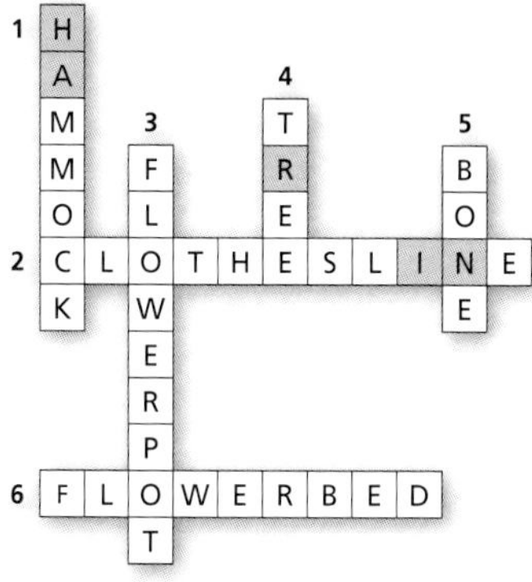

1b Vocabulary

Rihanna

2 Reading and grammar

1 *wasn't watering / was reading*
2 *wasn't playing / was playing*
3 *was sleeping*
4 *wasn't mowing / was climbing*
5 *wasn't hanging up / was sitting / was listening*
6 *was burying*

3a Grammar

a *Was Cassie watering the flowers?*
b *Were the boys playing football?*
c *Was Connor climbing a tree?*
d *Were Cassie and Connor looking at the dog?*

3b Grammar

1 *c* 2 *d* 3 *a* 4 *b*

4a Grammar and writing

1 *was getting up*
2 *were playing football*
3 *was talking on the phone*
4 *Dad was having a shower.*

4b Grammar and writing

1 *wasn't getting up. She was sleeping in a hammock.*
2 *weren't playing football. They were playing tennis.*
3 *wasn't talking on the phone. She was hanging up the washing.*
4 *wasn't having a shower. He was mowing the lawn.*

5 Writing

Students' own answers.

Lesson 7

1a Vocabulary and reading

1 *smoke*
2 *alarm*
3 *fire*
4 *saucepan*
5 *whistle*
6 *referee*

1b Vocabulary and reading

1 *alarm*
2 *referee*
3 *whistle*
4 *saucepan*
5 *fire*

2 Grammar

1 *was walking / came off*
2 *was reading / walked*
3 *was having / heard*
4 *was writing / broke*

3 Grammar and reading

1 *were travelling*
2 *saw*
3 *was*
4 *was going*
5 *were passing*
6 *noticed*
7 *was sitting*
8 *stopped*
9 *was driving*
10 *stopped*

4 Reading and grammar

1 *c* 2 *d* 3 *a* 4 *e* 5 *f* 6 *b*

5 Writing

Tom was walking to school when he saw a letter in the street. He was reading the letter when it blew away in the wind. He was running to catch it when he fell. He twisted his ankle. He was rubbing his foot when the letter landed next to him. He read the letter.

Lesson 8

1a Reading

1 *d* 2 *c* 3 *a* 4 *b*

1b Reading

1 *Rebecca broke the world record for the 800-metre freestyle swimming race.*
2 *Her parents watched her first race at home. / Her parents watched her second race in Beijing.*
3 *After her races, she wanted to eat a burger and chips.*

2 Writing

(Suggested answer)
Chris Hoy was born on 23rd March 1976 in Scotland. He won three gold medals at the Olympic Games in Beijing. He started cycling at six years old at a friend's house. He also did rugby and rowing at school. His childhood dream was to win an Olympic gold medal.

Learning diary

Study tip

(Students' own drawings.)

1
1 *jumped*
2 *twisted*
3 *broke*
4 *got*
5 *fell*
6 *bought*

2
1 *ran*
2 *didn't swim*
3 *threw*
4 *jumped*
5 *did*
6 *finished*
7 *didn't break*

3
1 *What did you do yesterday? I went to an exhibition.*
2 *Did Dan buy a football? No, he didn't.*
3 *What did you do last night? We watched TV.*
4 *What did Sally eat for breakfast? She ate fruit.*
5 *Did you read a book yesterday? Yes, I did.*

4
1 *were playing*
2 *was climbing*
3 *was listening*
4 *were riding*
5 *was doing*

Module 3

Lesson 9

1 Vocabulary

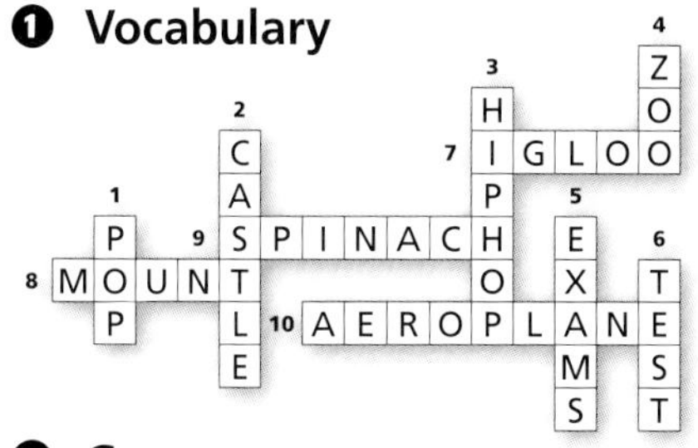

2a Grammar

1 *been*
2 *climbed*
3 *won*
4 *seen*
5 *eaten*
6 *ridden*
7 *travelled*
8 *flown*

2a Grammar

1 *'ve been*
2 *'ve ridden*
3 *'ve flown*
4 *'ve seen*
5 *'ve won*
6 *'ve travelled*
7 *'ve climbed*
8 *'ve eaten*

3 Grammar

1 *'ve played*
2 *haven't seen*
3 *haven't ridden*
4 *'ve danced*
5 *'ve tasted*
6 *haven't eaten*
7 *'ve listened*
8 *'ve jumped*
9 *haven't won*

4 Grammar and reading

1 *ridden*
2 *sailed*
3 *flown*
4 *been*
5 *seen*
6 *stayed*

5a Grammar

1 *Have you ever flown to India? No, I haven't.*
2 *Have you ever been to America? Yes, I have.*
3 *Have you ever travelled by train? Yes, I have.*
4 *Have you ever danced to hip hop? No, I haven't.*
5 *Have you ever climbed a tree? Yes, I have.*
6 *Have you ever won a prize? No, I haven't.*

5b Grammar

1 *I've never flown to India.*
2 *I've been to America.*
3 *I've never travelled by train.*
4 *I've never danced to hip hop.*
5 *I've climbed a tree.*
6 *I've never won a prize.*

6 Writing

Students' own answers.

Lesson 10

1 Vocabulary

1 *e* 2 *h* 3 *f* 4 *g* 5 *a* 6 *c* 7 *d* 8 *b*

2 Grammar

1 *She's won a swimming race, but she hasn't won a cycling race.*
2 *She's ridden an elephant, but she hasn't ridden a donkey.*
3 *She's met a king, but she hasn't met a queen.*
4 *She's written a travel book, but she hasn't written a recipe book.*
5 *She's climbed Mount Everest, but she hasn't climbed Mont Blanc.*
6 *She's eaten Mexican food, but she hasn't eaten Thai food.*
7 *She's skied in Switzerland, but she hasn't skied in Canada.*
8 *She's sailed around the world, but she hasn't sailed from Sydney to Hobart.*

3b Reading and grammar

1 *Has she been / No, she hasn't.*
2 *Has she lived / Yes, she has. She lived in an igloo in 1998.*
3 *Has she met / No, she hasn't.*
4 *Has she made / Yes, she has. She made a film in 1999.*
5 *Has she swum / No, she hasn't.*
6 *Has she flown / No, she hasn't.*
7 *Has she cycled / Yes, she has. She cycled to Morocco last year.*
8 *Has she broken / Yes, she has. She broke a world record in 2009.*

4 Grammar

1 *been*
2 *went*
3 *written*
4 *wrote*
5 *eaten*
6 *ate*
7 *swum*
8 *swam*

5 Writing

He's climbed Mount Everest. He's swum across the English Channel. He hasn't broken a leg or an arm. He's sailed to Antarctica. He hasn't made a TV programme.

Lesson 11

1 Vocabulary

1 *your hairstyle*
2 *a new job*
3 *an MP3 player*
4 *a friend to a sleepover*
5 *the kitchen*
6 *your back*

2 Vocabulary and grammar

1 *back*
2 *kitchen*
3 *hairstyle*
4 *kittens*
5 *sleepover*
6 *MP3 player*

3 Grammar

1 *I have just bought this new jumper.*
2 *Mum has just made a cake.*
3 *He has just fallen off his bike.*
4 *They have just finished their lesson.*
5 *We have just had lunch.*
6 *Ben and Vicky have just met.*

4 Vocabulary and grammar

1 *shopping / d*
2 *a prize / c*
3 *TV / f*
4 *a celebrity / b*
5 *a picture / a*
6 *lunch / e*

5 Grammar

1 *Have you ever bought*
2 *have*
3 *did you buy*
4 *bought*
5 *Have you ever been*
6 *haven't*
7 *did you go*
8 *went*

6 Writing

1 *Where did you go?*
2 *Who did you see?*
3 *What did she get?*
4 *When did they fly?*

Module 4

Lesson 12

1a Reading

1 *Dennis*
2 *snowmobile*
3 *igloo*
4 *fishing*

1b Reading

1 *c* 2 *d* 3 *f* 4 *b* 5 *g* 6 *e* 7 *a*

2 Writing

Students' own answers.

Learning diary

Study tip

Regular verbs:
I play/played/have played (tennis).
I dance/danced/have danced (hip hop).

Irregular verbs:
I do/did/have done (my homework).
I eat/ate/have eaten (pizza).

1
1 *He has done his English homework.*
2 *He hasn't finished his book.*
3 *He has started his project.*
4 *He hasn't written a poem.*

2
1 *Have you ever been to Germany? Yes, I have. When did you go? I went in 2007.*
2 *Has your dad ever played football? No, he hasn't.*
3 *Have your parents ever met an athlete? Yes, they have. Who did they meet? They met Usain Bolt.*

3
1 *has just fallen off*
2 *have just won*
3 *have just arrived*

Lesson 13

1 Vocabulary

1 *costume*
2 *guitar*
3 *microphone*
4 *stage*
5 *judge*
6 *audience*

2 Vocabulary and grammar

1 *will*
2 *won't*
3 *will*
4 *will*
5 *won't*
6 *won't*
7 *will*

3a Vocabulary and grammar

1 *dance*
2 *act*
3 *sing*
4 *do a magic trick*
5 *play the guitar*

3b Vocabulary and grammar

1 *'ll*
2 *will*
3 *'ll*
4 *won't*
5 *'ll*
6 *will*
7 *will*
8 *will*
9 *will*
10 *'ll*

4 Grammar

1 *e* 2 *d* 3 *a* 4 *f* 5 *c* 6 *h* 7 *g* 8 *b*

5 Grammar

1 *won't*
2 *will*
3 *will*
4 *will*
5 *won't*
6 *won't*
7 *will*
8 *will*

6 Writing

Students' own answers.

Lesson 14

1 Vocabulary

violin
accordion
amp
double bass
drums
recorder
flute
keyboards

2a Grammar and vocabulary

1 *b* 2 *d* 3 *f* 4 *c* 5 *a* 6 *g*

2b Grammar and vocabulary

a *3* b *1* c *4* d *2* e *6* f *5*

3 Grammar

1 *I'll carry your bags for you.*
2 *I'll take it away.*
3 *I'll get you a cold drink.*
4 *I'll show you on a map.*

4 Grammar

1 *I*
2 *you*
3 *I*
4 *lend*
5 *you*
6 *borrow*

5 Grammar

1 *Could I borrow yours, please?*
2 *Could you fix it, please?*
3 *Could I use your dictionary, please?*
4 *Could I have an aspirin, please?*
5 *Could you tell me, please?*

6 Writing and grammar

1 *I'll lend you some money.*
2 *I'll look for it.*
3 *I'll lend you some clothes.*
4 *I'll explain it to you.*
5 *I'll turn on the TV.*

Lesson 15

1 Vocabulary

a *puppet show*
b *folk music*
c *mime*
d *comedy show*
e *circus*
f *treet dance*

2 Vocabulary and reading

1 *f* 2 *b* 3 *c* 4 *a* 5 *d*

3 Grammar

1 *going*
2 *watch*
3 *to see*
4 *to listen*
5 *to do*
6 *I want to*
7 *to go out*

4 Grammar

1 *What would you like to do tonight?*
2 *I don't want to dance.*
3 *How about going to the theatre?*
4 *Let's play a game.*

5a Grammar and reading

6, 8, 2, 4, 5, 3, 7, 1

5b Grammar and reading

1 *having*
2 *do*
3 *walk*
4 *don't want*
5 *watch*
6 *don't like*
7 *see*
8 *listening*
9 *going*
10 *watching*
11 *do*

6 Writing

Students' own answers.

Lesson 16

1 Reading

1 *Aiden*
2 *Beth*
3 *Jack*
4 *Jack*
5 *Aiden*
6 *Beth*

2 Writing

Students' own answers.

Learning diary

Study tip

I'm; they'll; you won't; let's; I'd

1
1 *recorder*
2 *flute*
3 *keyboards*
4 *accordion*

2
1 *mime*
2 *audience*
3 *microphone*
4 *stage*

3
1 *Will / won't*
2 *Will / will*
3 *Will / won't*

4
1 *Could you open the window, please?*
2 *Could you get my coat, please?*
3 *Could you lend me your pencil, please?*
4 *Could you buy me a drink, please?*

5
1 *I'll turn up the radio.*
2 *I'll show you the way.*
3 *I'll buy you a ticket.*
4 *I'll fix your bike.*

Module 5

Lesson 17

1 Vocabulary

1 *a sore throat*
2 *a headache*
3 *a cold*
4 *a stomach ache*
5 *temperature*
6 *a cough*
7 *flu, medicine*

2 Vocabulary

1 *cough*
2 *stomach ache*
3 *cold*
4 *a headache*
5 *sore throat*
6 *medicine*

3 Grammar

1 *will / won't*
2 *carries / carry*
3 *is helping / will help*
4 *fail / pass OR study / don't study*
5 *are writing / write*
6 *are missing / will miss*

4 Grammar

1 *If she rides her bike too fast, she'll fall.*
2 *If he doesn't wear warm clothes, he'll get ill.*
3 *If Polly doesn't tidy her room, her mum will be angry.*
4 *If they eat all the sweets, they'll get a stomach ache.*
5 *If he doesn't study harder, he'll fail his test.*
6 *If he eats a lot of fruit, he'll be healthy.*

5 Writing

(Suggested answers)
1 *they won't let me go out*
2 *I'll get a place at university / I'll get my allowance*
3 *they'll invite me to their houses / they'll share their things with me*
4 *I'll put on weight / I'll be unhealthy*
5 *I'll put on weight / I'll be unhealthy / I'll get a stomach ache*
6 *I'll buy …*
7 *I'll get my allowance*
8 *I won't miss the bus / I'll be on time for school*

Lesson 18

1 Vocabulary
1 *warm clothes*
2 *insect spray*
3 *bull*
4 *tent*
5 *game*

2 Grammar
1 *may lose*
2 *may not sleep*
3 *may be*
4 *may rain*
5 *may fall*
6 *may not like*

3 Grammar and reading
1 *is going to*
2 *isn't going to / is going to*
3 *are going to*
4 *aren't going to / 're going to*
5 *is going to*
6 *is going to*

4 Grammar
1 *are you*
2 *may*
3 *may*
4 *'m going to*
5 *are you going to*
6 *may*
7 *may*

5 Writing
Students' own answers.

Lesson 19

1a Vocabulary
1 *f* **2** *c* **3** *b* **4** *e* **5** *a* **6** *d* **7** *g*

1b Vocabulary
1 *wet*
2 *muddy*
3 *stare*
4 *visitors*
5 *take off*
6 *present*
7 *rude*

2 Reading and grammar
1 *should*
2 *shouldn't*
3 *should*
4 *should*
5 *shouldn't*
6 *should*
7 *should*
8 *shouldn't*
9 *shouldn't*
10 *shouldn't*

3 Grammar
1 *e* **2** *b* **3** *f* **4** *c* **5** *a* **6** *d*

4 Grammar
1 *should*
2 *shouldn't*
3 *shouldn't*
4 *should*
5 *shouldn't*
6 *shouldn't*

5 Reading and writing
(Suggested answer)
You should eat more fruit. You shouldn't eat sweets or sugar. You should do more exercise. You should go to the gym or run. You should walk to school.

Lesson 20

1 Reading
1 *F* **2** *T* **3** *F* **4** *T* **5** *F* **6** *T*

2 Writing
(Suggested answer)
You should join after-school clubs. You should walk in the corridors. If you run, the teachers will shout at you. You should do sport. If you do sport, you will meet new people. You should do your homework. If you don't do your homework, the teachers will be angry. You should stand when the teacher walks in the classroom. You shouldn't sit. You should eat lunch in the cafeteria.

Learning diary

Study tip
1 *Mrs Brunel, my French teacher, is from Paris.*
2 *I live in King Street, near the River Cam.*
3 *There's a party on the first Sunday in June.*

1
1 *headache*
2 *medicine*
3 *temperature*
4 *sore throat*

2 **1** *b* **2** *e* **3** *d* **4** *a* **5**

3
1 *It may rain.*
2 *They may not eat meat.*
3 *There may be flies.*
4 *I may miss the bus.*

4
1 *should*
2 *shouldn't*
3 *should*
4 *should*

Module 6

Lesson 21

1 Vocabulary

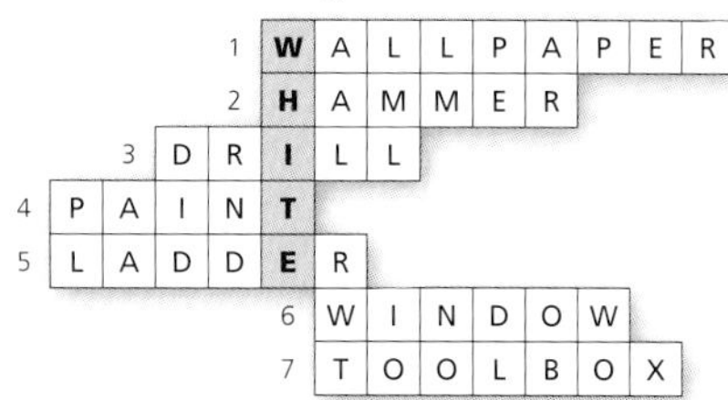

2 Vocabulary and grammar

1 *paint*
2 *wallpaper*
3 *toolbox*
4 *ladder*
5 *hammer*
6 *window*

3 Vocabulary

1 *break*
2 *spill*
3 *fall off*
4 *tripped over*
5 *dropped*

4 Grammar

1 *The waiter is going to spill the drink.*
2 *The child is going to trip over the bag.*
3 *The girl is going to give her friend a present.*
4 *The plates are going to fall off the table.*
5 *The man is going to pay the bill.*

5 Grammar

Students' own answers.

6a Grammar

1 *d* **2** *a* **3** *c* **4** *e* **5** *b*

6b Grammar

1 *is going to travel*
2 *'s going to drop*
3 *is going to fall over*
4 *is going to spill*
5 *is going to float*

Lesson 22

1 Vocabulary

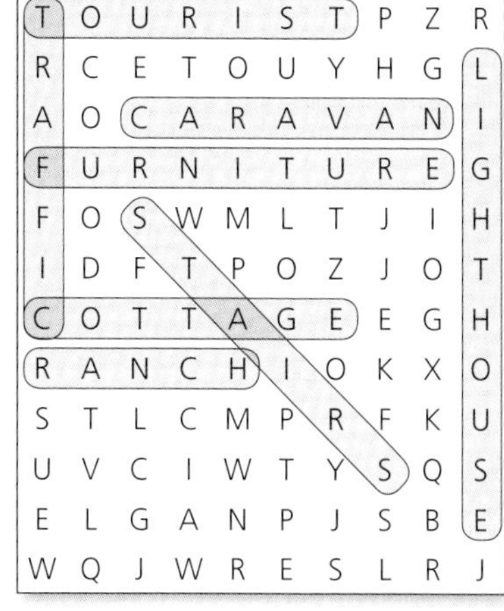

2 Grammar

1 *U* **2** *U* **3** *U* **4** *C* **5** *C* **6** *U*
7 *C* **8** *C*

3 Grammar

1 *enough friends*
2 *enough money*
3 *too many books*
4 *too much traffic*
5 *too many songs*
6 *enough space*
7 *too much homework*
8 *enough time*

4 Grammar

1 *aren't quiet enough*
2 *isn't warm enough*
3 *'re not old enough*
4 *isn't big enough*
5 *weren't good enough*
6 *'re not tall enough*

5 Grammar and reading

1 *aren't enough*
2 *'s too much*
3 *isn't enough*
4 *isn't enough*
5 *are too many*

6 Writing

Students' own answers.

Lesson 23

1 Reading and vocabulary

1 *village*
2 *kitchen*
3 *laundry*
4 *farm*
5 *food*
6 *wind turbines*
7 *recycled*

2 Vocabulary

1 *c* **2** *a* **3** *e* **4** *d* **5** *b*

3 Grammar

1 *c* **2** *e* **3** *f* **4** *b* **5** *d* **6** *a*

4 Grammar

5 Grammar

1 *is made*
2 *are collected*
3 *are washed*
4 *are dried*
5 *are cut*
6 *are used*
7 *are melted*
8 *is sold*

6a Reading and grammar

1 *are made*
2 *are washed*
3 *are dried*
4 *are put*
5 *is used*

6b Reading and grammar

a *5* **b** *4* **c** *3* **d** *2*

7 Writing

Students' own answers.

Module 7

Lesson 24

1 Reading

1 *Twelve people live at Brithdir Mawr.*
2 *The bathrooms are shared.*
3 *They eat together three or four times a week.*
4 *Fruit, vegetables, milk, eggs, cheese and yoghurt are produced on the farm.*
5 *The wind, sun and rain are used to produce energy.*
6 *You can visit their website.*

2 Writing

Students' own answers.

Learning diary

Study tip

Come here!

Do you like ice cream?

My favourite kinds of music are rock, pop and hip hop.

1
1 *ladder*
2 *hammer*
3 *paint*
4 *wallpaper*
5 *drill*

2
1 *It's going to rain.*
2 *He's going to drop that box.*
3 *He's going to fall off his bike.*
4 *I'm going to fall asleep soon.*

3
1 *enough*
2 *enough*
3 *too many*
4 *too much*

4
1 *one/a hundred*
2 *ten per cent*
3 *four and a half/four point five*
4 *1billion*

5
1 *are used*
2 *are cut*
3 *is thrown*
4 *are recycled*

Lesson 25

1a Vocabulary

1 *b* 2 *e* 3 *c* 4 *a* 5 *d* 6 *f*

1b Vocabulary

a *traffic lights*
b *road*
c *pavement*
d *car park*
e *motorbike*
f *crash helmet*

2 Grammar

1 *mustn't*
2 *must*
3 *mustn't*
4 *must*
5 *must*
6 *mustn't*

3 Grammar

1 *You must keep straight on.*
2 *You mustn't cross the road.*
3 *You mustn't cycle on the pavement.*
4 *You mustn't drive too fast.*
5 *You must turn here.*
6 *Bicycles must use the cycle lane.*

4 Vocabulary

1 *parking meter*
2 *traffic sign*
3 *pedestrian crossing*
4 *pavement*
5 *cycle lane*
6 *crossroads*
7 *traffic warden*

5 Grammar

1 *must*
2 *mustn't, must*
3 *mustn't, must*
4 *mustn't*
5 *must*

6 Vocabulary and reading

a *5* b *3* c *6* d *1* e *4* f *2*

Lesson 26

1 Vocabulary

1 *countryside*
2 *passport*
3 *profession*
4 *artist*
5 *pilot*
6 *licence*

2 Grammar

1 *lived*
2 *wanted*
3 *been*
4 *had*
5 *studied*
6 *known*
7 *liked*
8 *done*
9 *fallen*
10 *been*

3 Grammar

a *How long have you been a pilot?*
b *How long has Leila studied English?*
c *How long have they known each other?*
d *How long have you had a passport?*
e *How long has Ollie had that skateboard?*
f *How long have your friends been online?*

4a Grammar

1 *since*
2 *for*
3 *for*
4 *since*
5 *for*
6 *since*

4b Grammar

1 *b* 2 *e* 3 *d* 4 *c* 5 *a* 6 *f*

5 Grammar

1 *has had / for*
2 *has played / since*
3 *has studied /since*
4 *has wanted / for*
5 *have known / since*

6 Writing

Students' own answers.

Lesson 27

1 Vocabulary

1 *seeds*
2 *tomatoes*
3 *belt*
4 *rice*
5 *pots*
6 *guitar*

2 Grammar

1 *PS* **2** *PP* **3** *PS* **4** *PS*
5 *PP* **6** *PS* **7** *PP* **8** *PP*

3 Grammar

1 *have / been*
2 *'ve been*
3 *was*
4 *Have / lived*
5 *came*
6 *lived*
7 *Have / joined*
8 *had*
9 *did*

4 Grammar

1 *I've started horse-riding lessons.*
2 *When did you have your first lesson?*
3 *I had my first lesson last Tuesday.*
4 *What did you learn?*
5 *They taught me how to sit on the horse.*
6 *Yes. But I fell off.*
7 *What happened then?*
8 *I went home. And I haven't had another lesson since then.*

5 Grammar and reading

1 *'s going to buy*
2 *'s going to learn*
3 *'s going to practise*
4 *'s going to go*
5 *'re going to go*
6 *'s going to visit*
7 *'re going to play*

6 Reading and writing

1 *has started horse-riding lessons / went with her friend, Liz*
2 *has won a race / won the 100-metre race in July*
3 *has learnt Italian / went to Italy on holiday in August*
4 *has broken a record / won a swimming race in May*
5 *has joined a drama club / went every week last term*
6 *has got his first karate belt / passed the exam in April*
7 *'s going to paint her room*
8 *'s going to grow vegetables*
9 *'re going to form a rock band together*

Lesson 28

1a Reading

1 *c* **2** *b* **3** *a*

1b Reading

1 *Callum*
2 *Felix's dad*
3 *Mark Anderson*
4 *Yoko*
5 *Callum*
6 *Yoko*

2 Writing

Students' own answers.

Learning diary

Study tip

cross, stop, drive

1
1 *parking meter*
2 *crossroads*
3 *traffic lights*
4 *motorbike*
5 *pavement*

2 Students' own answers.

3 **1** *b* **2** *d* **3** *e* **4** *c* **5** *a*

4
1 *I've learnt to ski.*
2 *You've passed your exams.*
3 *We've visited the museum.*
4 *My brother has bought a moped.*

5
1 *I'm going to join a karate club.*
2 *My friend's going to have a party tonight.*
3 *My brother's learnt to dance.*

Module 1

Fast finishers

❶ Vocabulary and reading

1 *neybours / neighbours*
2 *creak / creek*
3 *beirs / bears*
4 *clapp / clap*
5 *hibirnating / hibernating*

❷ Grammar

1 *Rory is playing football.*
2 *Connor is going his homework.*
3 *Delia is watching TV.*
4 *Cassie and her friend are playing basketball.*

❸ Grammar

1 *mine*
2 *yours*
3 *hers*
4 *ours*
5 *their*
6 *his*
7 *mine*

❹ Grammar

1 *This jacket is cheaper than that jacket.*
2 *Your room is tidier than mine.*
3 *History is more interesting than maths.*
4 *Is your mother older than your father?*
5 *Are you worse at sports than music?*

Extra practice

❶ Vocabulary

1 *go*
2 *see*
3 *practise*
4 *visit*
5 *play*

❷ Grammar and reading

1 *'s seeing*
2 *'s visiting*
3 *'s going*
4 *are playing*
5 *are practising*

❸ Vocabulary

1 *a* 2 *d* 3 *c* 4 *b*

❹ Grammar

1 *his*
2 *hers*
3 *mine*
4 *yours*
5 *ours*
6 *theirs*

❺ Grammar

1 *the best*
2 *warmer*
3 *colder*
4 *nicer*
5 *cheaper*
6 *the most beautiful*
7 *the quietest*
8 *the noisiest*

Module 2

Fast finishers

❶ Vocabulary

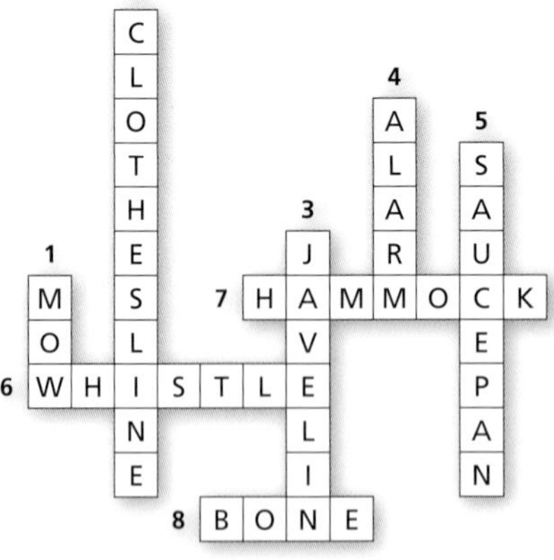

❷ Grammar

1 *Did Rebecca Adlington run in a race? No, she didn't.*
2 *Did she break a world record? Yes, she did.*
3 *Did her parents fly to Beijing? Yes, they did.*
4 *Did Chris Hoy win three gold medals? Yes, he did.*
5 *Did he start cycling at the age of ten? No, he didn't.*

❸ Grammar and reading

1 *happened*
2 *was walking*
3 *rang*
4 *was looking for*
5 *fell*
6 *broke*
7 *was driving*
8 *phoned*
9 *didn't go*
10 *went*

Module 3

Extra practice

1 Vocabulary and reading

1 *d* **2** *e* **3** *a* **4** *b* **5** *c*

2a Grammar

1 *Did Tom buy a CD yesterday?*
2 *Did Christina go to an exhibition?*
3 *Did your parents watch TV?*
4 *Did you do your homework?*
5 *Did Frank mow the lawn?*
6 *Did they win the football match?*

2b Grammar

1 *he did*
2 *he didn't*
3 *he did*
4 *he didn't*
5 *he didn't*
6 *he did*

3 Vocabulary

1 *whistle*
2 *bone*
3 *flowerpot*
4 *fire*
5 *saucepan*
6 *hammock*
7 *clothes line*

4 Grammar

1 *Connor was playing with the dog.*
2 *He was blowing the whistle.*
3 *The dog was looking at the bone.*
4 *Delia and Jess were sitting in the hammock.*
5 *Delia was talking on the phone.*
6 *Jess was reading.*
7 *Cassie was hanging up the washing.*
8 *Rory was cooking.*

Fast finishers

1 Vocabulary

1 *a mountain, a tree*
2 *rock, pop*
3 *spinach, an aeroplane*
4 *a castle, an igloo*
5 *basketball, a game*

2 Vocabulary

1 *zoo*
2 *castle*
3 *spinach*
4 *igloo*

3 Grammar

1 *has tidied*
2 *hasn't eaten*
3 *has changed*
4 *hasn't broken*
5 *have had*
6 *haven't invited*

4a Grammar and reading

1 *has broken*
2 *ate*
3 *has won*
4 *finished*

4b Grammar and reading

1 *Yes, she has.*
2 *in 2005*
3 *Yes, she has.*
4 *5 kilograms*

5 Writing

Students' own answers.

Extra practice

1 Vocabulary

E	E	P	T	R	O	F	N	T
B	E	N	C	A	M	E	L	R
C	R	Y	G	A	M	E	S	E
A	E	R	O	P	L	A	N	E
S	A	O	H	I	P	H	O	P
T	S	L	G	U	I	T	A	R
L	R	A	I	G	L	O	O	J
E	S	P	I	N	A	C	H	E

2 Vocabulary

1 *sails*
2 *ride*
3 *wins*
4 *play*
5 *break*
6 *take*

3 Grammar

1 *He has sailed a boat.*
2 *I've ridden an elephant.*
3 *She has won a prize.*
4 *They have played a game.*
5 *You've broken a record.*
6 *We've taken exams.*

4 Grammar

Present simple
go, write, see, take, eat, flt

Past simple
went, wrote, saw, took, ate, flew

Present perfect
have gone, have written, have seen, have taken, have eaten, have flown

5a Grammar

1 *Has Tom bought a new camera?*
2 *Has Sarah watched the DVD?*
3 *Has Mary found her school bag?*

5b Grammar

1 *Yes, he has.*
2 *Yes, she has.*
3 *Yes, she has.*

Module 4

Fast finishers

1 Vocabulary

violin
accordion
drums
flute
guitar

2 Grammar

1 *Will / live*
2 *will*
3 *will celebrate*
4 *Will / come*
5 *will*
6 *will / do*
7 *will write*
8 *will make*
9 *will / happen*
10 *won't be*

3a Grammar

a *Could you open the window, please?*
b *Could you drive me to school, please?*
c *Could I share your umbrella, please?*
d *Could you fix it, please?*
e *Could I sit down for a while, please?*

3b Grammar

1 *I'll turn it up, too.*
2 *I'll get you some medicine, too.*
3 *I'll hold it over both of us.*
4 *I'll turn off the heater, too.*
5 *I'll drive you home at 3pm, too.*

3c Grammar

1 *d* **2** *e* **3** *c* **4** *a* **5** *b*

Extra practice

1 Vocabulary

1 *audience*
2 *amp*
3 *violin*
4 *guitar*
5 *costumes*
6 *drums*
7 *recorder*
8 *microphone*
9 *judge*
10 *stage*

2 Grammar

1 *will*
2 *will*
3 *won't*
4 *won't*
5 *will*
6 *won't*

3 Grammar

1 *fix*
2 *be*
3 *lend*
4 *help*
5 *switch on*
6 *borrow*

4 Grammar

1 *Yes, I'll look at it for you.*
2 *Of course, I'll go to another room.*
3 *Yes, I'll get it out of my bag.*
4 *Yes, I'll look for them in the living room.*
5 *Yes and I'll open the curtains, too.*
6 *Yes, I'll give you a blue one.*

Module 5

Fast finishers

1 Vocabulary

1 *insect spray*
2 *bull*
3 *tent*
4 *insect*
5 *apple*
6 *visitor*

2a Grammar

1 *What will you do if you lose your bus ticket?*
2 *What will happen if you forget your books?*
3 *If you come late, what will your parents say?*
4 *What will you do if it rains tomorrow?*
5 *What will you do if you get a headache?*

2b Grammar

1 *will buy*
2 *will be*
3 *will shout*
4 *will go*
5 *will take*

3 Grammar and vocabulary

1 *The bull may get angry.*
2 *The tent may blow over.*
3 *There may be insects*
4 *I may get thirsty.*

4 Grammar

1 *should*
2 *shouldn't*
3 *should*
4 *shouldn't*

5 Writing

Students' own answers.

Module 6

Extra practice

1 Vocabulary

1 *Jess*
2 *Connor*
3 *Rory*
4 *Cassie*
5 *Delia*

2 Grammar

1 *c* 2 *e* 3 *d* 4 *b* 5 *a*

3 Grammar

1 *'ll*
2 *'ll*
3 *won't*
4 *won't*
5 *'ll*

4 Grammar

1 *are going to*
2 *may*
3 *is going to*
4 *'m going to*
5 *may*

5 Grammar

1 *d* 2 *e* 3 *b* 4 *c* 5 *a*

6 Writing

Students' own answers.

Fast finishers

1 Vocabulary

1 *hammer*
2 *drill*
3 *wallpaper*
4 *paint*
5 *ladder*
6 *toolbox*

2 Vocabulary

1 *a drink, water*
2 *a ball, a pencil*
3 *a glass, furniture*
4 *a table, a wall*
5 *a drill, a toolbox*

3 Grammar

1 *the bell is going to ring*
2 *the teacher is going to give us homework*
3 *we're going to pack our books away*
4 *I'm going to have a drink of water*

4 Grammar

1 *too many*
2 *enough*
3 *enough*
4 *too much*

5 Grammar

1 *Gold is found in South Africa.*
2 *Cars are produced in Europe.*
3 *The museum is visited by lots of tourists.*
4 *The children are taught at home.*

Extra practice

1 Vocabulary

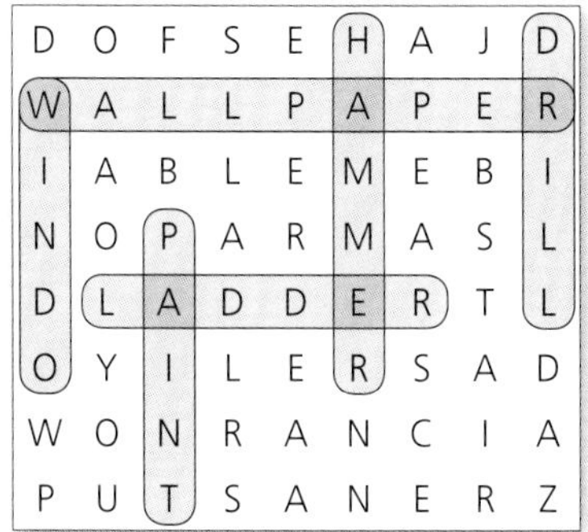

2 Vocabulary

1 *b* 2 *a* 3 *a* 4 *b*

3 Grammar and vocabulary

1 *'s going to trip over*
2 *'s going to fall off*
3 *'s going to spill*
4 *'s going to jump off*

4 Grammar

1 *isn't sweet enough*
2 *many*
3 *many*
4 *aren't*
5 *enough*
6 *well*

5 Grammar

1 *are read*
2 *are made*
3 *are sent*
4 *are written*
5 *are taken*
6 *are printed*
7 *are sold*

Module 7

Fast finishers

❶ Vocabulary

1 *d* **2** *h* **3** *b* **4** *a* **5** *c* **6** *e* **7** *f* **8** *g*

❷ Vocabulary and grammar

1 *must*
2 *mustn't*
3 *mustn't*
4 *must*

❸ Grammar

1 *have you been / Since / started*
2 *Have you known / for / have been / since*
3 *have you done / For / joined*
4 *have you lived / For*

❹ Grammar

1 *Delia is going to learn how to sail soon.*
2 *Connor planted a tree last week.*
3 *We haven't seen my aunt since December.*

❺ Vocabulary and reading

dentist

Extra practice

❶ Vocabulary

traffic warden
pedestrian crossing
car park
crash helmet
cycle lane
parking meter

❷ Grammar

1 *F* **2** *F* **3** *T* **4** *T*

❸ Grammar

1 *for*
2 *since*
3 *for*
4 *for*
5 *since*
6 *for*

❹ Grammar

1 *have you lived*
2 *did you move*
3 *have you been*
4 *have you and Jenny been*
5 *When did you meet?*

❺ Grammar

1 *is going to stay*
2 *is going to join*
3 *are going to start*
4 *'m going to grow*
5 *'re going to learn*

❻ Wrting

Students' own answers.

Searching for Speedy Smith

Module 1

1
Friday: *doing gymnastics*
Saturday: *going away (for the weekend)*
Sunday: *coming back*
Monday: *seeing the dentist*
Tuesday: *going shopping (for some new trainers)*

2
a *competition*
b *interview*
c *trainers*
d *race*

Can you remember?
a *E*
b *E*
c *O*
d *E*

Module 2

1
a *1*
b *3*
c *2*

2
a *walking*
b *carring*
c *going*
d *getting*

Can you remember?
a *E*
b *W*
c *O*
d *E*

Module 3

1
a *exciting*
b *ridden*
c *sailed / yacht*
d *did / sail*
e *did*

2
a *travelled*
b *been*
c *interviewed*
d *written*
e *sailed*
f *ridden*

Can you remember?
a *O*
b *I*
c *I*
d *O*

Module 4

1
b
c

2
a *4*
b *3*
c *2*
d *1*

Can you remember?
a *E*
b *O*
c *O*
d *E*

Module 5

1
a *She's taking sunglasses because it may be sunny.*
b *She's taking sweaters because it may be cold.*
c *She's taking an umbrella because it may rain.*
d *She's taking boots because it may be wet.*
e *She's taking insect spray because there may be insects.*

2
a *2*
b *3*
c *4*
d *1*

Can you remember?
a *O*
b *O*
c *E*
d *E*

Module 6

1
a *T*
b *F*
c *T*
d *F*
e *F*
f *F*

2
a *2*
b *1*
c *3*

Can you remember?
a *There aren't enough shops.*
b *The water isn't warm enough.*
c *There are too many old people.*
d *The village isn't big enough.*

Module 7

1
1 *He's going to be at the shopping centre.*
2 *He's going to meet his cousin Jake for lunch.*
3 *She must wear a crash helmet.*
4 *She's going to ride it in the park.*
5 *She fell off the skateboard.*
6 *He's an old friend from college.*

2
a *late*
b *interview*
c *invite*
d *find*
e *dangerous*

Can you remember?
a *E*
b *O*
c *J*
d *E*
e *O*

Hot Spot 3 Test CD

The Test CD contains editable tests and the recordings of the listening test activities. There are A and B versions of each test as well as answer keys

Contents of the Test CD

Tests

- Pre-Course
- Module 1
- Module 2
- Module 3
- Middle of Book
- Module 4
- Module 5
- Module 6
- Module 7
- End of Book

Audio tracklist

Track 1	Module 1 Tests A and B
Track 2	Module 2 Tests A and B
Track 3	Module 3 Tests A and B
Track 4	Middle of Book Tests A and B
Track 5	Module 4 Tests A and B
Track 6	Module 5 Tests A and B
Track 7	Module 6 Tests A and B
Track 8	Module 7 Tests A and B
Track 9	End of Book Tests A and B